D0597023

Advance Praise for
THOU SHALT NOT STAND IDLY BY

"*Thou Shalt Not Stand Idly By* is the story of one of the most important and improbable humanitarian initiatives of our time. In turn inspiring, heartbreaking, and exhilarating, this book is above all a testament to how a few determined people can change one tortured corner of the world. Anyone concerned with the future of the Middle East—with the future of humanity—should read this powerful book."

—YOSSI KLEIN HALEVI, Senior Fellow, Shalom Hartman Institute,
Author, *Letters to My Palestinian Neighbor*

"Georgette Bennett is not one to stand idly by, and when confronted with the Syrian refugee crisis of historic proportions, she dove in to find a way to help. She never took no for an answer, pulled out all the stops to corral governments, armies, organizations, and civil society to stop their real wars and their turf wars to cooperate, at least in 'the crevices,' to help people most in need on a huge scale, and in doing so building new relations across long-time enemies. This is humanitarian diplomacy at its best, engineered by a civilian Jewish woman of conviction in a region where any or all of those can get you in huge trouble. Not only is the blow by blow riveting, but here is a story to inspire all of us to use what we have at our disposal to help each other as humans, and to get past the rigidities which have left way too many as collateral damage."

—ANTHONY MARX, President and CEO, New York Public Library

"Georgette Bennett has turned her life story into a force for humanity. When she sees suffering, she takes personal and moral responsibility to do something about it. The Syria war is a stain on humanity and this book shows what it means to stand by Syrians suffering at the hands of their own government. The world needs more people like Georgette Bennett."

—DAVID MILIBAND, President, International Rescue Committee
and former UK Foreign Secretary

"Georgette Bennett is truly one of our better angels, caretaking all of us by caretaking those most in need: Syrian refugees. A child of the Holocaust, she is also the woman who established the Multifaith Alliance for Syrian refugees. Refugees everywhere need everyone's help all over the world and Georgette Bennett is on the front lines of it all. We owe her a debt of gratitude."

—MANDY PATINKIN, Actor, Activist on behalf of refugees

"This remarkable book is a testament to three things: first, the inhumanity that persists in the world, seen in the brutal treatment by the Syrian regime of millions of its own people. Second, the painstaking, behind-the-scenes and largely thankless work that goes into trying to help those suffering on a massive scale. And third, the difference that one person can make. It's the story of Georgette Bennett, private citizen with a steely determination to come to their rescue, who found the unlikeliest of benefactors, and to this day, simply refuses to give up."

—JUDY WOODRUFF, Anchor and Managing Editor, The PBS NewsHour

"Blessed are the peacemakers and blessed is Georgette Bennett. In this fascinating and well-written book she describes her dogged efforts to help those devastated by conflict and search for ways to bring people of differing faiths together. The stories she tells are an important reminder that we could all do more to try to make the world a better place."

—FAREED ZAKARIA, Host, CNN GPS

THOU SHALT NOT STAND IDLY BY

How One Woman
Confronted the Greatest
Humanitarian Crisis
of Our Time

Georgette F. Bennett, Ph.D.

WICKED SON

A WICKED SON BOOK
An Imprint of Post Hill Press

Thou Shalt Not Stand Idly By:
How One Woman Confronted the Greatest Humanitarian Crisis
of Our Time

ISBN: 978-1-64293-611-7
ISBN (eBook): 978-1-64293-612-4

Cover Design by Tiffani Shea
Interior design and composition, Greg Johnson, Textbook Perfect

Post Hill Press
New York • Nashville
posthillpress.com

Published in the United States of America
1 2 3 4 5 6 7 8 9 10

To my husband, Dr. Leonard Polonsky CBE,
who makes all dreams come true
and enabled me to pursue the dream
that resulted in this book.

CONTENTS

FOREWORD

Except for those times when the lifeless body of a toddler washes up on shore or when a camera captures a pair of traumatized children huddled together, the Syrian crisis slips out of public consciousness. But I could have been one of those children had my Syrian grandfather not brought my father to the US one hundred years ago to escape starvation. Ever since then, my family and I have felt unbounded gratitude for having been embraced by this country and spared the fate of our countrymen. Yet, I feel searing pain for the immeasurable suffering of our relatives still in Syria, whose lives hang in the balance.

When Georgette Bennett reached out to me, she gave me a way to get past my helplessness. I made a commitment to be the human face and voice for the Multifaith Alliance for Syrian Refugees, which she founded in 2013. I joined Georgette on her journey from bystander to activist on behalf of my people. That journey is described in this book, which brings to the fore the oft-forgotten people of Syria and the confluence of forces that brought them to this moment.

The Syrian crisis is the worst humanitarian tragedy of our time. Millions of decent, skilled, and educated people have fled their homes with nothing. In today's environment of fear, xenophobia, and Islamophobia, they are almost without hope. Because of my background, this is a very personal issue for me.

The journey began with Georgette's own background as a child of the Holocaust, a refugee, and a Jew.

When Georgette read a report on the Syrian crisis issued by the International Rescue Committee, she was struck by the parallels between her beginnings in war-torn Budapest and the devastation in Syria. The Hebrew scriptures make no fewer than thirty-six references to caring for the stranger. She felt commanded to do so and founded the Multifaith Alliance for Syrian Refugees. What began with a report resulted in nearly $200 million in aid being delivered to more than 2.2 million (and counting) Syrian war victims. I'm proud to be a part of that effort.

But this is more than a feel-good story of humanitarian activism. It is an exposé of how geopolitics makes pawns out of suffering human beings—in this case the 13 million displaced Syrians whose lives are being stolen from them.

As a Syrian American, I wish my community would do more to tell the world who they are—not only to share their contributions but to counter the phobic backlash against them. I don't think they are doing enough. It's time to speak out, and Georgette does that for them.

I'm extremely patriotic, but that doesn't mean I have to accept all the policies of my country. I have a right to criticize, and one of my criticisms is this: we seem to have lost the sensitivity and compassion that is a hallmark of America, a beacon. I don't see much of that lately. I see a lot of fear. Of course, that's not true only for the US. As this book shows, hearts and borders are closed to displaced Syrians in many countries. But the US needs to be the catalyst that moves other countries to do the right thing.

It seems to me that those who would lead by fear believe that the hearts and minds of good people can be closed to those who cry out for help. That's not who Americans are. That's not the country to which my grandfather fled for a better life, or the country for which my father worked so hard and sacrificed his two sons in the US military. America is the country that gave them hope and opportunity. We must not let our fears define us. This book powerfully addresses those fears.

We can take action right here in America by integrating Syrian families into our communities. The facts show that before long, Syrian refugees, who serve and contribute culturally and economically to this country, become one of us: they learn to speak our language, they generate jobs, and they embrace our values and our laws. Refugees are the standard bearers of the American dream. They personify the spirit, the diversity, and the values that made America the richest, most powerful, and greatest country in the world. But if we are sincere about enhancing our leadership in the world—and I believe we are still the world's leader—our moral compass must continue to set us apart. If we can find a way to combine our necessary vigilance with our trusting, loving, and generous nature, I sincerely believe the world would applaud and be grateful.

The insights, analysis, and recommendations in this book provide a roadmap for those who want to find a way to alleviate terrible suffering. Georgette's indefatigable dedication to saving Syrian lives through MFA's Herculean humanitarian efforts inspires me and countless others to be our best selves and to do good. Only she could have written this book.

—F. Murray Abraham

CHAPTER 1

IN THE BEGINNING

My Road from Budapest to Syria

The report was dated January 2013. It sat on my desk for five months, sinking deeper and deeper into a growing pile of papers. Being a typical overextended New Yorker, I didn't get around to opening it until May. But when I finally cracked it open, it changed my life.

The report, "Syria: A Regional Crisis," was issued by the International Rescue Committee. I joined the board of IRC after the death of my late husband, Rabbi Marc Tanenbaum. Marc, a pioneer in interreligious reconciliation and a world-renowned human rights activist, had a deep commitment to aiding refugees. To that end, he served for twenty-five years on the executive committee of the IRC. Founded by Albert Einstein to rescue Jews from the clutches of Nazism, it is now one of the world's foremost refugee rescue and resettlement organizations, operating in conflict zones around the world. From that base, Marc helped organize the international rescue effort for the Vietnamese "Boat People," having himself waded into the South China Sea to pull drowning refugees out of the water. Forty years later, the "boat people" were Syrian. Like the Vietnamese and the Jews before them, they were fleeing unspeakable horror.

And the silence of the world was deafening.

"Syria is tearing itself apart," said George Rupp, then-president and CEO of IRC, sounding the alarm. "Doctors are targeted specifically because they treat the injured. Women and girls are raped and brutalized...Homes, schools, and hospitals are destroyed."

I read about horrific torture, merciless bombings of civilians, mass displacement, and starvation by siege. By the time the IRC report was issued, the Syrian war had been raging for two years. Education had collapsed, with more than half of Syrian children no longer attending school. The loss of life was appalling, with 6 percent of the population having been killed or maimed—more than one million people.

Attacks on medical workers were being used as weapons of war. Physicians for Human Rights documented dozens of attacks on specifically targeted medical facilities. Doctors were being detained, tortured, and tried in military courts for having treated injured patients. The government killed hundreds of medical personnel.

Torture was rampant and gruesomely documented by a regime photographer who defected and came to be known as "Caesar."

Hundreds of thousands of people were living under siege, with food and essential supplies cut off.

Sarin gas attacks had taken place in Damascus, and more than a dozen chlorine attacks had been documented. In each case, the poison gas was embedded in barrel bombs that were indiscriminately used on civilian populations.

All of these are violations of the Geneva Convention and constitute war crimes.

But it was the gender violence that first gripped me and wouldn't let go.

I read about women and girls being repeatedly raped: fleeing rape in Syria and being raped again when they reached "safety." I read about young girls being forced into marriage to "protect" them from rape or because their families could no longer afford to shelter them. I read about pious women having to sell their bodies in order to survive.

Per the IRC report, rape was the primary reason that families fled the conflict, "yet there is an alarming lack of medical and counseling services to help them recover in the countries to which they have fled. They face unsafe conditions in camps and elevated levels of domestic violence." The report went on to say:

> "Many women and girls relayed accounts of being attacked in public or in their homes, primarily by armed men. These rapes, sometimes by multiple perpetrators, often occur in front of family members. The IRC was told of attacks in which women and young girls were kidnapped, raped, tortured, and killed. Roadblocks, prolific throughout Syria, have become especially perilous for women and girls.... Because of the stigma and social norms around the 'dishonour' that rape brings to women and girls and their families, Syrian survivors rarely report sexual violence. Many of those interviewed by the IRC said women and girl survivors also fear retribution by assailants. Others are afraid of being killed by family members if they report incidents, since a raped woman or girl is thought to bring shame to a family."

Sexual violence against women holds special resonance for me. At age eighteen, I was the terrified victim of a sexual assault in which I feared being killed. Later, in my career as a criminologist, I conducted rape research in several cities under the auspices of renowned sociologist, Amitai Etzioni. With Susan Brownmiller, the author of *Men, Women, and Rape*, I lobbied the New York City

3

police commissioner to establish a sex crimes unit—the first in the country—trained to deal with victims of gender violence.

So, the searing images of women getting brutalized in Syria and the host countries to which they fled hit me hard. But there was more.

At the time, more than 2.5 million Syrians had been uprooted by the conflict. Who could imagine that those numbers would shortly swell to 13 million—more than half of Syria's population? Of those who were refugees, more than 80 percent were women and children, and only 10 percent were finding their way to camps. The rest were urban refugees, squatting—unprotected and vulnerable—wherever they could find shelter.

And the silence of the world was deafening.

Syrians felt forgotten by the world—just as the Jews had during the Holocaust. In particular, they felt betrayed by the US. After President Obama encouraged the democratic stirrings of the uprising in Syria, the opposition assumed that they would receive meaningful aid from the US. But they didn't.

It was difficult to identify the good guys—although the war crimes were overwhelmingly committed by the regime. Finding the good guys was further complicated by shifting alliances, which often created strange bedfellows. There were times when the Syrian Free Army was allied with extremist groups. But this was rarely a matter of ideology. It was pragmatic. One of my colleagues related a story in which he visited a childhood friend in Syria. When he entered the friend's home, he found him wearing the heavy beard of an observant Muslim and sitting in front of a black-and-white banner, similar to the ISIS flag. The friend had never been religious, and my colleague was puzzled by this seeming transformation. The friend replied that he was the same person he had always been. He was simply sporting the trappings of extremists because "they get money and they get weapons," and the moderates don't get anything.

4

Some of the areas under siege were blockaded by the opposition and others by the regime. George Soros observed that both the Syrian government and the rebels were using the denial of humanitarian aid as a tool of war. Massive amounts of aid were coming into Syria via the UN and government channels, but the regime did not permit any of it to enter areas outside its control. Much aid was diverted to staunch supporters of the regime or sold for profit, and much more aid was needed. But the donor nations that had promised aid often failed to fully—if at all—pay their pledges.

The moderates, such as the Free Syria Army and others who were non-ideological, found themselves fighting on two fronts—against the Assad regime and against the extremists who were filling the vacuum left by the breakdown of Syria's social order. For many of the desperate people of Syria, ISIS and Jabhat al-Nusra (the Syrian branch of al-Qaeda) were the only source of relief. Just like Hezbollah in Lebanon and Hamas in Gaza, the extremists of Syria initially entrenched themselves by providing services that the government did not. The trade-off for food, money, and a modicum of order was to live under the reign of terror that came with them.

At an IRC dinner I attended in New York in November 2013, Madeleine Albright, Bill Clinton, David Miliband, Scott Pelley, and George Soros all raised the alarm about the acute urgency of the Syrian crisis. Samantha Power noted that the price tag needed from world governments was $4.4 billion. So far, she said, they had failed to step up to contribute what was needed.

All the speakers highlighted the unprecedented nature of the disaster and lamented the failure of the crisis to garner appropriate media and public attention. "We need to turn up the political pressure and shame" the world's governments into action, proclaimed Power.

Given my background, it's counterintuitive for me to have been riveted by the Syrian crisis. Yet, it's precisely because of that background that I was. For I, too, had been displaced in my early years, when my parents and I fled the chaos of postwar Europe as stateless refugees, to find a new life in America.

I am a child of the Holocaust, having been born in 1946, one year after the end of World War II. Most of my family had been killed in the war, and my mother endured seven miscarriages before she finally gave birth to me. The odds of my being born were heavily stacked against me.

During the siege of Budapest, surrounded by Red Army troops, 38,000 civilians died of starvation and bombings. One of my mother's miscarriages occurred as she lugged a sack of half-rotten potatoes home to 9 Madacz Utca, a bombed-out apartment building in what had once been an elegant neighborhood.

By the end of the war, Budapest lay in ruins. When I was born, our apartment was missing walls and food was scarce. I had to be fed on beer and canned sardines. Soon after my birth, my mother suffered a nervous breakdown and was temporarily separated from me. Today, it would be recognized as PTSD.

My mother's traumatic wartime experience began when Miklós Horthy's oppressive regime passed a series of anti-Jewish measures that mimicked Germany's Nuremberg Laws. Among other things, Jews could not own businesses. My mother was a custom lingerie designer, who, as a Jew, was illegally running her own salon in Budapest. Every day, she took a coffee break in a cafe across the street. One afternoon, a tall blond man entered the café with a woman. He spoke there of the horrors that he and his sister had escaped in Poland—of concentration camps and forced labor. The man's wife and two daughters had been shot in front of him by SS soldiers during the selections in the Tarnow ghetto. The patrons of the café accused the man of being an alarmist. My mother believed him. She took him and his sister into her home to give them shelter. That man was to become my father.

By then, air raids were a regular part of life in Budapest. The residents of 9 Madacz Utca would flee to the basement for protection. During one of these air raids, a fascist neighbor, who coveted my mother's apartment, noticed that she was accompanied by two strangers. She promptly denounced my Jewish mother to the Gestapo for hiding Jews. My mother was taken to prison and later to a Hungarian concentration camp.

The Hungarian resistance fighter, Hannah Szenes, was in the same prison, awaiting execution. Szenes was one of thirty-seven paratroopers sent by the British from Mandate Palestine to rescue Hungarian Jews about to be deported to Auschwitz. Szenes's mother was in another part of the prison. My mother, who had managed to get an inmate job cleaning floors, had access to their cells and carried messages back and forth between them. With every transfer, she put her life at risk. But she made it possible for the Szeneses to communicate with each other before Hannah was put to death.

My father was put on a forced labor train to Austria and escaped—again. Having been rescued by my mother, he was now determined to rescue her. His blond, blue-eyed good looks and fluent German gave him the look of an Aryan poster boy. Finding his way back to the camp in which my mother was interned, he came across a German officer, killed him, and stole his uniform.

Now in full Nazi regalia, he approached the commandant. "I have a girlfriend in this camp, and she's a very good seamstress. You could have her work for your wife in your home." The commandant liked the idea. So, my mother began a regimen of daily treks to his house. From there, my father engineered her escape. By the time my mother's absence was noticed and the dogs sent out to find her, they were both ensconced in the basement of a mansion in Budapest with a group of other hidden Jews. There they remained for a couple of months until the Nazis were defeated in Hungary.

When Budapest fell to the Soviet Union in February 1945, that mansion was taken over as the headquarters for the victorious Soviet army. Among the fugitives they found hiding in their basement was my very German-looking father. After the terrible losses they had suffered at the hands of the Nazis, Soviet soldiers were eager to confront any German they encountered, and my father's life was at risk. He immediately dropped his pants, shouting, "No, no! Look, I'm a Jew!" His circumcised penis saved his life.

My mother and father returned to the apartment at 9 Madacz Utca and resumed what life they could. But the same fascist neighbor who had reported them to the Gestapo now denounced my mother to the communist authorities. My mother was sent to prison again—on what pretext, I never learned.

Having now been in and out of Nazi and Soviet prisons, my parents realized that they would be persecuted as long as they remained in Hungary. With a child on the way, my father fervently hoped that they would eventually get to America.

Inhabitants of Iron Curtain countries could not travel outside the Soviet bloc, but they could travel within it. In 1948, my parents planned their escape. For Jews, doomed to wander throughout history, wealth always had to be portable. My parents packed a suitcase for a "vacation" in Czechoslovakia and stashed our little hoard of gold inside my diaper. We boarded a train to Prague and, from there, made our way to Paris and freedom.

That gold was to be our survival and our future. But somehow, according to my mother, it had fallen out of my diaper and been lost *en route*. My parents now had to start life all over again.

My father, ever resourceful, went into business manufacturing shearling coats. But he soon became ill and, to my child's mind, disappeared from our home. Then I became ill and had to be put in a sanitarium in Switzerland, where, at the age of two, I was separated from both my parents. My mother, finding this arrangement unbearable, spirited me away to Nice so that I could recover in the warmth of the Riviera before returning to Lyon.

In 1952, our immigration papers came through. We boarded the *Ile de France* in Le Havre for the trans-Atlantic journey to New York. All I remember of that trip is being given orange-grapefruit juice that made me nauseous. The passenger manifest listed our nationality as "Stateless." I have kept the suitcase we carried with us to this day, as a reminder of our journey and my own severed roots.

Although we had little money, my mother insisted that we settle in a nice neighborhood with a nearby school. For us, that was Kew Gardens, Queens—a neighborhood with a large number of central European Jews, many of them Holocaust survivors.

But moving into that solidly middle-class reserve, and paying the exorbitant rent of $250 a month, was frightening for my father. He was fifty-one years old, unaccustomed to American business methods and unskilled in English. Although quick-witted and successful in Poland and France, he could do only menial work in New York. Sadly, he never had the chance to improve his circumstances because he died of cancer at the age of fifty-two, when I was six years old.

My mother was now a thirty-six-year-old widow, in a strange country, with no close family and no husband to help her support a young child. It was also the McCarthy era—the time of the "red scare." We were in the US legally, but as a refugee from Hungary, a Communist country, my mother lived in constant fear of deportation. Government buildings displayed signs for "alien registration." Each routine visit to the post office brought me face to face with those signs. That was me. An alien. I felt I didn't belong. I spoke with an accent; my father was gone; even my clothes set me apart.

My mother found a part-time job at DePinna, a fashionable Fifth Avenue women's clothing store, and later started her own custom lingerie business. She acquired a prestigious clientele, among them Happy Rockefeller, the wife of New York's governor.

Eventually, life stabilized. I became a "real" American and lived the American dream. I received scholarships to attend Vassar College, went on to earn a PhD at NYU, and later received an executive banking degree.

As a product of the '60s, my penchant for activism began at Vassar and became the connecting thread in both a diverse career and my choice of life partners.

Vassar students are required to do a senior thesis. In 1967, the year I graduated, the culture was awash in drugs. It happened that Timothy Leary's commune was located in Millbrook, New York—minutes from the Vassar campus. As a sociology major, one who was already eager to get behind the headlines, I decided to do my thesis research in Millbrook on LSD as a social movement. As a participant-observer, I regularly encountered Leary. I have an amusing memory of the two of us pruning tree branches and then picking up a couple of them to fence with each other. Not being a druggie myself, I used to come to the main house with blueberry muffins for the residents. Being a friendly—albeit stoned—lot, they warmly encouraged me to come with them to turn on with the cows. That not being my thing, I declined and stuck with the blueberry muffins.

Soon after I graduated, I attended a demonstration in Kew Gardens in support of the seventeen indicted members of the Revolutionary Action Movement, a militant civil rights group, and was quoted in the Daily News: *"[Y]ou can't get a realistic point of view...from textbooks...alone. I'm interested in seeing things first hand and unearthing my own truth."* These words, spoken at age twenty, would define my career as a change agent and "action" sociologist.

In graduate school, inspired by the searing black-Jewish conflict spawned by the Ocean Hill-Brownsville experiment in giving control of schools to local communities, I wrote a 600-page doctoral dissertation on a New York City ghetto school.

I started teaching before I completed my PhD and was invited to join the Women's Advocacy Committee, a group of a dozen activists: Eleanor Holmes Norton, Betty Friedan, Elinor Guggenheimer, Ronnie Eldridge, Carol Greitzer, and other icons of the women's movement.

My colleague, Ellen Mintz, and I were assigned to work with the New York City Police Department to address the plight of women as victims, criminals, and colleagues in the NYPD.

My journey took me from the NYPD to the New York City Office of Management and Budget. From there, I became a broadcast journalist with stints as a correspondent for NBC News and a host of Walter Cronkite's program *Why in the World*. Then it was on to PR and marketing, which led to a sojourn in financial services. I wrote several books along the way, one of which was nominated for a Pulitzer Prize.

In 1982, I married Rabbi Marc Tanenbaum, the man who would foreshadow the great turn that my life would take a decade later.

A poll of religion editors ranked Marc one of the four most respected and influential religious leaders in the country. With the American Jewish Committee as his institutional home, he became known as "the secretary of state for the Jews," "the human rights rabbi," and the Jews' "foremost apostle to the gentiles." As such, he had an enormous impact on contemporary Jewish life and on the broader world. In the words of his biographers, Gerald and Deborah Strober, "For him, addressing injustice was synonymous with being alive."

In the '60s, Marc had been the only rabbi to be an observer at Vatican Council II, where he was a crucial back channel in reversing 1,900 years of the teaching of contempt against the Jews. He sounded the alarm and organized a response to the starvation in Biafra, helped organize the campaign to free Soviet Jewry, supported Cesar Chavez in ameliorating the plight of Mexican farmworkers, fought apartheid in South Africa, and became deeply immersed in the Civil Rights Movement.

In 1963, when Marc organized the first National Conference on Religion and Race, he gave Martin Luther King Jr. one of his first national platforms. It was there that he introduced Dr. King to Rabbi Abraham Joshua Heschel.

In the '70s, Marc joined an IRC mission to raise awareness of the Vietnamese Boat People and Cambodian refugees who were being ravaged by famine and disease induced by the inhumane policies of brutal dictators, like Pol Pot. Marc, along with Elie Wiesel, Liv Ullmann, Bayard Rustin, Joan Baez, and soviet Refusenik Zion Alexander Ginzburg, brought medical teams to refugee camps in the region. Marc would come to call the victims they encountered, "the Jews of Asia."

I hadn't yet met Marc in 1978, when he was literally pulling drowning boat people out of the South China Sea. It would be another three years before a mutual friend would introduce us. During the Vietnam war years, I was still an academic. My activism took the form of leading anti-war teach-ins and sit-ins. I was an unlikely "radical," in my Jackie Kennedy-style pillbox hat and prim, A-line dresses.

By then, Marc, who was twenty-one years older than me, had been deeply immersed in combating all forms of bigotry and in humanitarian crises around the world. In the decade I shared with him, we had very different careers and operated in different spheres. But I absorbed the methods and techniques that he used.

- He formed multifaith coalitions to address key issues.
- He called out the politics of purity that cause us to view the other as evil rather than someone who simply holds a different point of view.

- He debunked myths with facts by popularizing the relevant history.

- He mobilized the moral authority of the clergy.

- He challenged politicians' claims of piety if they behaved in ways that contradicted the principles they espoused.

- He listened deeply to the fears that underlie hate, spoke powerfully to address those fears, and used the media to amplify his message.

These are all methods that I incorporated into the intergroup efforts and humanitarian activism that would come to dominate my life.

Marc died in 1992, at the age of sixty-six, due to complications from open-heart surgery. I was in my eighth month of pregnancy with our only child.

That year, I founded the Tanenbaum Center for Interreligious Understanding to combat religious prejudice and religion-based violence. The Tanenbaum Center focuses on four core areas: schools, workplaces, health-care settings, and areas of armed conflict. The latter is implemented through its Peacemakers in Action program, which was inspired by conversations with the late Ambassador Richard Holbrooke, architect of the Dayton Peace Accords that ended the war in Bosnia. The Peacemakers in Action program demonstrates that religion can be a solution to conflict, not just a cause of it.

In the same year, I assumed Marc's seat on the IRC board and joined the program committee.

* * *

And that brings me back to 2013 and the fateful Syrian refugee report waiting patiently on my desk.

I was stunned by the magnitude of the tragedy. Some years before, with the sanction of Bashar al-Assad, the Tanenbaum Center had gone to Damascus to train sixty women in conflict resolution. They spanned a range of ages and beliefs, and all were activists committed to intergroup relations and mutual respect. Our then-CEO, Joyce Dubensky, served as the trainer from Tanenbaum and was the only Jew present. "One woman," conflating Judaism and Israel, reported Joyce, "wanted to talk to me…about Israel and how angry she was." Another woman said, "I've never met a Jew before, and now I've met you. When I travel throughout the world, I always try to talk to Christians to learn more about what they're thinking. Now I will also try to talk to Jewish people."

I was aghast at what had happened since that time. These new boat people, trying to land their fragile vessels on the shores of Turkey and Greece, with borders closing all around them, reminded me of the *St. Louis*—the doomed ship that left Hamburg in May 1939, carrying 937 mostly Jewish refugees. The *St. Louis* tried landing in Havana, but the Cuban government refused permission. It continued to the US and Canada. Both countries turned the ship away. Having no choice but to return to Europe, one-third of the passengers were killed in the Holocaust.

The silence of the world was deafening.

By this time, I had been remarried for twelve years. My husband, Dr. Leonard Polonsky CBE—who makes all dreams come true—has always been supportive of my passion for conflict resolution, bridge-building, and intergroup relations. I was no longer a refugee child growing up in near-poverty. With Leonard's backing, I was in a position to take action.

The gruesome "Caesar" photos mentioned above documented the torture of Syrian civilians—eviscerated corpses, starved bodies with burn marks, dislocated limbs—a ghoulish gallery of death. The photos were first exhibited at the National Holocaust Museum in Washington, DC, in December 2017 under the rubric: "Syria: Please Don't Forget Us." A defected Syrian forensic photographer for the military police, code-named "Caesar," had smuggled 55,000 photos out of Syria on discs and thumb drives, brought them to the US, and testified to Congress in 2014 about what he had witnessed. "Caesar" had been in charge of documenting the dead in Military Hospital 601 and Tishreen Military Hospital in Damascus. There were three categories of corpses: those killed in government custody, including victims of torture; dead soldiers and members of the security regime forces; and crime scene photos of those killed in explosions, assassinations, fires, and car bombs. Those in the first category showed evidence of violent blunt force trauma, suffocation, starvation, and torture. They included one woman and one hundred boys. I was given thirty-three of the photos. As I looked at them, I recalled the skeletons unearthed in Nazi concentration camps, where so many of my family had been murdered.

When I saw the real-time destruction of Aleppo, I was transported back to the bombed-out city of my birth. The idea of starvation being used as a weapon of war brought me back to my parents' wartime deprivation. As I watched millions of displaced Syrians pouring across borders, I recalled my own repeated displacement as a child. I felt a duty to step up.

But my impulse was deeper than that. As a Jew, I felt *commanded* to respond. Leviticus 19:16 kept reverberating in my brain: "Thou shalt not stand idly by while the blood of your neighbor cries out from the earth."

Intellectually, I knew that many, if not most, of these Syrian refugees would just as soon see every Jew dead and Israel driven into the sea. I had grown up believing that Israel was the only truly safe haven for Jews—even more so than America—the one place where we could feel protected and free of persecution. But how could I, as a Jew, not respond to the terrible suffering of Syrians—which so echoed that of my own family? How could I, in good conscience, sit at my seder table every year reminding our family and friends, "Once we were strangers too," without remembering my own experience of being a stranger in McCarthy's America? And how could I not feel compassion for the Syrians who were now strangers in many lands, including my own? If I was to be true to the post-Holocaust admonition, "Never again," then "Never again" had to include my fellow human beings in Syria. If I was to be true to Judaism, I had to make it my business to care for the stranger—even if that stranger was my enemy. I would later learn that there was a name for the vague stirrings that were driving me to inhabit a role I had yet to define: humanitarian diplomacy.

CHAPTER 2

ON-THE-JOB TRAINING

Understanding the Worst Humanitarian Crisis of Our Time

The Syrian civil war began in March 2011 after a few teenage boys, perhaps emboldened by the Arab Spring, scribbled the words, "It's your turn, doctor" on a wall in Daraa, a city in southern Syria. The boys were arrested and tortured, sparking mass protests. That's the part you read about in the formal accounts. Here's the part that was related to me by a Syrian, which you won't find in a Google search: After the boys were arrested, the frantic parents went to the police to inquire about their children. The parents were told, "Forget about your children. Go home and make more children. And if you can't do that, I'll send my men to your house to make them for you." Those were explosive words that triggered huge demonstrations in Damascus and Aleppo.

In another version of events, humiliation sparked the protests. A tribal delegation met with Atef Najib, the head of the political security branch in Daraa, asking him to release the imprisoned children. Consistent with tribal tradition, the delegates removed their headbands and left them on the table pending resolution of the matter. Headbands are a powerful tribal symbol of masculinity and honor. Instead of responding positively, as expected, Najib tossed the headbands in the trash. This offense was unforgivable.

The protests were non-violent, but the regime's security forces opened fire on the unarmed demonstrators, killing dozens and arresting six. The nation was stunned.

Callous and crude treatment of concerned parents of disappeared children wasn't the sole cause of the uprising. And it's not an accident that the protests began in Daraa, a drought-stricken, rural, tribal province. Bedouin tribes inhabit 55 percent of Syria and make up 15 percent of the population. Former president Hafez al-Assad had co-opted the ruling clans among the tribes to help him suppress the Muslim Brotherhood. But al-Badia (desert region) Bedouins and farmers in the countryside had been marginalized and impoverished.

Given the complexity of the Syrian conflict, it is necessary to explain its fundamental outlines, beginning with the accession of Syrian president Bashar al-Assad.

When Bashar succeeded his father as president in 2000, there was hope that the unassuming ophthalmologist with a London post-graduate degree would be a reformer. Instead, reform was slow in coming, and Syria spiraled into ever-deepening inequality and repression. By 2003–2004, more than 5 million Syrians were living below the poverty line, with 2 million unable to meet their basic needs. Although Assad did move to privatize an economy that had been dominated by the state, the main beneficiaries were cronies of the regime.

Then there was the matter of religion. The ruling Ba'ath Party is secular. But a country that is more than 70 percent Sunni was being ruled by an Alawite minority that was aligned with the Shiite world. Ten percent of the population was Christian, mostly clustered in Damascus, clinging to Assad for protection and fearful of rule by the majority Sunnis.

Even before the graffiti episode and its aftermath, Syria was teetering toward instability with widespread crop failures, rising food prices, mass migration from rural areas to urban centers, and deep sectarian divides. By September 2011, the protests had spread, as had the brutality of the crackdown. Armed opposition groups formed after the Syrian city of Idlib was bombed by regime forces, and the civilian insurgency became militarized by early 2012. The first opposition fighters emerged in Homs, Idlib, and Damascus and were made up primarily of local fighters and defectors from the Syrian army. After 2012, hundreds more such groups formed.

By the time the armed insurgency morphed into full-blown civil war, there were a number of combatants: On the regime side, there were the Syrian Armed Forces and its allies. On the opposition, the Turkish-backed Free Syrian Army (FSA); the jihadist militant group, Hay'at Tahrir al-Sham; the Kurdish-dominated Syrian Democratic Forces (SDF); and the Islamist terrorist group ISIS, which had formed in the aftermath of the Iraq War and had ambitions of establishing a caliphate across the Middle East. What ultimately emerged from this confusing multisided conflict was a proxy war between Iran and Russia on one side and Saudi Arabia and the US on the other. Turkey, Saudi Arabia, and Qatar were arming the rebel groups based on tribal kinship ties. Iran propped up Assad by sending weapons, Hezbollah, and the legendary General Qasem Suleimani, head of the Revolutionary Guard Corps Quds Force. (Suleimani would be killed in Iraq in a targeted US operation in January 2020.) The US, feeling gun-shy after the debacles in Vietnam, Iraq, and Afghanistan, withheld direct support at first but eventually relented and modestly equipped and trained a few carefully vetted groups. The major players were Russia, which conducted the air war, and Iran, which led the ground war.

The government forces concentrated on urban centers and lines of communication. The opposition forces made their major inroads in the countryside. Like the regime—but to a far lesser degree—they, too, engaged in torture, kidnapping, and sieges.

By late 2012, the Assad regime had changed tactics and shifted away from mobilizing its mostly-Sunni infantry in ground attacks. Too many recruits had used these battles as an opportunity to defect. Instead, the main strategy was "*tansheef al bakhar*," or drain the sea to kill the fish. Based on interviews with war victims, a 2015 UN Human Rights Council report identified four components of this strategy:

- *Encircle the restive area and set up checkpoints.*
- *Impose a siege* to prevent the flow of food, medical supplies, water, and electricity.
- *Aerial bombardment.* This included the use of cluster bombs, barrel bombs, thermobaric bombs, and missiles, often used against schools and hospitals. Later, barrel bombs were regularly dropped on areas where civilians congregate— bakery lines, transportation hubs, apartment buildings, markets, and aid distribution centers.
- *Arrest and disappear wounded persons* trying to leave the area for medical treatment or smuggle in supplies.

The earliest besieged areas were Daraa, Homs, and the Yarmouk Palestinian refugee camp in Damascus.

Jabhat al-Nusra, the offshoot of al-Qaeda in Iraq, made its appearance in January 2012 and attracted many foreign fighters. ISIS tried to romance al-Nusra into an alliance but was spurned in April of the following year. Going out on its own, and using terror tactics, ISIS soon held thirty-five municipalities under partial or total control. These included significant natural resources, which gave the group a stable flow of income.

Regardless of the combatants, civilians were intentionally targeted and bore the brunt of the fighting.

In hindsight, there were a lot of "coulda-shouldas." Had Assad responded to the protests with meaningful reform, had the US stepped in early, had President Obama enforced his famed "red line" militarily rather than handing Syria to a marginalized Russia, things might have turned out very differently. But that is not what happened.

Here are the grim numbers as of August 2020—a decade into the conflict: 80 percent of the country has descended into poverty. The inflation rate is 25 percent. Life expectancy has dropped from eighty to fifty-six. Six and a half million refugees have fled, most to low and middle-income countries—Jordan, Lebanon, and Turkey—that can't afford to host them. Another six and a half million are internally displaced. Eleven million urgently need aid inside Syria. Over 500,000 have been killed. By the time this book is published, the numbers will be even worse.

Out of 70 million displaced persons in the world, Syrians today make up nearly 20 percent. They comprise fully one-quarter of refugees, making theirs the largest refugee crisis in the world.

Among these are 300,000 of the more than half-million Palestinian refugees living in Syria—now twice displaced. Ironically, Palestinian authorities have denied them admission to either the West Bank or Gaza, lest they give up their "right of return" to Israel.

What was I, a private citizen, to do? What could *any* individual do about a crisis of such magnitude? I could not stand idly by. Neither could I focus on the big picture, which would only paralyze me. Yet I felt I must do something.

When I first read the IRC's January 2013 report, I knew hardly anything about the scale of the Syrian humanitarian crisis or what was being done about it. That was an education I acquired along the way. As I plunged into further research, hoping to find a single thread that I could pull in this great tapestry of suffering, I learned that the early response had involved a range of stakeholders—government actors, the UN, donor nations, and NGOs—both Syrian and international. What I saw was a confusing patchwork of efforts, some effective, some not, and all plagued by a variety of roadblocks and frustrations.

State actors were involved in three ways:

- Diplomacy, which had achieved a number of ceasefires and created deconfliction zones along the way—most of which didn't hold.

- Refugee admissions, which initially were more generous but diminished when borders closed as the conflict dragged on. It was mostly Western countries that admitted refugees. Notably, the wealthy Arab Gulf states did not. Nor did most Eastern European countries, which had centuries-old Muslim indigenous populations.

- Funding for humanitarian aid.

Support for humanitarian aid was largely dependent on thirty-eight donor countries. The largest contributors were the US, the European Union, Kuwait, and the UK.

The biggest recipient of funding was the UN and its agencies, foremost among them the UN High Commission for Refugees. In 2013, UNHCR had published a 300-page Regional Response Plan calling for more than $830 million for the neighboring countries of Jordan and Lebanon, where most Syrian refugees had fled. By 2014, the need increased to $1.3 billion, of which only 60 percent was funded. That's because a large percentage of the amounts pledged by donor nations went unpaid. (This is not unusual. Since adopting Global Needs Assessment [GNA] as the framework for its budgeting process, UNHCR has averaged a funding gap of about 43 percent, part of which is the result of unpaid pledges.) In the case of the Gulf states, much of their funding was channeled through non-UN organizations, such as UAE Red Crescent Authority, Khalifa bin Zayed Al Nahyan Foundation, and the Abu Dhabi Fund for Development.

UN agencies, such as the World Food Program, had to suspend food vouchers for 1.7 million Syrian refugees because it didn't have $64 million to cover the cost. Of the $1 billion needed, WFP had received less than half.

UNHCR, which was responsible for running camps, delivering aid, and doing initial processing of refugees for resettlement, was overwhelmed, underfunded, and understaffed.

Even with full funding, Chapter 7 of the UN charter creates roadblocks to the delivery of aid. If the UN wants the unrestricted ability to deliver humanitarian aid across a nation's borders without government consent, the UN Security Council must pass a resolution that invokes Chapter 7. Chapter 7 allows the UN to use all possible means, including economic sanctions and military action, to enforce a UN resolution.

Easier said than done.

The US, France, and the UK repeatedly called for a resolution under Chapter 7 regarding Syria. But Russia, a close ally of President Assad, consistently vetoed those resolutions. That meant that all the aid deliveries had to go through the regime—and the regime prohibited the delivery of aid to any area it did not control. As the 2015 Human Rights Council report so aptly stated: "Humanitarian aid has been instrumentalized for military gain." This was true for all sides of the conflict.

In July 2014, the Security Council finally adopted a resolution under Chapter 7, which activated aid access at four border crossings in Turkey, Iraq, and Jordan. Finally, aid could be more broadly distributed without the consent of the Syrian government. The

UN pledged that it would deliver aid to as many as two million refugees and IDPs. But by the end of 2014, they had succeeded in delivering food to only 208,000, medical supplies to only 250,000, and water/sanitation equipment to only 86,000. (The UN challenges these numbers and claims to have reached 1.6 million as of January 2015.)

While you might think that UN agencies are the gold standard for the delivery of aid, I was surprised to learn that non-UN organizations have been more efficient. Mercy Corps, for example, managed to send 688 trucks into Syria, compared with only 422 sent by all the UN agencies combined. According to the Syrian American Medical Association (SAMS), Turkish Red Crescent sent 297 trucks in just two weeks, compared to 207 sent by the UN in four months. The Syrian government's obstruction was a roadblock to the UN's ability to access areas of great need. But NGOs can often work in the crevices.

The lesson for me was that my efforts were more likely to have some impact if I focused on the NGO sector. Fortunately, I already had a strong connection with one of the world's premier private humanitarian organizations.

The NGO with which I was most familiar was the IRC, with its team of over 30,000 staff and volunteers across nearly forty countries. IRC gets about 75 percent of its funding from grants and contracts from the US government, the UN, and other international agencies. IRC started work in Syria in 2012, operating in Raqqa, Idlib, and Deir ez-Zor. In 2013, when I was first trying to figure out where to focus, IRC needed $13,300,700 for its Syria relief operations, only half of which was covered by the UNHCR Regional Response Plan.

Given the regime's frequent and premeditated attacks on medical facilities, IRC was operating with cross-border teams in Iraq and Jordan to support clinics and mobile health teams, with a special focus on women and girls who had survived assault and abuse. Working with partners, such as the Syrian American Medical Society (SAMS), IRC provided medical supplies and child protection services to more than one million Syrians each year.

IRC was the largest provider of health care in northeast Syria and the only agency to provide mental health services in all its medical facilities. IRC was also providing job training, cash and vouchers to buy food and other essentials, and documents to access services. And IRC was one of the nine agencies in the US contracted by the government to resettle refugees. As such, they were major advocates for increasing the number of Syrian admissions.

A big chunk of their funding was tied to those numbers. As Shelly Pitterman, UNHCR regional representative for the US and Caribbean, observed: IRC's credibility is compromised because they have a vested interest in resettlement. Therefore, advocacy could be more convincing coming from religious leaders.

So far, the key takeaways were:

- *Humanitarian aid depends heavily on diplomacy.*

- *Working with local NGOs can be more efficient than working through the UN and can enable one to bypass barriers.*

- *Medical care is a top priority in a country where the medical infrastructure has been destroyed.*

- *Southwest Syria is less accessible and has received less attention than other parts of Syria.*

- *Religious leaders are a resource in advocating for aid and resettlement.*

These lessons would become my guideposts in engaging with the Syrian crisis.

No one can be everywhere at once, so I next needed to choose a country on which to focus my efforts. The four countries most impacted by the crisis are Egypt, Jordan, Lebanon, and Syria—of which only one, Egypt, is a signatory to the 1951 Convention on Refugees.

I had few contacts in Egypt, where I'd only visited as a tourist. The closest I'd been to Lebanon was the Israeli border, where— wanting to experience every corner of the country during my first trip there—I'd traveled on my honeymoon during the 1982 war. (Coincidentally, Marc and I were married on June 6, World War II D-Day, and also the day of the Israeli-Lebanon invasion.) The Tanenbaum Center had done work in Syria years before, but our link to the country was now living in exile. That left Jordan, where I'd been numerous times and had existing relationships.

Then there was Israel, which shared a border with all these countries. Israel is viewed as a pariah in many parts of the world. Nevertheless, the Israelis had a real interest in ameliorating the crisis, and they had the resources to do so. Fundamental Jewish values drove the humanitarian agenda, but maintaining a stable and secure border with their neighbor to the north was also of strategic value. But who in the region would work with them? Not believing that they could provide aid directly, they were interested in working through the UN or other such bodies.

It's widely believed that the Chinese character for "crisis" is comprised of the words for "danger" and "opportunity." That happens to be a mistranslation. Nevertheless, there was a huge opportunity in this crisis, along with a high degree of risk. One could mobilize Israel's vast resources—advanced technology, medical research, abundant agriculture, search and rescue expe- rience, and trauma expertise—on behalf of the 1.4 million Syrian refugees in Jordan.

Much of my career has been devoted to building bridges and doing back-channel work, and that's where I realized I could be of use. My ultimate hope was to harmonize national interest, human- itarian need, and the NGO sector in service of Syrian war victims. By pursuing these goals in partnership with interested political and diplomatic actors in a hybrid approach that has come to be called humanitarian diplomacy, I learned that one could build bridges between enemies—in this case, Israel and Syria. Such bridges could potentially outlast the crisis. But building them could also risk lives.

I stared at a map, and my eyes kept returning to Jordan. Officially, the governments of Jordan and Israel were at peace, but nothing had been done to prepare the Jordanian people to accept peace with their perceived enemy. Therefore, it was a cold peace in which the people remained enemies. Nevertheless, it was an open secret that the governments had developed cooperative ties at many levels. And I had connections in Jordan from the Tanenbaum Center's previous conflict resolution and bridge-building activities.

At an IRC party for its directors and overseers, I cornered Farooq Kathwari, an astute Kashmiri-born Muslim activist and CEO of the quintessential American furniture chain, Ethan Allen. Farooq has emerged as a leading Muslim voice in the US and a great immigrant success story. I had tried for two years to recruit him to the board of the Tanenbaum Center, but he joined the IRC board instead. (Years later, we found ourselves on the same board again—this time, the Muslim Jewish Advisory Council.) Because of his sophistication and demonstrated commitment to both refugees and intergroup relations, I wanted to bounce my "radical" idea off him. Was I being a Pollyanna thinking that Israel could be "accepted" as having a role in alleviating the Syrian refugee crisis?

Farooq was not encouraging. Nevertheless, I thought the IRC would prove to be a useful platform for my efforts going forward.

Jordan is a country of about 9.5 million people—most of whom are refugees. Prior to the influx of Syrians, 750,000 Iraqi refugees fled to Jordan. Before them came the Palestinians, who make up 70 percent of Jordan's population. Two million of those are still living in camps that have become small cities. The royal family is western-educated and westward leaning. But they must carefully navigate the ideological gap between themselves and the Jordanian street.

Here, a little background is needed to understand the fraught relationship between Jordan and Israel.

At the end of 1947, the British Mandate terminated, and the UN Security Council adopted a partition plan for Palestine that called for the creation of independent Arab and Jewish states. The Arabs rejected the plan, and when Israel declared its statehood that year, the former emirate of Transjordan joined Lebanon, Iraq, Syria, and Egypt in attacking the fledgling state. The invading armies failed to drive the Jews into the sea, but Transjordan did capture the West Bank and later annexed it. That annexation was viewed as illegal by the Arab League, but it was recognized by Britain, Pakistan, and Iraq.

President Harry S. Truman gave diplomatic recognition simultaneously to Transjordan and Israel. Truman viewed Israel as the place to absorb Jewish refugees from Europe and those driven from Arab lands. He envisioned Transjordan as the place to absorb displaced Palestinian Arabs who had fled or been driven out of the new state of Israel. Already at that time, there were private discussions between Transjordan's King Abdullah I and Golda Meir, who was then head of the political department of the Jewish Agency.

In 1967, Jordan again joined other Arab countries in attacking Israel. This time, Israel regained control of the West Bank. This triggered another flood of Palestinians into Jordan, which now had to contend with the growing threat of Palestinian militants using their host country as a base of anti-Israel operations. In 1971, Jordan expelled the so-called *fedayeen* and recognized the Palestinian Liberation Organization as the sole legitimate representative of the Palestinian people, but it ended its political ties to the PLO in 1986. In 1988, Jordan renounced any claim to the

West Bank but backed the Palestinian uprising, known as the first *intifada.*

During the first Gulf War in 1991, Jordan supported Saddam Hussein, breaking with other Arab countries and costing it the financial aid of the US. Palestinians in Jordan burned the Israeli flag (along with the US and Soviet Union's) and cheered while Saddam Hussein rained thirty-nine Scud rockets on Israel. Nidal Rahwy, a twenty-six-year-old clothing salesman whose family had arrived in Jordan as refugees from Palestine, was quoted in the *New York Times* as saying: "We like Saddam very much because he returns glory to the Arabs…All people look at Saddam Hussein as a hero. They look to him to liberate Palestine." *Times* reporter John Burns went on to observe, "There, as at today's rally, the fragility of King Hussein's position is immediately apparent."

After Iraq's defeat, Jordan, Lebanon, Syria, and Palestinian representatives entered into direct talks with Israel. A peace treaty was signed between Jordan and Israel in late 1994. But the fragility of the monarchy persisted throughout the 1990s, induced by food riots, a 25 percent unemployment rate, and boycotts of parliamentary elections.

In 1999, the beloved King Hussein died and named his son, Abdullah II, to succeed him.

There are many stories of secret communications and meetings between Hussein and the Israeli government. There was a Mossad warning to Hussein about a planned assassination attempt. During Hussein's war against the PLO, Syria invaded Jordan, and Israel conducted overflights to protect its neighbor and drive the Syrians back to their own territory. Then there was the time Hussein warned Prime Minister Golda Meir about Syrian and Egyptian threats in the lead-up to the 1973 Yom Kippur War.

Then-Crown Prince Hassan himself, who was born the year before the 1948 Arab-Israeli War, had many encounters with Israelis. "I had the privilege of meeting Golda Meir at a tender

29

age for me, not for her, of course, and Yigal Allon, Moshe Dayan, and many of the leaders of the State of Israel," he would recall many years later. "I try, informally, to reach out in my meetings with…Israeli civil rights groups and Israeli Palestinian groups, who straddle the families of the bereft." Years after the late prime minister was assassinated in Israel, Hassan recalled: "I spent thirty years of my life in so-called secret negotiations with Yitzhak Rabin. It was a 'gentleman's agreement.' 'You will say no to the right of return, and we'll say yes to the right of return, and we'll all look good with our constituencies.' But let's get on with the job of signing a peace and moving from final status to permanent status."

When, in Abdullah II's reign, the Syrian civil war cut off normal trade routes, Israel helped Jordan get goods to Turkey and Iraq. There are joint desalination projects and Qualified Industrial Zones that use Israeli inputs to send exports duty-free to the US. And there's much more, enough to fill another book.

Nevertheless, Israel's peace with Jordan is a cold one, with little people-to-people engagement.

Ironically, Jordan leans heavily on back-channel coordination with Israel to maintain stability. Publicly, it must maintain distance because of its roiling Palestinian population. Some years ago, research was done in a group of western and Middle Eastern countries to explore what kind of messaging shifts attitudes toward Israel. Jordan was the only country in which there was *no* messaging that could move the needle. Such is the depth of hostility in the Jordanian street toward Israel.

Now, a flood of Syrians was threatening to destabilize Jordan—a country that is economically insignificant but diplomatically crucial to the region. At the time, Senator Lindsey Graham opined, "If [the Syrian civil war] doesn't end soon, the king of Jordan is going to be the casualty." If Jordan falls, that would be a geopolitical disaster for the region as well as for the US.

In its volatile corner of the Middle East, Jordan has been an island of moderation, a balanced intermediary, a key ally to the US, and a partner—albeit a cold one—in peace with Israel. Should Jordan collapse, the Muslim Brotherhood is likely to prevail, and porous borders would permit the infiltration of bad actors from Syria. This would leave Israel surrounded by Hezbollah in Lebanon, the Muslim Brotherhood in Jordan, and Hamas in Palestine/Palestinian Territories. Palestinian refugees in Jordan could be emboldened to make common cause with extremist elements in neighboring countries. The US would lose a foothold in the region, and Iran's and Russia's spheres of influence would expand.

It could also be a health disaster. Polio had been absent in the Middle East for fifteen years, but in 2014, the virus resurfaced in the face of poor medical care, hygiene, and sanitation caused by the war. Conditions ripe for polio exist in Jordan's overcrowded cities and towns, where most of the refugees abide. It would just take a few infected people to trigger a medical cataclysm. (The same applies to the coronavirus, COVID-19, which has crept into Iraq and threatens the weak health systems of Syria, Yemen, and Afghanistan.) The Gates Foundation responded to this challenge by providing $3 billion for the Global Polio Eradication Initiative, a public/private initiative led by WHO.

Jordan was a strategically promising partner. I had already, for some years, been engaged in promoting interfaith activities with people at the highest levels of the Jordanian monarchy. Therefore, it felt natural to play a role in bringing such a partnership about.

As I wended my way through the maze of the Syrian crisis, I had to find an entry point for doing something meaningful. That meant mapping a route that, however circuitous—and it turned out to be circuitous, indeed—would get me to my landing place. At this phase of my journey, it looked like that place would be Jordan.

The opportunity to do some good through Jordan seemed self-evident to me. But I hadn't taken sufficient note of the geopolitical hurdles that would follow.

CHAPTER 3

LOOKING OVER JORDAN

The Search for an Entry Point

My engagement with Jordan began in 2002 when I attended a speech by Prince Hassan bin Talal at the Oxonian Society in New York. At the time, he was serving as a moderator for the World Conference of Religions for Peace and was the only Muslim member of the Oxford Center for Hebrew and Jewish Studies. Hassan founded the Royal Institute for Inter-Faith Studies, the Foundation for Intercultural and Interfaith Research and Dialogue, and the Arab Thought Forum and served on the boards of the Center for Peace Studies and Conflict Resolution at the University of Oklahoma, the Parliament of Cultures, and the International Tolerance Foundation for Humanities and Social Studies. Because my husband is, like Hassan, an Oxford man, I was admitted to that event.

Prince Hassan had been for years a passionate advocate of interreligious dialogue. And as the founder of the Tanenbaum Center, I was very keen to hear what he had to say. I was enthralled by this urbane, eloquent, witty, and slightly rotund Arab's powerful message of reconciliation and mutual respect.

As Hassan walked down the center aisle to leave, I planted myself squarely in front of him and handed him my card. I was determined to get to know him, and in 2003, because of his life-long commitment to dialogue between religions, the Center honored him with the Rabbi Marc H. Tanenbaum Award for the Advancement of Interreligious Understanding.[1]

During his lecture and subsequent interview with Peter Jennings, Hassan echoed many of the themes I had heard at the Oxonian Society regarding the importance of interfaith activity. That year, Hassan also hosted religious leaders in Iraq and emphatically declared: "I would like to harness centrism—whether Jewish centrism, Christian centrism, or Muslim centrism…in the cause of peace…and put our money where our mouth is and initiate a program of education of the other…. What about doing something *for* a culture of peace in the region, rather than just working *against* terror…."

Our audience was completely wowed by Hassan, and following the award ceremony, he joined one of the Tanenbaum Center's advisory councils. Since then, we have occasionally met for lunch. At one of our meetings, I mentioned that I was in the process of reading the Quran but had been slogging through a translation with antiquated language. Hassan presented me with a recent translation that was much more readable. I read both translations from cover to cover. But it was Hassan's gift that gave me more clarity about this widely misunderstood religion.

In 2006, my husband, son, and I were invited to visit Hassan and his wife, Princess Sarvath, at the Royal Palace in Amman. The visit was supplemented with a tour of Mt. Nebo, where Moses caught his first glimpse of the Promised Land and where he would

---

[1] Recipients in other years included UN Secretary-General Kofi Annan, Ambassador Richard Holbrooke, Notre Dame President Father Theodore Hesburgh, Senator Joseph Lieberman, Bosnian Co-President Haris Silajdžić, Nobel Laureate José Manuel Ramos-Horta, and President Bill Clinton, among many other distinguished recipients.

die without ever setting foot in it. We also went through Madaba, the capital of a governorate in Central Jordan that is known for Byzantine and Umayyad mosaics. Throughout, we were escorted by a colorfully uniformed palace guard.

Two years before, Hassan had hosted our Peacemakers in Action retreat in Amman. One of our peacemakers was an Orthodox Israeli settler rabbi, Menachem Froman, who had dared to cross boundaries to work for peace with Yasser Arafat. He was strongly urged to remove his yarmulke, lest he be attacked in the streets of Amman. He refused and continued to wear his prayer shawl and skull cap for the duration of our meetings.

Later that year, I received a request from the office of Jordan's Cambridge-educated Ambassador to the UN (later UN High Commissioner for Human Rights) Prince Zeid Ra'ad Al Hussein. Would the Tanenbaum Center receive a delegation from Jordan to discuss interreligious programs? The high-level delegation included a diverse group of Jordanian leaders: Sheikh Izzedin al-Khatib At-Tamimi, chief Islamic justice and the king's adviser on Islamic affairs; Sami Gammoh, former minister of finance; Father Nabil Haddad, Jordan's leading voice for Arab Christians; and a female member of Parliament—all associated with the Jordanian Interfaith Coexistence Research Center (JICRC).

They explained that they had been sent by King Abdullah. Their ultimate mission was to stop World War III, which the king believed would be triggered by interreligious conflict. JICRC's mission was implemented primarily through interfaith dialogue events. But they also organized more activist groups, such as Imams for Coexistence, Women for Coexistence, Youth for Coexistence, and Media for Coexistence. They were eager to learn about Tanenbaum's education and Peacemaker in Action programs.

Surprisingly, the group also affirmed its desire to do cross-border work with Israel. They proudly showed us the brochures they had created—which were focused on the need for Muslims and Christians to co-exist. When we asked why there was no mention of Jews, they replied, "Because there are no Jews in Jordan." We pressed further: "How can you talk about cross-border work if there's no understanding of Judaism and its links to Islam or what it means to be a Jewish state?" They immediately revised their material and, some months later, brought a group of rabbis to Jordan. Sheikh Tamimi had explained that he could not go to Israel to meet with rabbis because he would be accused of collaboration. But he was happy to welcome rabbis to Jordan and meet with them there to advance interreligious dialogue.

I met Sheikh Tamimi, Father Nabil, and Sami Gammoh again in 2005, when I was invited to speak at a conference organized under the patronage of the king to mark the first anniversary of the "Amman Message." The Amman Message had been issued by King Abdullah with the goal of clarifying to the modern world the true nature of Islam. This document, an unflinching and courageous statement, coming from a Hashemite king—a direct descendant of the Prophet—should have been of immense interest in the West. Yet, it received almost no attention here. The Amman Message made three key assertions:

- There is no justification in Islam for violence and extremism.
- Islam must engage with the modern world.
- Islam is a religion that respects pluralism.

Fatwas endorsing the Amman Message were issued by Islamic scholars and clergy throughout the Muslim world, across various sects, including those in Arab, Asian, African, and European countries. However, it was not uniformly accepted. Correct Islamic Faith International Association (CIFIA), a Wahhabi organization based in Pakistan, for example, ruled that the Amman Message was contrary to the teachings of Islam.

Just how courageous it was for Abdullah to issue this statement is demonstrated by the coordinated hotel bombings that took place in the lobbies of the Amman Radisson, Grand Hyatt, and Days Inn just a few days after our conclave.

Per the mission statement, the attendees at the conference were there to promote coexistence. In fact, there were almost no participants from the West. But the Tanenbaum Center obtained statements from prominent US clergy that were displayed on large screens during the opening ceremony. For providing these statements of support, Father Nabil whispered to me, *"Georgette, you are a great friend, not just to me, but to Jordan. And every contact I have in Jordan knows about it."*

I was one of only two women with a role in the conference. My job was to give a Jewish perspective on the Amman Message to an entirely Arab audience during Ramadan. As I entered the conference room, I was intercepted by a Jordanian journalist asking whether I was in Amman with the permission of Israel. I had to explain that I'm a Jew, not an Israeli, and I don't need Israel's permission to speak at a conference in Amman.

But once the deliberations began, the entire emphasis was again on coexistence between Arab Muslims and Christians. There was no mention of coexistence with Jews. Where did that leave me and the one other Jew in the room—Ephraim Isaac, an Arab Jew from Yemen and Ethiopia?

While coexistence was being discussed inside the confines of that meeting room, Jordanian television was airing *Al Shatat* ("Diaspora"), a twenty-nine-part Syrian-produced Ramadan special based on the discredited forgery, *Protocols of the Elders of Zion*. Ramadan is like "sweeps week" in the US. It's the peak audience time when everyone gathers around their TV set after the *iftar* (the evening meal that breaks the Ramadan fast each day). What, I posited, was the point of airing a series that served no purpose other than to incite hatred of Jews, while we're in this room discussing co-existence?

After our meeting, I sought out Prince Hassan to ask what could be done about the series. At the same time, Marc Gopin, then-chair of the Tanenbaum Center's Religion and Conflict Resolution Program Advisory Council, reached out to his contacts in Jordan. When the king heard about the content of the series, *Al Shatat* was taken off the air in Jordan.

By the time I read the IRC's 2013 report on the Syrian crisis, I had established relationships in Jordan. I had the ear of Prince Zeid. Prince Hassan had been charged with addressing the influx of Syrian refugees. I had worked with and provided an intern for Father Nabil. Jordan and Israel were in close coordination, and it seemed to make sense to start there. I hadn't considered the political landmines that would line my path.

My first stop was Ido Aharoni, then-Israeli consul-general in New York City. Ambassador Aharoni, a twenty-five-year veteran of Israeli's foreign service, was its longest-serving consul-general in New York. Tall, jocular, and charismatic, Ido was a ubiquitous presence in Jewish New York. After his diplomatic career ended, he became Israel's head of brand management. "No place, no person, no organization, wishes to be solely defined by its problems. Every place has a DNA, a personality, just like a human being," asserts Aharoni. He was very open to hearing about how counterintuitive assistance by Israelis to Syrians could add another dimension to the brand.

I had heard vague stories from a couple of knowledgeable Israelis about Israel opening the Golan border to admit Syrians needing medical treatment into their country. As of this writing, more than 5,000 Syrians have received such services in Israel. When Israel first started treating Syrians in the Golan Heights, they did so in a military field hospital made up of a cluster of what looked like repurposed cargo containers. The boxes had been turned into treatment rooms, operating theaters, and hospital rooms.

People may think that the Israeli military deals only with war, but IDF soldiers are also trained to respond to humanitarian and natural disasters. Since 1953, the IDF has sent twenty-seven humanitarian missions around the world, and they are often among the first on the scene. So when Syrian civilians began to appear at the border needing medical help, it was consistent with the soldiers' training to call for a military ambulance.

By mid-2014, the al-Nusra Front, an al-Qaeda affiliate, had successfully defeated the forces of Bashar al-Assad and "liberated" the Quneitra crossing on the Israel-Syria border. Through a web of ad hoc agreements between locals and al-Nusra fighters— sometimes based on family relations, sometimes tribal ties, and sometimes based on bribes to make them look the other way— they cooperated in bringing injured or ill Syrian men, women, and children through the border fence via ambulance. They arrived on stretchers, covered with green medical blankets and wrapped in their traditional Arabic rugs, many with oxygen masks, with injuries to limbs, heads, eyes. Once in the compound, medics—some in IDF uniforms, others in white scrubs—tended to the wounded.

While a TV crew was there, a child getting his ears checked was handed a giant green balloon and patted on the head by an Israeli doctor. An elderly man, his head wrapped in a *keffiyeh*, was tended to by a doctor who made him more comfortable by giving him a blanket roll to lean against. An Arabic-speaking Israeli interviewed him. Another had a gash in his scalp above his abraded ear, on which a medic carefully applied a sterile dressing. Soon afterward, the first Syrian baby was born in Israel.

The Assad regime was quick to condemn this initiative in the UN. A *New York Times* article on August 7, 2013, reported that the Syrian spokesperson accused Israel of aiding rebels by returning them to Syria after they'd completed their medical treatment. An Israeli diplomat confided that such complaints from the regime were regular occurrences.

In fact, the IDF field hospital asked no questions; they simply treated whoever was brought in—civilian or military. The unknown part of the story was the risk being undertaken by the IDF soldiers who rescued the wounded Syrians, as well as the resources that were diverted from residents of northern Israel to send ambulances to the border for the Syrians.

In general, IDF soldiers felt safe going to the border fence once a week to meet fifty or sixty Syrian children with their mothers. But bringing in men with gunshot wounds was a different story. One day, a Syrian brought a bleeding and unconscious friend to the border. Given the shrapnel permeating his body, a medic immediately transported him to the operating room. When the doctors cut away his pants and shirt to prepare him for surgery, they heard the clang of metal hitting the floor. When the surgeon looked down, he saw between his legs an unexploded grenade that had fallen out of his patient's pants pocket.

All this was heroic and commendable. But it was reactive. My pitch was that Israel needed to be *proactive* in providing aid for Syrian refugees in Jordan. Because of the cold peace with Jordan, Israelis themselves might not be welcome in Jordan to deliver aid. But the IRC had boots on the ground in Jordan, and I thought that Israel might be able to work through them.

Accordingly, I arranged for Ido to meet in May with George Rupp, then-president of the IRC. After exploring various options, they decided to try a pilot in which Arabic-speaking Israeli trauma counselors could be deployed under the IRC umbrella.

Two weeks later, I got a call from George. His staff in Jordan had sounded an alarm: "If we're in any way seen to be in partnership with Israel, our lives are in danger." IRC could not go forward with the plan.

But there was another way. If this couldn't be accepted as an Israeli response, perhaps it could instead be a Jewish response.

In June 2013, I was in Israel with my husband for the Hebrew University, where he served as a board member for decades. Alan Gill, then head of the Joint Distribution Committee (JDC) happened to be in Jerusalem at the time. I knew that JDC co-chaired a group of fifty Jewish communal organizations that had pledged to respond to humanitarian and natural disasters. Alan was, therefore, the key to mounting a coordinated effort in this area. As we sat—incongruously—on blue velvet sofas in a corner of the historic King David Hotel lobby, I made my case for a Jewish communal response to the crisis. "You're right," Alan replied. "I'm going to get right on it."

The following month, I was back in Jerusalem for the opening of the Polonsky Academy for Advanced Studies in the Humanities and Social Sciences, which our family had built. The Polonsky Academy was created to fill the gap created as Israel became a "start-up nation"—the tech and R&D (research and development) behemoth that it is today. The focus on STEM (science, technology, engineering, and mathematics) was leaving the humanities undervalued and underfunded. To address that gap, our family created a post-doctoral research facility for the most promising early-career scholars from around the world. At the same time, we hoped to stem the brain drain in Israel by providing post-docs with fellowships of up to five years.

Because many of our friends and colleagues were coming from overseas to attend the ceremonies, we arranged several tours in Israel from which they could choose. One of the groups went to the Golan Heights. Those who chose that tour reported hearing gunfire from battles raging immediately below, in Quneitra Province in southwest Syria.

The reality of the war, so near at hand, gave special impetus to my meeting with Alan, who, in the meantime, had checked with the JDC leadership and received approval to create a sub-committee of sixteen organizations called the Jewish Coalition for Syrian Refugees in Jordan. Thus began a partnership in which we raised money for organizations providing direct services to Syrian war victims on the ground.

The Jewish Council for Public Affairs (JCPA) immediately sent out a call to action. JDC had infrastructure in place through which I could work with Alan and the co-chair of the Jewish Coalition, Will Recant. It had processes for evaluating grant requests and monitoring their implementation; it had payment mechanisms for distributing funds; and it had the ability to vet the grant applicants to ensure that they weren't fronts for terrorist groups. The coalition received grant requests from a wide range of organizations—both faith-based and secular. Among these:

- *International Rescue Committee* requested support for Syrian refugee survivors of sexual assault to provide medical and non-medical clinical services in Jordan.

- *Brit Olam* requested funds for a psycho-social program for Syrian refugees in Jordan.

- *UNICEF* asked for money to support education in the Zaatari refugee camp in Jordan.

- *Save the Children Canada* applied on behalf of the Multi-Activity Centre (MAC) program to provide young refugees with informal education and life skills activities.

- *Ziv Medical Center* sought a grant to treat Syrian casualties in Israel.

- *Jordanian Red Crescent* needed support to distribute hygiene kits and an Arab trainer for a community-based first aid program.

- *World Jewish Relief* wanted to construct and run two child-friendly spaces where more than 320 Syrian refugee children could play and receive therapy, education, and protection services.

- *IRAP* (International Refugee Assistance Program) needed funds to locate and document Syrian refugees who desperately need resettlement and quickly assist particularly vulnerable refugees.

- *HIAS* applied for help to send a qualified representative to Jordan to aid in resettlement and reprocessing assistance, specifically for refugee children with medical conditions.

Meanwhile, I tried repeatedly to reach Prince Hassan. He had recently hosted a conference on refugees and had a long history of interfaith involvement. Naively, I thought that his refugee portfolio and lifelong devotion to building bridges meant he'd be keen to sign on to this effort. I was wrong. No response to my emails. No response to my phone calls. Complete radio silence. Faisal Hassan, a Tanenbaum board member, also reached out but received no response. "Completely unlike him," Faisal observed. Fortunately, Faisal was able to reconnect me to his close friend Prince Zeid, with whom we met at the end of July.

Elegant, bearded, bespectacled, and trim, Zeid warmly welcomed Faisal and me into his comfortable living room on East 72nd Street in New York. It was an ironic setting for a discussion about human suffering half a world away. But at least the discussion was taking place!

I explained that my motivations were both humanitarian and diplomatic. My goal was to convince him that our humanitarian activities could provide urgently needed help to a desperate population while helping to stabilize Jordan and build bridges between hostile neighbors. In short, humanitarian diplomacy. I briefed Zeid on the Jewish Coalition for Syrian Refugees in Jordan, including the allocation that had been made to Jordanian Red Crescent. I also cited Israeli civil organizations, such as the Truman Institute for the Advancement of Peace at Hebrew University, which was hosting a joint Israeli-Jordanian working team focused on issues of environment, alternative energy, and water.

Water rights were a key point in the Israeli-Jordanian peace agreement of 1994, which specified that the parties were to cooperate in an effort to alleviate their mutual water problems. Water was an even more dire issue now because of the increased demand triggered by the influx of Syrians. Because of the flood of refugees, as well as the dry year, Israel had recently agreed to double the amount of water allocated to Jordan under the peace agreement. Among many rumors circulating at the time was one about a Syrian agent who attempted to poison the water so that Israel would be blamed for killing the Arabs who consumed it. Fortunately, he was caught. Or so I was told. But true or not, it illustrates a conspiratorial mindset that is prevalent in the region.

I encouraged the Truman Institute to find a way to link water and other environmental issues to the Syrian refugee crisis. However, as Naama Shpeter, then head of the Truman Institute reported, "the Jordanians did not respond enthusiastically to our offer to be involved."

I had several asks of Zeid:

- A public endorsement of our efforts
- Input on the areas of greatest need and how to proceed
- A briefing from him for a group of organizations to engage them in addressing the Syrian crisis
- Government-to-government request of Israel for proactive aid

Zeid listened intently and expressed his sincere gratitude for the initiatives being undertaken by the Jewish community. But *realpolitik*—and a reality check for me—intervened.

Jordan is not a signatory to the 1951 Convention on Refugees or the 1967 Protocol Relating to the Status of Refugees. Therefore, it has no obligations to them under international law. However, Jordan does abide by the International Covenant on Civil and Political Rights as well as the International Covenant on Economic, Social, and Cultural Rights. Accordingly, that small country took in 1.4 million refugees fleeing the horrors of Syria. As his country's leading diplomat, Zeid did not want the Syrian refugees to be seen as Jordan's problem; the refugees needed to be positioned as an international responsibility.

"Not even the strongest global economies could absorb this demand on infrastructure and resources," King Abdullah II told the United Nations in September 2013. "My people cannot be asked to shoulder the burden of what is a regional and global challenge."

Zeid also provided a valuable lesson in the realities of refugee resettlement. Although his country wanted them to leave, Zeid acknowledged that the Syrian refugees would likely never return home and that Jordan would have to find some way to absorb them. That meant treading a fine line between hosting the refugees humanely and not making them so comfortable that the world felt free to ignore them.

According to UNHCR, the average duration of displacement is twenty-six years. The Brookings Institution cites an average of ten to twenty-six years. The World Bank challenges that number as measuring the average duration of the conflict or disaster that drives the displacement rather than the actual years that people remain displaced. But regardless of the length of displacement, later Brookings Institution research reveals statistics that have more serious implications for host countries such as Jordan.

There are three solutions for displacement: return home, resettlement, and local integration. Per the Brookings Institution: "In 2016, less than 3 percent of the world's refugees found one of those solutions. Only 2.5 percent of refugees (552,000 people) were able to return to their home countries that year and even fewer, 0.8 percent (or 189,300), were resettled through formal resettlement programs."

That means the Syrians were most likely never going home.

This did not shock me. After all the years of working in conflict resolution—and the years of hearing my late husband talk about intractable conflicts—I was well aware that the odds of refugees going home were increasingly slim. That fact reinforced my determination to find ways to aid displaced persons where they are.

Many Syrians didn't even register as refugees for fear of reprisal by the Assad regime. That left most of them scattered in urban areas, without access to services. In Jordan, only about 10 percent were distributed among the Zaatari, Azraq, and Mrajeeg al Fhood refugee camps. Tens of thousands more Syrians languished in twenty-three camps in Turkey, ten in Iraq, and dozens of camps in Greece and Macedonia.

Under Jordanian law at the time, it was illegal for refugees to work outside the camps. (As of 2017, they have been allowed to apply for work permits in certain sectors, such as agriculture, if sponsored by a Jordanian.) But because they must survive, many work under the radar. That leaves them vulnerable to exploitation and abuse. They are known to be overworked, underpaid, unpaid, and beaten. Women, who mostly find only domestic work, are repeatedly subject to sexual harassment. Because they are working illegally, they have no recourse to remedy their situation.

"Four out of five Syrian refugees live in Jordan's cities and towns, where, being banned from working, they take black market jobs for low wages." The government says this has pushed down wages for Jordanians, too. "The potential seeds of conflict are really there," observed Musa Shteiwi, who heads the University of Jordan's Centre for Strategic Studies.

Because they need shelter, homeless Syrians crowd into whatever space they can find, driving up housing costs for Jordanians. There is also the strain on Jordan's limited resources. Nearly 50 percent of the Syrian refugees are under the age of fifteen, compared to only 34 percent of Jordanians. Schools have been operating in two shifts to accommodate the newcomers. But that's not enough to serve all the children, and a generation of Syrian children are at risk of being lost. At the same time, medical care has to be provided for a traumatized population. (In 2014, Jordan canceled free medical services to 90 percent of Syrian refugees living outside the camps. By 2018, subsidized care was canceled, and Syrians were charged the "foreigner rate," which, for most, is unaffordable.)

All this breeds resentment of the refugees for the pressure they put on scarce resources and a weak economy. And that resentment is further exacerbated by the fact that the small businesses created by refugees in the camps pay neither rent nor taxes, while Jordanian-owned small businesses must pay both.

During the early years of the Syrian war, the unemployment rate in Jordan jumped from 12.2 percent to 14 percent. Despite the pressure, Jordan's GDP actually increased from 2.6 percent to 3.5 percent in 2015, a time when the inflow of Syrian refugees was at its peak. The GDP has since declined from that level by about 1 percent but continues to grow.

Nevertheless, according to a 2014 report issued by the Konrad Adenauer Foundation, Jordan suffered a huge net loss, and its poverty pockets increased by more than half. Assistance pledged by the international community, much of which failed to materialize, covered only 75 percent of the needs. The rest was left to Jordan and the UN system to cover. By 2013, Jordan had to increase borrowing and raise both prices and taxes to cover its growing expenses.

You'd think that Jordan would welcome any help it could get. But Zeid was a pragmatist. Jordan is a constitutional monarchy with a parliamentary form of government. Democracy is limited because of the constant threat of extremism. Among the most potent threats is the main opposition party, the Islamic Action Front, the political arm of the Muslim Brotherhood in Jordan.

Zeid knew he had a conservative Parliament that could create obstructions and feared a backlash if he got too far ahead of his government. Politically, a Jewish communal initiative would be dicey in a country that has no Jews and whose people are so antagonistic to Israel.

Zeid offered that things would be easier if there were a way to channel funds through USAID or the UN, while acknowledging that their source was the Jewish community. But dealing with these massive bureaucracies is, in itself, an obstacle.

Alternatively, Zeid suggested that we scale up to a multifaith initiative, under the Tanenbaum Center umbrella. The Middle East gave birth to three of the most influential religions in history: Judaism, Christianity, and Islam. Through their basic belief in the Golden Rule, those great religions have a great deal in common— which would be one way to obviate political sensitivities.

Political considerations aside, now it was time for them, and other people of faith, to join forces and resources to come to the aid of our Syrian brothers and sisters. Given that I had spent the last twenty years building on my late husband's legacy of interreligious engagement, this was yet another way in which I felt I could be of use.

In a conversation with UNHCR's Shelly Pitterman, he averred that his organization is very focused on the multifaith dimension of refugee work. The high commissioner had been promoting this concept in the belief that the leadership of states will need to be influenced by public opinion and religious leaders. One of the fundamental precepts of all religions is the concept of asylum.

Pitterman saw resettlement as an area of potential intervention for a multifaith group—and it was, indeed, an area on which I came to focus.

I knew from my own experience that religious actors and institutions bring important assets to the table. They have vast constituencies, sophisticated communication networks, convening ability, and street credibility. Above all, they bring moral authority and can serve as the conscience of the world at a time when the world is in great need of a conscience.

I checked in with JDC and got an enthusiastic response to the idea of a multifaith approach, and most of the Jewish Coalition went along with it. In a subsequent call, there was some feeling about this having started out as a Jewish initiative that now needed cover. But in September 2013, the Multifaith Alliance for Syrian Refugees (MFA) in Jordan was born.

Zeid provided a private briefing at the launch dinner for MFA. The invitation had to be carefully worded so as not to create the impression that Zeid was doing formal lobbying for his government—something he had not been authorized to do. But he assured me that there were Jordanian communities throughout the US that could contribute and which he would later "embroider" into the project. Given Jordan's history of inter-faith work, it would be natural to support such an initiative.

Once the embassy staff returned to Washington, DC, Zeid offered to send me a list of Jordanian Americans who might be eager to support this effort to help their native country. That list never materialized. Nor did any private Jordanian funding for MFA. Nor did any Jordanians or Jordanian organizations join MFA.

Nevertheless, having set the wheels in motion, I was committed to seeing it through. This was no longer a simple undertaking, though: there was a start-up organization that needed to hire staff, get funding, and start operating on its own. And I realized I would receive no help beyond the kick-off briefing for MFA. In fairness, Zeid and his wife had been struggling intermittently with serious medical problems. Still, after having received so many accolades for being "a friend to Jordan," I felt abandoned.

But that didn't mean the end of my relationship with Jordan.

By 2015, Jordan's interfaith activities were stewarded by Prince Ghazi bin Mohammad, son of Princess Firyal, with whom I served on the board of the International Rescue Committee. The venerable Sheikh Tamimi had died and Ghazi, a Princeton and Cambridge-educated scholar, succeeded him as Abdullah's chief advisor for religious and cultural affairs. Nominated three times for the Nobel Peace Prize, Ghazi also served as Abdullah's personal envoy and occasional regent when the king was absent from Jordan. In short, Ghazi is one of the most influential figures in Jordan.

That year, Ghazi hosted a gathering of world leaders in inter-religious relations, to which I was invited. The event could not have been more timely.

By then, ISIS was firmly entrenched in Iraq and Syria, partly due to the cynical non-action of Bashar al-Assad. The regime withheld bombing the ISIS base in Raqqa to demonstrate that there were greater threats than his Alawite government. As loath-some as their repressive and violent ideology is, ISIS and the (now rebranded) Jabhat Fatah al-Sham, provided some measure of stability, security, income, and services in areas that had been destroyed by war. It served Assad's purpose to tolerate the pres-ence of ISIS—and that of other extremist groups—in order to support his claim that he was battling terrorists, not civilian opponents.

Days before the Jordan meeting, ISIS shocked the world with an act even more gruesome than their notorious beheadings. The previous month, ISIS had taken hostage Muath al-Kasasbeh, a Royal Jordanian Air Force pilot whose plane crashed near Raqqa, the ISIS stronghold in Syria. ISIS offered to spare Muath's life in exchange for a failed suicide bomber who had been sentenced to death in Jordan. But the government insisted on their pilot's release. Instead, ISIS released a video on February 3, showing Muath being burned alive in a cage. In all likelihood, this hideous immolation had taken place weeks before, while ISIS was negotiating in bad faith with the Jordanian government.

Five months before, in the wake of a meeting with then-US Secretary of State John Kerry, the monarchy had announced its plan to expand its activities to combat ISIS. According to the *Jerusalem Post* of September 14, 2014: "…Jordan had pledged support for the international coalition and offered to provide a base for future US strikes against Islamic State in neighboring countries. Jordan said it would also open its airspace to Western warplanes headed for strikes in Iraq and possibly Syria."

By the time of Ghazi's 2015 interfaith meeting, Jordan did more than provide a base: it took direct military action. On February 5, King Abdullah ordered Operation Martyr Muath, a three-day series of airstrikes over ISIS-held territory in Syria in which fifty-five ISIS fighters were killed.

Ghazi's convening of interreligious leaders opened at the secluded Kempinski resort on the Dead Sea the day after the last airstrike. In the wake of Muath's murder, ostensibly in the name of Islam, our meeting was not an empty exercise. In a note to David Ford, a highly respected theologian from Cambridge University, who had been working closely with Ghazi, Colonel G.A.J. Macintosh, OBE (Order of the British Empire), military advisor to the Jordanian Armed Forces, observed:

> The situation here is sombre and resolute, certainly for now DAISH's [ISIS] actions have unified and strengthened the country. There is the need for strong leadership, loud rhetoric and demonstrations of intent but I personally worry that

51

as time goes on people (west and east) see the problem as a military one and that the solution is therefore military. As you know more than most the fight is ideological and this is the ground we must own. Violence begets violence—this is what DAISH wants after all.

The ideological response was the focal point of Ghazi's meeting. Tall, sleek, and movie-star handsome, Ghazi swept into the ornate conference room bedecked in stately gold and brown royal robes and red-checked keffiyeh. At the top of his agenda: selling the concept of "religicide" to the UN. The four-page resolution, drafted with the shadow help of Zeid, read in part:

> ...threatening, propagating, planning, initiating, executing the killing, cleansing, displacement, destruction, desecration, of religious groups, sects, and communities, constitute a particular form of genocide targeting a religious group when such acts are...deliberate...systematic...and purportedly justified by religious or sectarian aims, or as part of a campaign of offensive religious or sectarian conquest—this crime herein and henceforth being referred to as 'religicide.'

The "religicide" concept spun off from another initiative—the Global Covenant of Religions—that was spearheaded by Ghazi, Ford, Jerry White (Co-Nobel Laureate for founding the International Campaign to Ban Landmines)—all of whom had also helped draft the religicide resolution—and Peter Ochs (a professor of Judaic Studies at the University of Virginia, with a specialty in inter-religious violence and peacebuilding). GCR's mission was to delegitimize the use of religion as a justification for violence and extremism. "Religicide" took it a step further, making it an international crime against humanity. Eventually, GCR came under the umbrella of Global Covenant Partners, for which I served as a founding board member and treasurer. GCR aspired to work closely with religious actors, scholars, and civil society in the Middle East, including the royal family of Jordan, which is what had brought us to this meeting.

By this time, Zeid was the UN high commissioner for human rights—a courageous and wise one, who called out Syrian atrocities and the failure of the international community to respond. After his first year in office, he wrote in his report to the UN: "Unless we change dramatically in how we think and behave as international actors—Member States, inter-governmental organizations, and non-governmental organizations alike—all of us, in the human rights community, will be inconsequential in the face of such mounting violations."

That year, Jordan had been elected to serve a two-year term on the Security Council. Ghazi was satisfied that, as written, the document would pass muster in the UN. Many of us had misgivings, including an ambassador, who counseled that such moves must first be circulated among Security Council members and reviewed through many iterative drafts. But Ghazi insisted it was non-negotiable and preferred a "cram-down" approach because he had the king's approval. We came to realize that our presence at the Kempinski was to be our seal of approval for this document. (We thought we were there to advance the Global Covenant of Religions.)

In the end, the religicide resolution failed to make it to the UN Security Council. A close colleague, who had served in the US State Department, explained: It became clear that the US, UK, China, and Russia would block this Jordanian initiative, even though there was sympathy for Jordan after the immolation of Muath al-Kasasbeh. The US opposed language suggesting new rights for religions. The UK, like the US, preferred to stick with an individual human rights model, rather than invoking new collective rights. China and Russia, where discrimination and violence against Muslims were well known, were struggling with their own religious minorities. Zeid himself confided to a GCR colleague that the resolution wouldn't fly and opined that it might be better to take a more patient approach and make a future run via the UN General Assembly. As of this writing, that hasn't happened; but my colleague still thinks it might. Nevertheless, the need to take a firmer stand against religious extremism was vividly underscored by the Muath video. As a fellow participant observed: "Extremism put into action is terrorism."

Muath's father had issued a declaration asking Arab states to unite to battle against the brand of extremism practiced by ISIS. A Jordanian colleague, with whom I was reunited at the Ghazi meeting, quipped: "Change 'religicide' to 'religiside,'" imploring that we show respect for religion by combatting those who are hijacking religion."

One of the documents distributed at the Ghazi meeting was the "Open Letter to Abu Bakr Al-Baghdadi," the leader of ISIS. (Baghdadi was killed in 2019 in a joint US/Kurdish operation.) This scholarly treatise, signed by hundreds of Islamic thinkers, rebutted ISIS ideology point by point, documenting all the ways in which ISIS violated Islamic principles. However, in order to understand the letter, you needed to be an expert in the Quran and Islam. It would be very difficult for a layperson to grasp its nuanced arguments and wade through its numerous scholarly citations. Accordingly, this, too, did not receive as much attention in the West as it deserved.

Following our deliberations at the Dead Sea, which provided for Ghazi the backing of religious leaders for the religicide resolution, but led to no further action, our group transferred to Amman. There we were joined by King Abdullah and Prince Charles of the UK. In a stately room of Arabic design, they sat beneath a dignified, benign portrait of Abdullah's father, King Hussein. Abdullah spoke movingly of his country's grief in the wake of this latest ISIS atrocity and strongly affirmed his commitment to combatting this cruel abuse of Islam. "This is a struggle within Islam. We can no longer accept crimes in the name of religion...or against minorities." It would have been a good time to re-release the "Amman Message," which, unlike the "Open Letter to Baghdadi," was direct, simple, and easy to understand.

* * *

Following the close of our meetings, three of us, including David Ford and Sarah Snyder, the director of the Rose Castle Foundation in England, traveled to the Zaatari refugee camp. Zaatari, with a population hovering around 80,000, is now Jordan's fourth-largest city and was then the largest refugee camp in the world.

This was my first visit to a camp for Syrian refugees and I felt somewhat uneasy about it. Zeid had warned about the perils of "refugee tourism" and the humiliation camp residents feel when seen in such demeaning conditions. I wanted to be sensitive to that. Nevertheless, to do my work, I needed to move beyond abstractions and high-flown sentiments, expressed in elegant settings, to meet the real people in their real world.

It's difficult to gain access to refugee camps, but our visit was organized by Colonel Macintosh, and we were guided by two very knowledgeable camp workers from Northern Ireland and a Jordanian officer. Zaatari occupies a former Jordanian armed forces field on a vast desert plain in the north of Jordan, near the Syrian border. The camp opened in July 2012 with 15,000 refugees and skyrocketed to 156,000 by March 2013 before settling at half that number in the years since. The once empty space is now filled with endless rows of tents that are gradually being replaced with rows of metal-sided caravans. It's a dreary place, but it is teeming with resilient people. I described my experience in an article for the *Huffington Post*.

I expected to see a place of abject misery—and there was much of that. Syrian refugees are essentially prisoners. If they are caught outside the camp, without having been bailed out by a Jordanian citizen, they are subject to deportation. So they languish among ramshackle temporary structures built on dusty earth. Large families live in small tents or caravans with sparse furnishings. Although I did not personally witness these, there have been many accounts of fires, theft, riots, and worse.

What I did witness was a startling affirmation of life and the building of a spontaneous self-organizing community—a testament both to the resilience of Syrians and the hospitality of Jordanians.

As David, Sarah, and I walked through the camp, almost all the young boys and girls shouted "hello" in English. Some went so far as to say, "How are you?" The adults were more guarded. Yet everywhere there were signs of life.

There is an unpaved main street in Zaatari, which runs the length of the camp. It is known as the "Champs Elysees." The residents stroll or ride donated bicycles up and down the street, which is densely lined with shops on both sides. You can buy almost anything here: baked goods, electronics, bridal gowns, produce, shoes, appliances, hardware, toilets. There are also cafes. All these makeshift shops are made from bits of leftover building material. We ate lunch in a restaurant, constructed of corrugated siding. Its walls and ceilings were painted in vivid hues, and the entrance featured a spurting fountain on which soft drinks were displayed.

In visiting one refugee family of eight, we were greeted with a colorful "Mikey Mous" cartoon painted on their caravan. We were immediately offered coffee, and the children shyly gathered around. I asked the man of the house through an interpreter: If the Syrian civil war is not resolved soon, would he apply for resettlement or stay in the refugee camp? He said he would rather stay in the camp because it is close to home. "We breathe the same air as Syria. The Jordanians are our brothers." But, just the day before, he told us, one of his younger daughters said to him: "I don't want to die in Jordan. Please let's go home."

Unfortunately, that's highly unlikely to happen, given the lengthy average time of displacement for those who flee their homes.

The Syrian refugees are under strict Jordanian jurisdiction. They are policed by Jordan authorities, and while they can form community councils, they are not themselves permitted to serve in an official capacity.

Jordan has permitted some refugees to acquire licenses to operate their own small businesses within the camp. These businesses have created an internal economy that generates a GDP, according to unverified numbers given by our guides, of more than $10 million a month. That's a startling number—but not when you consider that the thousands of aid workers in the camp also need a cup of coffee and chargers for their iPhones.

UNHCR, which runs Zaatari with the Syrian Refugee Affairs Directorate, has nearly sixty staff on site. It works with four governmental agencies and forty-two humanitarian partners, including IRC, Mercy Corps, Syrian American Medical Society (SAMS), and many other UN agencies. According to a 2014 Affordable Housing Institute study, "the 530-hectare camp costs $500,000 per day to operate, paid for by the United Nations (UN), partner organizations, and the government of Jordan."

Each organization operates differently in terms of its ratio of native to ex-pat staff. The workers distribute food, build infrastructure, provide counseling, medical care, education, and the full panoply of goods and services that are essential for survival.

Jordan has introduced community policing within Zaatari and has outsourced its implementation to Siren, a highly experienced Northern Irish firm. Ironically, I had done much of the pioneering work in community policing in my own early career as a consultant to the New York City Police Department. Yet here I was, nearly forty-five years later, in a remote part of the world, being briefed on a program that I had been intimately involved in developing.

The Zaatari community policing stations are designed in such a way that there are private rooms for residents to speak with officers. The officers serve as a liaison between the refugees and the many NGOs providing services within the camp, as well as Jordanian officials. It has taken a great deal of confidence-building, but the colonel who runs Zaatari proudly told me that he has received several hundred reports of gender violence—an indication that the most vulnerable are now willing to come forward with their problems.

The scale of gender violence in the Syrian war was one of the horrors that lured me into the vortex of the crisis. So I was particularly keen to learn how Zaatari was dealing with this issue. Despite the enlightened policing, the camps are known to be dangerous places—especially for women. And, as previously mentioned, women and children make up 80 percent of the refugee population.

Domestic violence has increased due to the stresses of displacement and changes in gender roles. Twenty percent of households in Zaatari are headed by women. That percent is higher inside Syria because of the deliberate targeting of fighting age males—including minors—for arrest, torture, enforced disappearance, and death.

In Syria, where medical workers and facilities are targeted as a weapon of war, women often are forced to give birth unaided and in unsterile conditions. Due to a dearth of childcare options, women are often trapped in the home. Those who can work are subject to sexual harassment.

Women are vulnerable to human trafficking, specifically forced prostitution, child marriage, and "temporary" marriage.

According to a July 2013 article in *The Guardian*, Zaatari even has its own brothel and bar district, where the local boss "has requested that UN officials launch patrols to control gangs of young men wreaking havoc in the camp and harassing women. Groping and lewd name-calling during food distributions and in the public latrines are common."

Many arrived in Zaatari after having been raped and sexually assaulted in government detention. For those who have been raped, there are few services to address their health needs or trauma. Transgender and queer women are the most vulnerable of all. Cultural factors discourage women from seeking help. When a woman is raped, she is the one who is blamed for bringing dishonor to the family. Most will not admit to being raped, even if it means they could be fast-tracked by a resettlement agency—if, that is, the woman is even registered. When it comes to resettlement, women often register in the name of their oldest male relative rather than their own. That means that they cannot be processed for resettlement and a possible escape from their dire situation.

Children, too, suffer abuse. Many have witnessed or been the victims of horrific violence. By virtue of being in Zaatari, perhaps some have been spared the fate of their peers in Syria. There, children have been detained, tortured, and exposed to sexual violence while in government custody. They have been instrumentalized and recruited as fighters and suicide bombers by extremist groups. Five thousand schools have been destroyed and more than half of school-age children have been deprived of school for years. Even in Zaatari, child labor is rampant. Instead of going to school, many must work in order to contribute to the family's income.

While UNICEF, Mercy Corps, and Save the Children provide schooling in the camp, not all children attend their schools. Nor are they required to. What happens when the smiling young children who greeted us with "hellos" become teenagers who have grown up in the confines of Zaatari? If they see no future, they will become vulnerable to manipulation and radicalization.

As reported in *The Guardian* in 2017, researchers at Quilliam—a think tank—ISIS was offering up to $2,000 to recruit in refugee camps in Jordan and Lebanon, while Jihadi groups bombarded refugees with propaganda. Unaccompanied children are the most vulnerable.

A 2015 Brookings Institution report raised another alarm: "The risk of radicalization is especially heightened where IDPs and refugees find themselves in protracted situations: marginalized, disenfranchised, and excluded." In other words, the longer they are left in limbo, the greater the odds of radicalization.

My visit to Zaatari was my first encounter with the people behind the numbers. It reinforced for me the need to humanize the conflict and the parties involved in it. Moving beyond baked-in stereotypes would later prove to be the key that led to a big breakthrough in humanitarian diplomacy.

* * *

The "Amman Message," the Global Covenant of Religions, the religicide initiative, the unprecedented outreach of "A Common Word," (which reinforced the link between Christianity and Islam), the prominent interfaith institutes in Jordan—they all are testaments to King Abdullah's commitment to interreligious engagement. For this, he was awarded the prestigious Templeton Prize in 2018.

As I wrote in my letter in support of the award, the king deserved this handsome gesture for: "His leadership. His courage. His grace under fire. His unwavering commitment to expanding the boundaries of interreligious understanding." But

Jordan never came through as a partner in MFA's work on behalf of refugees.

So I went forward with MFA, without Jordan as my partner. Today, MFA is comprised of more than one hundred organizations across the religious spectrum—including Hindus, Sikhs, and Buddhists—who are committed to undertaking activities on behalf of Syrian war victims via MFA's multi-part mission:

- Mobilize the interfaith response to the Syrian Crisis.
- Raise awareness of the facts and the needs.
- Advocate for sensible and humane refugee policies.
- Cultivate partnerships in the region to plant the seeds for future stability.

With a small budget and a small staff, based in New York, Detroit, and Washington, DC, MFA mobilizes tens of millions of dollars in aid while energetically advocating on behalf of Syrian war victims.

It was the Jews who stepped up first. For many years, I've served on the board of the Jewish Funders Network (JFN), which I eventually chaired. JFN is an international association of Jewish funders, who are driven by Jewish values in their philanthropy. The organization casts a wide net, including both the largest Jewish foundations and modest individual donors, to guide them in giving more effectively, to help them form partnerships, and to harness the power of the collective in addressing the major issues of our time.

At our Fall Board Retreat in 2013, I shared my vision of Israeli/Syrian-Jewish/Muslim humanitarian diplomacy with several JFN members. Among them was Charlene Seidle, head of the Leichtag Foundation, a progressive San Diego institution. She immediately "got it." For a year or two following our conversation, Leichtag dedicated its resources to the Syrian refugee crisis. Linda Mirels of the Kirsh Family Foundation was also part of our spontaneous group. The foundation her father started had provided seed funding for 10,000 small business ventures in Swaziland. She, along with her sister, Wendy Fisher, became major supporters of MFA's work. And we had JDC as a stalwart partner.

For the first few years of MFA's operations, in partnership with JDC, we focused solely on Jordan. But after a year or two, we outgrew the focus on Jordan and dropped Jordan from our name. We also expanded beyond a sole focus on refugees to providing aid to Syrian war victims both outside and inside Syria.

As the applications for grants came in, we noticed numerous Israeli organizations—Israeli Trauma Coalition, Natan, IsraAid, Israeli Flying Aid—applying for grants. That's how we learned that Israeli NGOs were operating both above and below the radar to provide assistance. Although Jordan's stability is of strategic interest to Israel, Jordan could not openly accept aid from Israel because of the threat from Salafists and the Syrian government.

* * *

Only a few days before the Ghazi convocation, I received a note from Shachar Zahavi, then-head of IsraAid, which had been providing treatment in a gender-based violence center for women in Mafraq. "In Arab culture, they are not given much freedom of movement, and young girls and women may need to be accompanied by a male member of the family. They generally have to be careful of their behaviors because of the need to protect the family honor, and any slight hint of impropriety can bring serious repercussions. Because of this, they may feel trapped and not be able to access community services," wrote Zahavi.

"The refugees living in Mafraq suffer from the traumas of war and displacement. Additionally, poverty and severe unemployment lead to frustration, low self-worth, and despair. These trends often lead to a breakdown in social structures and norms of behavior, substance abuse and Gender Based Violence, thus perpetuating the cycles of violence, fear and isolation within the camp."

Hence, the urgent need to build a Women's Center for Syrian Refugees. Starting in November, IsraAid had been sending trauma therapists to build capacity to deal with the psycho-social needs of refugees in the Mafraq Governorate, where the Zaatari camp is located.

Zahavi reported that the Jordanians had asked IsraAid to continue its work there. So did the Israeli government, which well understood the importance of keeping the Jordanian channel open. But it could not openly acknowledge the work of its NGOs without putting their activities at risk.

NGOs, such as IsraAid, led us to a completely unexpected phase of our work and affirmed my notion that a Jewish and Israeli response to the crisis could build lasting bridges between historic foes.

My hopes for a partnership between IRC and Israeli trauma specialists had been dashed, driving me to pivot from an Israeli response to a Jewish communal response. At Prince Zeid's behest, I had converted that into a multifaith initiative. Despite that, Jordan didn't come through for me. In the end, it was JDC and the Jewish community that first supported my efforts. And that's how I learned about Israeli NGOs that were already operating on the ground in and around Syria.

Of these, one organization stood out—Israeli Flying Aid— and that's where our first serious foray into humanitarian diplomacy began.

CHAPTER 4

ENTER ISRAEL

Forming an Unlikely Partnership

M*arch 2015. Three hundred people are crammed into a large conference room. They sit on windowsills and any other nook where they can find a space into which to squeeze. The attendees are Israelis on the campus of the Hebrew University in Jerusalem, and they're here to hear a lecture by a Syrian refugee—the first Syrian most of them have ever seen. The Syrian is risking his life by addressing this audience. He forbids any filming of his face because, by being in Israel, he has put a target on his back.*

The Syrian is Shadi Martini, Sunni Muslim, and scion of a prominent and wealthy Syrian family. A former hospital administrator in Aleppo, he was forced to flee after his network for aiding injured civilians was discovered. But now, in 2014, three years into the Syrian uprising, he is in Jerusalem to promote the unlikely humanitarian partnerships in which he has been engaged with Israelis.

I sit off to the side, retracing the path that had led me to Shadi a few months earlier and brought him to Israel now. My partnership with Shadi was a turning point in my work. His deep knowledge of history and the situation on the ground, his credibility, and his extensive network of contacts enabled me to penetrate circles to which a nice, middle-class Jew from New York would not otherwise have access.

When I first embarked on my Syria work, I called Josh Block, then CEO of The Israel Project (TIP). TIP, a non-partisan organization focused on providing the media with accurate information about Israel, shut its doors in 2019. But in 2013, Josh and TIP were a valuable resource, and I turned to them for help and advice. Josh made several important introductions, including the heads of Syrian NGOs in Washington.

Block's most pivotal introduction was Nir Boms, an Israeli research fellow at the Dayan Center for Middle East Studies, Tel Aviv University. So, while in Jerusalem in the summer of 2013, I reached out to Nir. Prior to that, we had spoken only on the phone.

Before his return to Israel, Nir served as vice-president of the Foundation for the Defense of Democracies (FDD) and as academic affairs officer at Israel's Embassy in Washington, DC. He had extensive experience in policy, government, and scholarship. At the same time, he was an activist, who operated at the nexus of government and civil society in Israel. By the time we met, he had been deeply enmeshed in Israeli responses to the Syria crisis.

It was Nir who told me of an Israeli NGO that had gotten authorization to send goods directly into Syria via a tested channel over the Golan Heights. He also told me of a Syrian refugee who had been working with that Israeli NGO. This unnamed refugee had arranged to bring a Syrian boy to Israel for heart surgery at Save a Child's Heart—a well-known humanitarian organization that provides life-saving cardiac treatment for children who cannot get adequate care in their own countries. Because of his intervention, that child is alive today.

I had no inkling that this Syrian would soon become my trusted partner. Nir also introduced me to the Israeli general who, three years later, facilitated the work that resulted in MFA funneling more than $120 million of humanitarian aid directly into southwest Syria—aid that helped to stabilize an entire region.

It was also Nir who had introduced me to the concept of "humanitarian diplomacy." In May 2013, the World Health Organization had adopted a resolution blaming Israel for the health conditions of the Syrian population in the occupied Golan. In a December 2013 post in the *International Journal of Security Affairs*, Boms wrote:

> Interestingly enough, this condemnation came just as yet another group of wounded Syrians had crossed the Syrian-Israeli border to be treated in a military hospital that was set up for that precise purpose in the Golan....
>
> Syrians—some of them as young as four years of age— have crossed the common border between the two countries seeking humanitarian assistance. The medical services available on the Israeli side of the Golan have become sufficiently well known that one of the recent injured, suffering from a bullet wound to the chest, arrived with a detailed doctor's note in Arabic pinned to his shirt. Lending a hand to the Syrians has not been limited to the military-medical channel. Israeli NGOs have been engaged in humanitarian work from the beginning of the Syrian civil war in March 2011, operating, at times under the auspices of a non-Israeli organization, in Jordan, Turkey, and elsewhere. Via this vehicle, hundreds of tons of equipment (including medical aid, clothing, baby food, tents, and sanitary utensils) have found their way to refugee communities inside and outside Syria.

On an official level, of course, Israel didn't want to take sides in the Syrian war. But, as early as 2012, 300 Israeli civilians marched, in solidarity with their Syrian neighbors, from Habima Square to Meir Park in Tel Aviv. They carried signs reading, "No More

Silence," "Israelis Stand with Syria," "10,000 Syrians Murdered." (The number eventually ballooned to 500,000.)

In March 2015, MFA gave a briefing at the Institute for National Security Studies, Israel's security think tank. In contrast to those marchers, their analysts told us that the northern border was quiet and that it was best to let sleeping dogs lie. To our delegation, that seemed like shortsighted old-think.

Boms understood there was a real risk that the conflict could spill over into Israel's borders. In both 2014 and 2018, for example, Israel shot down Syrian warplanes that had entered its airspace in order to bomb southwest Syria. Nor, per Boms, could Israel risk the Syrian arsenal ending up in the wrong hands.

At the same time, Jewish values required that the Jewish state not stand by and "watch these atrocities from afar." Boms cited seventy tons of clothing collections by the Israeli youth movement at a time when Syrians were freezing to death. The success of Operation Human Warmth was widely reported in the Israeli press. So successful was the effort that the warehouses were filled to capacity and the collections had to stop. He pointed to 900 tons of aid that had been distributed to Syrians by Israeli NGOs as of 2013. The particular NGO he had in mind was Israeli Flying Aid.

In the last paragraph of his blog, Boms eloquently adds:

> When a Syrian rebel, whether a mother or a father, encounters an "enemy" lending a hand, it is a confusing moment. I have personally seen the looks in the eyes of those Syrians who realized that help is coming from the least expected source. This is not an easy encounter, but it is a unique one that enables a rare dialogue that has not taken place to date. While Israelis and Palestinians have been speaking for over thirty years, Israelis and Syrians have never really "met." Paradoxically, Syria's tragedy has at long last afforded the chance to begin that conversation.

My July 2013 stay in Israel was in many ways a life changing experience. Yes, there were the catalytic meetings with Alan Gill and Nir Boms, without whom my Syrian work could not have gotten off the ground. But there was another meeting, not directly related to Syria. That was my encounter with Sari Nusseibeh.

The Nusseibeh family is the oldest Muslim dynasty in Jerusalem, dating back to the seventh century at the very dawn of Islam. So important is the Nusseibeh clan that they hold the keys to the Church of the Holy Sepulcher in Jerusalem.

As a reader, I had been surprisingly moved by Nusseibeh's book, *Once Upon a Country*, in which he wrote about his family's losses in the 1948 war that followed Israel's declaration of statehood. For a person who had suffered so much dislocation, his account was remarkably free of vitriol.

In 2013, Nusseibeh was president of Al-Quds University in Abu Dis. He picked up Leonard and me at the King David Hotel and drove us to the campus, where we spent the day together. As we entered Abu Dis, we were unnerved by the gray separation wall that loomed over the grounds. The wall was originally planned to bisect the campus, but Sari had succeeded in getting it moved to the outer edges. As of now, the cluster of beige stone buildings, burbling fountains, and green shade trees remain an undisturbed oasis in the hillside Arab village.

Before visiting the various faculties, Sari took us to the Abu Jihad Museum for Prisoner Movement on the campus. The Museum commemorates various aspects of the Palestinian experience in Israeli prisons. Leonard and I were surprised by the absence of anger. Yes, there was one wall devoted to torture. But the rest of the museum displayed the writings and crafts that had been produced by the prisoners during their sojourns in Israeli jails. As we wandered among the artifacts and absorbed their impact, Sari said to us: "You know, the thing the Israelis don't understand is that their best partners for peace are former prisoners." Years later, I would hear the same refrain echoed at the launch of the Arab Council on Regional Integration, where one of the delegates said: "Leaders for peace usually come out of prison. They are a resource."

I was struck by this statement because it put me in mind of a fateful meeting in Belfast in 1998, shortly after the signing of the Good Friday Agreement.

The agreement, which ended the nearly thirty-year conflict between the Catholic IRA and Protestant Loyalists, contained a key provision that was extremely difficult for the citizens of Northern Ireland to swallow: the release of all political prisoners. Saying "yes" to that condition meant agreeing to the release of the murderers of their loved ones. Yet, despite the ruinous decades of the Troubles, voters were able to reach beyond their losses and check the "yes" box.

I had been sponsored in Belfast by the late Alan Slifka, a long-time benefactor of the Tanenbaum Center. My purpose there was to attend a conference on conflict resolution and the implementation of the Good Friday Agreement. I was also there to interview two of Tanenbaum's Peacemakers in Action, Father Alec Reid, known as the IRA priest, and Rev. Roy MaGee—both now deceased. Senator George Mitchell, Gerry Adams, and other boldface names received all the media attention. But it was these two clergymen who were responsible for negotiating the ceasefire between the IRA and the Loyalist paramilitaries that made the peace agreement possible.

During my stay in Belfast, I found myself in a meeting flanked by released IRA political prisoners on one side and Loyalist Para-military political prisoners on the other. I marveled that they could sit in the same room to discuss reconciliation and the rebuilding of their communities. Ironically, the released prisoners had become their community's leaders. How did that happen?

These prisoners had been sentenced as common criminals for acts they deemed to be political. Their years of hunger strikes and protests were focused on changing their status from criminals to political prisoners. In the process, they had acquired negotiation and leadership skills that positioned them to be constructive forces in their communities. But that meant being able to put aside their enmity.

Like Northern Ireland's political prisoners, Palestinian inmates were in daily contact with Israelis. While in prison, they gained familiarity with the culture, the language, and the habits of their captors. As a result, I was convinced that rapprochement could be achieved between Syrians and Israelis, Jews and Muslims, through humanitarian diplomacy.

Nir arranged for me to meet Gal Lusky, founder of Israeli Flying Aid. She is a real life "wonder woman." We were joined in our meeting with one of her volunteers, Asaf Hazani, an IDF reserve Lt. Colonel working for the Reut Institute and facilitating Jordan-focused operations.

Their team had been working with Jordanian Red Crescent and other local contacts to deliver aid. Collecting goods in Israel would have been easy to do. But distributing Israeli goods in Jordan could invite disaster. For example, during Operation Human Warmth, all traces of the clothing's origins had to be removed before being distributed to Syrians. In distributing medicines, it was very important to check the expiration date, lest Israelis be accused of trying to kill Syrian patients with tainted drugs. As such, the safest approach was to purchase all the supplies in Jordan, which had the added benefit of supporting the local economy.

When I had my first encounter with IFA volunteers, they had been to Jordan numerous times. Per Gabrielle Charnoff, a representative of one of the mission's donors, "The Jordanian Red Crescent knew we were Jewish and Israelis. The refugees did not."

My first meeting with Gal took place in a modest café in Pardes Hanna, a town in the Haifa district in Israel. I recall my first impression of her—model slim in skin-tight jeans and draped blouse, with dark eyes, long dark hair pulled back into a simple ponytail, and a 1,000-watt smile. An article in the *Daily Beast* had dubbed Gal "Syria's Israeli Guardian Angel," and it was easy to see why. IFA's focus is solely on life-threatening situations. Its mission is to provide search and rescue teams, medical and lifesaving aid, emotional trauma treatment, and mass feeding projects in countries that don't have diplomatic relations with Israel or where regimes prevent the provision of aid.

Syria falls into both categories. In the case of Syria, the government withholds humanitarian aid from the opposition-held areas that are under siege or no longer in its control. But as Gal repeats in many of her speeches, "Nobody asks permission to kill. We don't ask permission to save lives."

Gal's inspiration is her grandfather, an Orthodox rabbi, who taught her core values of Judaism: the sanctity of life, human dignity, the obligation to help others, and to never be indifferent in the face of suffering. The particular biblical verse that he emphasized over and over again became the guiding principle of Gal's life: "Devote yourself to justice, aid the wronged, uphold the rights of the orphan, defend the cause of the widow." (Isaiah 1:16–17)

With its 1,200 volunteers, IFA uses medical clowns to overcome language barriers and religion-based sensitivities when treating little girls who have been raped. ("Are European NGOs brave enough to fund a clinic that will treat women who want to abort after rape," Gal was later to challenge an EU official.) It provides life-saving surgeries. It collects urgently needed supplies for the internally displaced. All of this applied to Syria.

Because Israel is, *de jure*, in a state of war with Syria, Gal was technically committing a crime by aiding the enemy. It is against

Israeli law for its citizens to enter enemy territory. But she risked her freedom in other ways too. By spiriting aid into enemy territory in disguise, and under cover of night, she could be caught and held hostage at any time. During one operation, she entered Jordan in hijab, disguised as a Muslim woman. During another operation, boxes of supplies were carted into Syria overland on donkeys.

Happily, Gal was never tried for violating Israeli law. On the contrary, she was honored by her government. Even more fortunate, although arrested twice in Jordan, Gal was never stranded in enemy territory. She was, however, denied future entry to Jordan by the Jordanian authorities. And for security reasons, the Israeli authorities asked her to shut down IFA's website.

By the time I met Gal, IFA had been operating in Jordan for two and a half years and was looking for additional funds to supply food and sanitary products to Syrian refugees. The goal was to go to Jordan once a month with $5,000 to buy supplies for hundreds of families on a list provided by Jordanian Red Crescent. For that initial grant, and others later on, I served as IFA's advocate with the Jewish Coalition for Syrian Refugees in Jordan. I sensed in Gal a kindred spirit who shared my passion for building bridges between enemies. After all, IFA had been practicing humanitarian diplomacy since its founding.

Gal told me more about Shadi Martini, the mysterious Syrian refugee who had been working with IFA. He sounded like a huge asset in reaching out to Syrians both inside and outside their country. Gal generously offered to make an introduction.

After graduating from university in Beirut, Shadi had gone to work in Sofia, Bulgaria, where he met his Eastern Orthodox wife. His dual passports—Bulgarian and Syrian—enabled him to move freely between the two countries and run his businesses in each. It was in Bulgaria that Nir connected with Shadi through the Sankar brothers from Damascus. At the time, Nir explained, the Sankars were known activists who were ready to work with Israelis and helped Gal open an early channel for delivering humanitarian aid.

During World War II, the Bulgarian government was allied with Hitler. But when the time came to deport its Jews, Bulgarians rose up in mass protest, and that country's Jews were rescued. Some historians viewed this as an act of heroism. Others conclude it was an act of cynicism, lest Bulgaria end up on the wrong side of history if the Nazis lost the war. Regardless of the motivation then, when the Syrian refugees arrived nearly seventy years later, they were greeted with hostility. According to a 2013 UNHCR report—which covered the period when Shadi and the Sankars were there—2,000 Syrians had already arrived in Bulgaria, with fifty new arrivals each day. Bulgaria was overwhelmed by the influx and the refugees faced dire conditions. Up to one hundred families shared a bathroom. People were sleeping in corridors and cooking on flimsy burners in overcrowded dormitories. The processing of asylum applications typically took a year, while refugees languished in detention centers.

After we started working together, Shadi related the story of a town in which refugees had been placed. They were initially viewed with suspicion, so he arranged a meeting in which the locals would get to know the Syrians. After a while, the townspeople noticed that the village hotel and shops were thriving. Because Bulgaria was only a stopping place for the refugees, whose ultimate destination was Germany and other northern countries, they eventually moved on. At that point, the town folk asked when they would get more of the refugees who had been such a boon to the local economy.

Their initial suspicion was not a surprise, given prevailing attitudes towards Muslims in Eastern Europe. As of 2010, Europe was home to 13 million Muslim immigrants and 44 million total Muslims—6 percent of the population. Most live in Eastern Europe. Many Muslims in Western and Northern Europe are relatively recent immigrants, but most in Russia and Eastern Europe belong to populations that are centuries old. Nevertheless, favorable attitudes toward Muslims are much higher in Western Europe than in Eastern Europe—and most Syrian refugees are Muslims.

Gal was with Nir in Bulgaria to meet the Sankars, and they were also eager to work with Shadi. A friend later explained why: "It was your family, religion, ethnicity, your connections, your ability to speak several languages, your open-mindedness, and your ability to travel freely." Clearly, Shadi brought a lot to the table. As such, it seemed fortuitous for Nir to bring Shadi and Gal together while both were in Bulgaria.

As a Syrian, Shadi had been raised to believe that Israel was an implacable enemy that aspired to drive Syrians off their land and kill them. He believed "we have to kill them before they kill us." And he was inculcated with the notion that Jews are the devil because they support Israel.

He later recalled to me one episode in high school that stuck with him to this day. Seven new students had entered his grade. They were "*Yahud*," Arabic for "Jew." They kept to themselves and no one else approached them. One day, they disappeared as suddenly as they had appeared. Shadi was relieved that the "Israeli spies" were gone from his school.

Now here he was in Bulgaria, being offered help by Israelis. What did they want from him? Were they Mossad? After learning that Gal's group had been secretly delivering aid for two years, he found her completely credible. He could find no motive, other than a desire to help. And for the first time in his life, he was forced to question everything he had been taught about Israel. It wasn't the Israelis who were driving Syrians off their land and killing them. It was his own government. The Israelis were the ones coming to the rescue. If the Israeli monster was a lie, what else was a lie? Suddenly, all the certainties he had been fed were turned upside down.

Shadi was of a generation of young Arabs, finding their voice in the Arab Spring of 2011, whose minds could actually be opened up. Ed Husain, Senior Fellow for Middle Eastern Studies at the Council on Foreign Relations, gave a powerful illustration of this change in attitudes during a 2013 webinar hosted by the Jewish Funders Network. He cited the years, 2003–2006, in which he lived in Syria and taught at the University of Damascus.

I remember one day drawing a map in that classroom white-board, and I rather innocently put Israel right next to Syria.... I was familiar that most Syrians have animosity toward Israel but didn't really recognize the depth of it until I drew that map. Almost to a person in that classroom of twenty-six students, men and women were in an uproar as to how dare I put Israel on that map...It was a huge wakeup call that any discussion of Israel, any discussions of the Jewish people, almost always elicited a negative response.

Husain went on to postulate that the Arab Spring had modu-lated the obsession with Israel as an evil interloper. Up until the popular uprisings, Arabs had been indoctrinated to believe that all their problems were caused by the Israeli occupation of Pales-tine. They were taught that they needed to build strong armies in order to liberate Palestine and drive the Jews into the sea. The uprisings had limited Israel's utility as a tool to be used by dicta-tors to prop themselves up at the expense of educating, feeding, and opening up their oppressed societies.

The breakdown of strict censorship enabled freer thought and led to the realization that armies that were supposed to liberate Palestine were instead being turned against fellow Arabs.

Now younger Arabs were turning inward to focus on "bread and butter issues, as well as political transparency in their own coun-tries." This, concluded Husain, "provides an ideal opportunity for

Israel to recast itself and its image among this young generation of Arabs."

Shadi had, to his surprise, become one of those young Arabs.

But this needs to be seen against the backdrop of other elemental shifts in the Middle East. These were powerfully brought home to me in November 2019, when I was a witness to a historic two-day meeting in London: the launch of the Arab Council for Regional Integration.

The attendees were thirty-two Arab delegates from thirteen Arab countries in the Middle East North Africa (MENA) region. Among the participants were journalists, academics, educators, imams, politicians, artists, and other influentials. The best known of these was Mohamed Anwar El-Sadat (nephew of President Anwar Sadat and now a member of Parliament in Egypt). In many of the countries from which they hailed, "normalizing" relations with Israel is, literally, a crime.

Since that time, a number of Arab countries have opened full diplomatic and economic relations with Israel. But back then, they were considered traitors by some of their fellow Arabs. They had assembled at the Millennium Gloucester Hotel in Kensington to forswear ideology in favor of pragmatism; fantasy in favor of reality; insularity in favor of inclusivity. At the same time, they were there to assert the human rights of *all* the peoples of the region—a notion that, in some quarters, was equally radical.

The output of the conclave was a declaration, signed by each participant, that called for the end of boycotts against, and isolation of, Israel and full integration of that nation for the good of the entire region.

Because these were Arabs speaking to Arabs, the discussion was astoundingly candid. What I heard were stirrings of ideas that had not yet been made public, but which heralded new hope for the Middle East.

"The Arab Spring demonstrated that our problems are Arab-Arab conflicts, not Arab-Israeli conflict. We thought the Palestinian cause would unite us, but it didn't. We need to focus on local issues."

"Arafat accepted Iraq's occupation of Kuwait. Iraq is occupied. Syria is occupied. No one is talking about these occupations. Why do we focus only on Israel's occupation of Palestine?"

"There is a culture of hatred in the Arab world—a culture of extremism, conflict, and revenge rather than development."

"It is not enough to say that we tolerate 'Jews;' we must come to terms with the largest Jewish community in the world, which is Israel. Israel is the only country in the region whose existence we refuse to accept, and whose population we brand as 'traitors' because they serve in the army. Why do we not say the same about Iranians or Turks?"

"We must look at this in a balanced way. What happened in Palestine is unique. Millions were transferred and it was reciprocal. 900,000 Jews were forced to migrate from Arab countries and we lost our professional population. It's shameful that Jews fled our countries and now Christians are doing the same. We must preserve the indigenous Jewish heritage of the Middle East."

"We engage in political hypocrisy. Our governments deal with Israel under the table, but our children are being taught hatred and extremism."

These statements are astonishing against the backdrop of an escalating BDS (Boycott, Divest, Sanctions) movement. In their deliberations, the members of the Arab Council had forcefully refuted demonization of the Jewish state; advocated for applying the same standards to judging the actions of Israel as they do other countries; and unambiguously accepted the legitimacy of Israel's presence in the region.

Just before the signing of the declaration, Tony Blair addressed the group via video and summed up the importance of the Arab Council's mission in a few key points.

> Integrating Israel in the region will benefit all parties. It's the countries that have never been involved in a war with Israel that don't have a peace treaty. This is based on the mistaken assumption that it would interfere with the peace process. Ultimately, this has deprived important countries of the ability to influence and assist the process. Every fifth Israeli is an Arab, and they have full rights. The benefits of full integration are clear. The hope is they will translate into political gains.

This groundbreaking meeting and the movement it engendered must be seen in the context of seismic—formerly unthinkable—shifts taking place in the region. Within less than a year of the Arab Council's declaration, Israel and the UAE normalized diplomatic relations. The first El Al flight from Tel Aviv landed in Abu Dhabi, with permission to cross Saudi airspace, on August 31, 2020. This was shortly followed by Bahrain. Bahrain was considered the stalking horse that would open the way for Saudi Arabia to do the same. Sudan and Morocco got there first.

Given the realignments that later took place, one might think the Arab Council's work was now irrelevant. In fact, it became even more relevant. They were preparing the ground at the grassroots with civil society leaders in order to avoid the failings of the earlier peace agreements between Israel and Egypt, Israel and Jordan. Those agreements, between governments only, neglected to prepare their people, and all the decades-long hostility remained. But the Arab Council was doing what MFA was also doing: people-to-people diplomacy.

What a difference a decade makes! When I was invited by the government of Oman in 2010 to meet with its ministers about interreligious programs, they had suspended relations with Israel in response to the second intifada. Yet, in 2018, Israeli Prime Minister Benjamin Netanyahu was welcomed to Oman, and his visit was broadcast on state television.

In his monograph, *Reclamation*, Joseph Braude cites other examples: a Sudanese minister called for civil partnership with Israel; a Kuwaiti writer asked why Arabs should not live in peace with Israel and benefit from its technological achievements; Egyptian-Israeli security cooperation is at an all-time high; the king of Bahrain denounced the Arab boycott of Israel, and its foreign minister affirmed the right of Israel to defend itself against Iran.

Because the interests of Sunni Arab countries are now aligned against Iran, there is ongoing contact between Israel and Saudi Arabia. In 2019, an Israeli General introduced me to a Saudi philanthropist to discuss funding to distribute an Israeli device to visually impaired Syrian refugees and IDPs (Internally Displaced Persons). The General suggested that Israel's involvement be downplayed. The Saudi protested. For him, Israel's role was a key attraction in the story. Who could have imagined this?

There were no Syrians at the Arab Council meeting because they could not get visas to enter the UK. But partnerships like Shadi's and Gal's demonstrate that Syrians would likely have signed on if they'd been present.

Shadi and Gal started working on joint operations about a year before I met him. There were gifts for Syrian IDPs and refugee children in Bulgaria. They brought a Syrian child into Israel for medical treatment. Deliveries of food, search and rescue equipment, and firefighting equipment were smuggled into Aleppo through Shadi's contacts. The materials were packed and shipped from neighboring countries, but not from inside Israel. Their network included people on the border and inside the country.

Gal stressed "the importance of having good friends over the border. Trust must be established from start to finish."

Gal was invited to present IFA's Syria mission on stage at former Israeli President Shimon Peres's ninetieth birthday celebration, and she asked Shadi if he would be willing to send greetings. Wishing to express his gratitude to his former enemies, Shadi recorded a video. Wearing a short-sleeve black t-shirt, with a nondescript backdrop and his face blurred out, Shadi somberly intoned:

> *A Salaam Alaikum,* and *Shalom,* Ladies and Gentlemen. It was a day I couldn't imagine, the day I saw this wonderful Israeli lady, with her wonderful smile, telling me, "We are helping the Syrian people in their hour of need, and we want your help." I was stunned, as a Syrian who just got out of Syria and witnessed the brutal crackdown of the government on a population that was fed up with the status quo and wanted change. Well, ladies and gentlemen, we started working with friends joining us from both sides. In this work, I saw hope for the future, a future with no dictatorship in Syria, where we were taught that Israelis are inhuman and only care about killing. Ladies and Gentlemen, it's a long road and a bumpy one, and people will lose their lives, and the forces of evil will try to hinder us at each step, but it is a battle for humanity, and it is worth dying for. God bless you, Gal, and God bless you all. And God bless you, Mr. President, for this opportunity and for the good deeds you are doing to achieve "Ha Mizrach Ha Tichon [a new Middle East]." And please accept this flag as a sign of this hope.

At that point, Gal's graceful fingers enter the frame, and Shadi hands her a Syrian flag. Those Israeli hands fold the flag with the utmost gentleness and respect and Gal holds it up to the camera in the closing frame. Gal played the video and then handed the flag to Israel's greatest living statesman.

I don't know whether the people who watched that video understood what a tremendous act of courage it was. Shadi, working underground with Israelis, was at risk of being killed by fellow Syrians if his activities were revealed. His aged parents were still in Aleppo, and he had a wife and two children. "I was so terrified when I did this video," Shadi confessed a few years later. "It was still 2013, and I wasn't sure that it was the right move at the time. Now, in hindsight I think it was the right one. It opened so many doors that I couldn't imagine it would."

Having heard from Nir that Shadi was willing to talk to Jewish audiences, I invited him to Miami for the 2014 JFN Conference, where I had organized a workshop on the Syrian crisis. And that was where I finally met this mysterious figure whose courage, in my mind, had reached almost mythic proportions. I'm not sure what I expected. What I found was a dark-haired, fair-skinned man with a shy smile, twinkling dark eyes, a slight wariness, and a contagious sense of humor. When he arrived in the lobby of the Eden Roc Hotel—that slightly frayed, former grand dame of Miami Beach—I happened to be chatting with Rolando Matalon, the senior rabbi of Congregation B'nai Jeshurun on the Upper West Side of New York City, where I am a member. When I introduced them, Roly gave Shadi a big hug and exclaimed that his family, too, was from Haleb (Aleppo).

The panel made a powerful visual statement. Arrayed at the long table were Nir Boms (an Israeli), Alan Gill (an American Jew and head of JDC), and Shadi Martini (a Syrian Muslim). I served as moderator.

Present in the room was Marty Kalin, a Washington, DC-based fan and friend of Shadi's. Marty shared with me that Shadi had drained his fortune in order to pay for the humanitarian work he was doing. He also was using his own money to cover travel to speak at venues such as ours. Marty wanted to explore whether we might do something for Shadi. Indeed, we could: Soon after,

I retained him as senior Syria advisor for MFA. Marty did his bit by making several grants to MFA. Shadi would later be hired as MFA's director for humanitarian relief and regional relations. As of this writing, Shadi has been promoted to executive director.

Eventually, this brought Shadi to Israel for the first time to speak at the Hebrew University. That lecture was one of four that he gave at universities throughout Israel. It was also part of a series of meetings that Gal had arranged with every level of government, civil society groups, and interested individuals, in Israel.

Another key person was also present at our panel in Miami: Roberta Bonazzi, executive director of the European Foundation for Democracy. Roberta was intrigued by the nascent partnership between Syrians and Israelis and thought Europeans needed to know about it. She offered to organize a reveal for the European Parliament and European Commission in Brussels. That's where our work took a serious turn into people-to-people diplomacy—and it's where a Syrian powerhouse entered the arena.

Gal, Shadi, and I formed an ad hoc alliance, which would lead to two years of bringing together influential Syrians and Israelis and making grand plans. Some were thwarted by politics, some by money, and some by friction that would periodically erupt between Gal and Shadi. In the end, Gal would go her own way, and Shadi and I went ours. But together, we prepared the ground for the leap forward that was to come.

CHAPTER 5

BRUSSELS

An Improbable Trio Hits the Road

It is September 2014. Shadi, Gal, and I are in the headquarters of the European Parliament in Brussels. One can only marvel at the huge glass and steel complex with nesting arches that is the hub of the European experiment. The approach to the main entrance is lined with the flags of the twenty-eight (now twenty-seven, with the UK's exit) member states as they lead to the EU's blue flag with its ring of twelve stars. We're here to meet with Members of the European parliament and have been here since 8:00 a.m. We're now about to meet with Spain's MEP, Javier Nart. Having been greeted so graciously by others, we're unprepared for the punishing meeting that awaits us in his office.

True to her word, Roberta Bonazzi had arranged for us to take our Syrian/Israeli/Jewish American show on the road in Europe. The unprecedented partnership between Syrians and Israelis was something on which we agreed we should build. And we could do so in two ways. The first was to raise awareness of the crisis in Syria. The second was to get backing to nurture the nascent partnerships via people-to-people (known in the trade as "Track 2") diplomacy.

At this stage, we were still finding our way. We started with the EU because the opportunity had been presented to us by Roberta. But we quickly realized that there was a convergence of interests between the aid and advocacy we wanted to provide and the governments to which we were giving briefings about our work. Without that convergence, humanitarian diplomacy—or "soft power," as some would call it, cannot be put into practice.

The EU is on the receiving end of large flows of Syrian refugees. At the same time, EU countries are targets of terrorist attacks—almost none of which are perpetrated by Syrians. What happens in the Middle East doesn't stay in the Middle East. And that's why our EU interlocutors were interested in what we had to say. The optics of our improbable trio itself conveyed a powerful message of overcoming hatred.

There was a very practical case to be made. International efforts, focused primarily on finding a political solution, excluded one of Syria's most powerful neighbors: Israel. Technically in a state of war with Syria, Israel's official response had been muted. However, there was an extraordinary untold story of humanitarian assistance to be told, one that belied the one-dimensional perceptions that tend to dominate the global media narrative. (The fact that Israel was then engaged in a war with Gaza didn't help the situation.) The germ of the project we were fertilizing was a necessary dimension of Syrian-Israeli civil society peacemaking.

Israel shares a border with the four countries most affected by the war: Syria, Jordan, Lebanon, and Egypt. As such, it is uniquely positioned to be a staging area for the outbound delivery of international humanitarian aid. Its geographical advantage, infrastructure, and resources mean that aid can be delivered quickly and reliably with goods shipped to Haifa or Ashdod and transshipped over the Golan Heights or directly into Jordan.

In our briefing for the European Commission Humanitarian Aid and Civil Protection Department (ECHO), which took place at the end of our first day, we pointed out that government donations are often directed to refugee camps, but that's not where most of the refugees are found. Between 90 and 95 percent of Syrian refugees are "urban refugees," sheltering in cities or in isolated, desolate areas. Shadi added that aid delivered by European countries goes directly to the Assad regime—under Chapter 7 of the UN Charter—and is not reaching those who really need it. Indeed, much of the aid was ending up on store shelves outside the camps, where it was being sold for profit rather than given to the intended recipients.

Several studies had also pointed out that NGOs delivered larger amounts of aid more quickly than the UN's various humanitarian aid arms. Therefore, we argued, some of the funding that goes to UN agencies might be better spent on NGOs working closely and efficiently with local partners. We were assured that ECHO works only with NGOs and never with governments. Gal was queried on how her aid is delivered and on whether IFA had partners waiting at the Syrian borders. She explained the importance of having good friends over the border and that trust must be established from start to finish, especially between Israeli and Syrian counterparts. Shadi added that their network included people on the border and inside the country.

Because of the multiplicity of humanitarian crises, we were advised that funding for Syria was declining but was still a significant part of the ECHO budget. The main issue faced by ECHO was access to people. Access was something we thought we could offer, and I again emphasized the value Israel could bring to the table in alleviating the humanitarian situation in Syria. But we were told at another meeting with an EC agency that they had no budget for working with Israeli ministries.

Our next meeting was with the MEP from Germany, and I couldn't help being curious about how he would react to this new and unlikely channel between Syrians and Israelis. It turned out that he was a staunch proponent of interreligious dialogue, who was also deeply concerned about rising anti-Semitism in Germany. He was enthused about our story and proposed to talk to other MEPs about linking the issue of Syrian refugees to Syrian-Israeli cooperation.

Afterward, we met with Tunne Kelam, MEP from Estonia, who dubbed our partnership the most inspiring story he'd heard to come out of the world's worst crisis. Kelam was haunted by the question of whether the West should have intervened earlier. Shadi explained that Syrians had been encouraged by the positive outcomes of the revolutions in Tunisia and Egypt. But the West's non-intervention in Syria left a vacuum, and it was this vacuum that allowed ISIS to infiltrate his homeland. ISIS offered money and social services, but ISIS was cynically using Syrian suffering as a way to gain ground in the region and complete the establishment of their caliphate.

The MEP inquired about ISIS's main sources of funding—oil and kidnapping—and called out Iran's deep interest in strengthening terrorist groups.

But ISIS wasn't the only enemy. Shadi pointed out that Syrians saw Iran as an occupying force in their country.

As was well known, the air war in Syria was being fought by Russia, but the ground war was being fought by Iran and its proxies. Qasem Suleimani, the Major General of the storied Islamic Revolutionary Guard Quds Force, was in Syria directing his troops. The 2014 Naame Shaam report, "Iran in Syria," confirmed Shadi's assertion that Iran had, indeed, moved from being Syria's ally to an occupying power.

One of Suleimani's first moves was to create the so-called Syrian National Defense Force—known as the *shabbiha*—to sow terror and do the dirty work of suppressing mass protests. Modeled on the Iranian Basij Force, a volunteer paramilitary organization that counters perceived threats to the regime, the shabbiha are particularly associated with the crimes of looting and rape—both used as recruitment incentives for the NDF.

Iran's proxy, Hezbollah, once revered in Syria for its singular focus on destroying "the Zionist entity," was now sending its fighters to Syria to prop up Assad. Hezbollah, and other Iranian-backed militias, played key roles in securing the Damascus-Homs-Lebanon corridor for the regime in 2013. If Damascus were to fall, the regime would be perceived to have fallen. Therefore, securing Damascus had great symbolic value. Once admired, Hezbollah was now viewed with loathing by the Sunni majority in Syria.

"Iran in Syria" also revealed links between Syria, Iran, ISIS, and al-Nusra. The authors claim that both regimes "infiltrated, collaborated, and used these al-Qaeda-affiliated groups to derail the Syrian revolution…to justify their military actions against Syrian protesters and rebels." The reality was that, as an occupying power, Iran was violating the Fourth Geneva Convention for protecting civilians, while promoting itself and its allies as partners in the fight against Islamist terrorism. The authors proposed action against Iran as an occupying power by the EU, the US, and other international actors. However, the main strategy invoked by the US was to let Iran get mired in its own Vietnam and do a "slow bleed" of money, resources, and lives that would eventually lead to Iran's collapse. So far, Iran has been able to hold out longer than the Syrian people who suffer the consequences.

In my view, that made the potential role of Israel all the more important. When I asked Kelam whether the European Parliament would be willing to host people-to-people dialogue between Syrians and Israelis, he indicated an interest in introducing the idea to a broader base. But, he warned, the European Parliament is biased and the approach to Israel is unbalanced. The Israeli government is perceived as a "problem."

The extent of the unbalanced approach was evident when we reached the office of Spanish MEP Javier Nart, a former journalist and politician with a full mane of long silver hair.

As we sat down at his conference table, I introduced myself and explained my personal story as a Hungarian refugee to provide context for my engagement with Syrian war victims. He immediately asked whether I was aware of the Spanish Ambassador, Angel Sanz Briz, who provided assistance to refugees escaping the Holocaust during World War II. Nart was sharing his knowledge of the Holocaust, but Briz's story was new to me.

I later learned that Briz had been appointed to the post of chargè d'affaires at the Spanish Legation in the summer of 1944. Known as "the Angel of Budapest," he saved 5,000 Hungarian Jews from deportation to Auschwitz by setting up a series of Spanish safe houses and International Red Cross-branded facilities in the Nazi-occupied city. His deeds are enshrined at the Yad Vashem Holocaust memorial in Jerusalem as one of the Righteous Among the Nations.

Briz's story put me in mind of Bassam Barabandi, a heroic Syrian diplomat whom I had met in Washington, DC. Working out of the Syrian embassy in Washington, he had secretly provided passports for nearly one hundred Syrian activists, enabling them to flee their country and campaign against the regime that Barabandi officially represented. Barabandi eventually applied for asylum in the US and now heads People Demand Change, whose mission is to provide short-term aid and long-term support to build up the civil society sector in the Middle East. PDC would later become one of MFA's key partners in delivering aid to northern Syria.

In a note of introduction Barabandi sent to a colleague, he explained:

The Syrian crisis changed a lot of concepts and ideas, and one of them is to get direct help from the American Jewish community to the Syrian refugees.

The point is not only humanitarian but also big step for the future relations between the Jewish and the Arabs and especially the Syrian. When Iran and Russia send the weapons to kill us the Jewish should send us the food and the medicine....

But Nart had his own preconceptions. As Gal started explaining the work that IFA was doing in Jordan, he kept interrupting with questions: Can Israeli NGOs work freely in Jordan? Do they have to use pseudonyms? Do they have to work with other NGOs? Can they use their Israeli passports in Jordan? Gal explained that some Israeli NGOs have to use foreign organizations to deliver aid. It was clear that Nart was disinclined to believe anything Gal said.

I pointed out that it's not only Israeli NGOs that are providing aid. It was also the Israeli government, via the field hospital on the Golan Heights run by the IDF for the express purpose of aiding injured and ill Syrians who cross over the border at night.

Nart was skeptical. He was shocked that the Israeli authorities allowed civilians to cross the border. He said he had extensive experience working in Syria and expressed his passion for that country. "I don't believe that Israel is opening the border. I've been to the border fence. I've seen the separated families crying." And he was outraged by Israel's actions in the Gaza war that had been raging that summer.

Until Shadi stepped in, Nart would not believe that Israel was actually taking care of Syrians in need of medical care.

"Sir," retorted Shadi, "I share your concern about what's going on in Gaza. I see outrage from the West about the war in Gaza. But where are the protests in the street about what is happening in Syria? Don't you understand that when all your energy is devoted to bashing Israel, the world is ignoring what is happening to Syrians?"

That got Nart's attention, and he became much more conciliatory. "I'm ashamed of the cynical approach of the European Union and the European Parliament to the Syrian crisis," Nart acknowledged. He was incensed that only now, with the emergence of ISIS, did the world become concerned, and he emphatically agreed with double standard Shadi had pointed out. "The crimes committed in Gaza, which everyone is more interested in today, are not more important than the crimes in Syria." Nart slammed the hypocrisy of focusing so much condemnation on Israel and so little on other aggressors in the region. "The West should have helped the Syrians three years ago. Military intervention then would have been much better than dealing with ISIS now... As a result of this crisis, Syrian society will be irreparably fragmented."

Nart had suddenly shown a complete change of heart. "Cooperation between Syrians and Israelis is a truly revolutionary approach, and I believe it can work," Nart concluded.

We believed it too—especially after a wholly unexpected dinner the evening before.

The Martini clan is vast, with relatives in seemingly every country. One of Shadi's cousins, Dr. Mohammed Ammar Martini, heads Orient for Human Relief. The founder and sole funder of Orient for Human Relief is Ghassan Aboud, a hugely successful Syrian entrepreneur who, like Dr. Ammar, hails from Idlib. The Ghassan Aboud Group is an international conglomerate engaged in several business sectors—automotive, logistics, media, hospitality, real estate, retail, and catering. But it was Ghassan's ownership of Orient Media Group that would prove to be critical for our nascent partnership.

Orient Media, the only private channel operating in the Syrian Arabic dialect, began broadcasting in Syria in February 2009. On July 27, Orient was on the air when armed Syrian Internal Security

Forces raided the Orient offices in Damascus and Aleppo, shut down its broadcasts, and forcibly ejected all the journalists and photographers, whose only weapons were pens and cameras. Ghassan's house and personal property were confiscated, and he became the target of frequent threats.

Ghassan moved Orient Media—and his family—to Dubai, where he could broadcast freely and was often critical of the regime. He also bought a mansion in Brussels, the former home of an ambassador, where he was in residence at the time of our EU meetings.

The evening before our meeting with Nart and the other MEPs, Shadi had wrangled a dinner invitation from Ghassan. Departing from the civic center of Brussels, Gal, Shadi, and I found ourselves taking a long taxi ride to the city's wooded outskirts. When we finally arrived at Ghassan's gated estate, he greeted us effusively, along with his gracious wife, Nahed, who had prepared an abundant spread of traditional Syrian lamb, stewed chicken, rice, dips, and vegetable dishes. After dinner, we adjourned to the living room. Reclining on velvet seats, with many varieties of rich Syrian baklava arrayed before us, I settled in to listen to Ghassan expound on his vision of a new Syrian-Israeli relationship and the message he wanted Gal to carry back to her government. That message was spelled out in an astounding letter he sent two-days later:

> In 1996, there were vibes that a peace treaty between Hafez Al-Assad's regime and Israel can be brought up to existence; Major General "Ali Heydar," an Alawi, and the leader of what is known as the "Special Forces," had gathered a large number of Alawi military officers to express his dissatisfaction, saying: "the Alawite control of Syria will come to an end someday, twenty or thirty years from now maybe, but eventually the majority, Al-Sunna, will govern the country again, but

Al-Sunna will remind us for generations and generations that we were the ones to raise the Israeli flag on an Israeli embassy in the heart of Damascus, and the following Alawi generations will bear the consequences. If Sunna were to build connections with Israel, let them do it when they are in charge of the country; we as minorities cannot bear this responsibility."

In other words, it's unrealistic to think that the Alawites, as a minority in Syria, could take the risk of signing on to an unpopular peace with Israel, for which the government had laid no ground to prepare its people. As such, any peace treaty with the current government was doomed.

He went on to cite a visit that Kamal Al-Labwani had paid to Israel the previous month—a visit that had been denounced mostly by Syria's educated minorities, but by few Sunna. By contrast, he mentioned a meeting between the Syrian regime's Grand Mufti Ahmad Hassoun and Israeli's Chief Rabbi David Lau, which had attracted no criticism. It was strange to see Rabbi Lau's name brought up in this context. My late husband had laid much of the groundwork for the Vatican-Israel accords that were ratified at the end of 1993. The following year, the Tanenbaum Center co-hosted the first post-Accords conference in Israel, and it was there that Lau had, for the first time, agreed to meet with Catholic prelates. All these years later, it took this letter from Ghassan for me to learn that he had also met with the Syrian Mufti. Lau had come a long way in interfaith engagement!

Ghassan took these as indicators that the Sunna were the most promising partner for building "strategic, long-lasting connections between the Syrian and Israeli people." Far more productive than working through the dictatorships whose survival was based on hatred of Israel.

On the Israeli side, Ghassan opined that the most compatible partners were likely on the left. But, as has so often been the case in the Middle East, the most progress would end up being made by the right.

He went on to argue that it is in Israel's interest to establish a safe zone for Syrian war victims. Without that, ISIS could easily access Israel with chemical and other weapons of mass destruction.

He then cited the field hospital that the IDF had set up to provide medical treatment for injured Syrians on the border and said that this operation had resonated through the medical media in Syria. Indeed, Orient's TV channel, radio, and website had covered this development and received no criticism for doing so. Therefore, Ghassan could envision Magen David Adom (Israel's national emergency medical, disaster, ambulance, and blood bank service) providing medical assistance to Syrians—paving the way through an international organization.

If I were to summarize Ghassan's point, it is this: Whatever the outcome of the Syrian civil war, Israel will always have a Sunni majority on its northern border. During all the years of peace negotiations that went nowhere, Israel has been dealing with the Alawite minority that controls the government. It is in Israel's interest to develop a relationship with the Sunna because only a majority can make peace with Israel legitimate. The current crisis has provided the opportunity to do so. And Ghassan had detected signals among the Sunna that there was a reduction in resistance to dealing with Israel.

"I have the power of money and media, but I need a roadmap," Ghassan asserted as we sat with him. Whatever positive action Israel takes, and at tremendous risk to himself, Ghassan said he would attend a press conference and use his media empire to publicize the results. At the same time, he insisted that we needed more than NGOs. He needed a signal from the Israeli government in order to go forward. These signals might include enforcing the agreement of 1974 and establishing a no-fly zone forty kilometers from the Syria-Israeli border. Or helping to develop the agricultural economy of the Horan area between Israel and Jordan. This would ensure that local tribes would be a buffer against extremists and also help stabilize Jordan. Ghassan was ready to bring together ten businesspeople to help if Israel would send its Arab citizens to help. Finally, he pressed for a free trade zone in the Golan.

We tried to make the case in Brussels for humanitarian engagement with Israel. But in 2014, there were no takers. Israel was politically toxic, and government entities were not willing to rise above politics. Politics was one issue, but there was also the effectiveness of the donations that were being made.

Fortified by the power of Ghassan's vision—and Javier Nart's about-face the next day—Gal, Shadi, and I felt encouraged to embark on a series of historic people-to-people meetings that brought a small group of influentials together from both sides to create the road map that Ghassan was seeking. The outcome was a two-year process that identified six areas of Syrian-Israeli partnership, of which we were able to jump-start two. With this foundation, we achieved a major breakthrough—albeit not with our original partners.

CHAPTER 6

BUMPS IN THE ROAD

People-to-People Diplomacy

"Today, religious and ethnic identity play a huge role in setting the world's agenda... I have had occasion to witness the powerful and positive force of religion in promoting peace in communities torn apart by intractable conflicts... Religiously motivated men and women are a necessary component of Track 2 diplomacy."

—AMBASSADOR RICHARD HOLBROOKE,
Foreword to Tanenbaum Center's *Peacemakers in Action: Profiles of Religion on Conflict Resolution,* 2007

I came to know the late Dick Holbrooke, who served on the board of IRC, after he was honored by the Tanenbaum Center in 1997. It was Holbrooke who inspired what eventually became one of our signature programs: Peacemakers in Action. He impressed on me the importance of publicly identifying religious peacemakers for recognition, support, and training. He felt strongly that public awareness of their work would provide these courageous grassroots leaders with a measure of protection and make it more difficult to marginalize or kill them.

Peacemakers in Action was distinct from most of the work that had been done on the role of religion in conflict resolution. While most prior work focused on the role of institutions, the Tanenbaum Center focused on the pivotal role of individuals. As such, our work filled a void in the field. Today, the Tanenbaum Center has a network of peacemakers, operating in conflict zones around the world, and two books have been published to highlight their work.

Their effectiveness derives from their position in their communities. They have "street cred" because they are indigenous. They understand the suffering of their people and have standing to speak to all sides. Nearly all work at the grassroots level, yet they have a profound sense of isolation. Rather than run from what they find painful, they work to alleviate the pain of others. Some of the peacemakers created zones of peace in which violence was suspended. Others used interfaith mobilization as a tool. Still others used the media to raise awareness of humanitarian crises.

Although the peacemakers program predated, by years, my "aha moment" about the Syria crisis, the lessons learned from it laid the groundwork for the people-to-people diplomacy on which I was embarking with my new Syrian and Israeli partners.

Syria and Israel were technically in a state of war since 1948—the year that Israel declared its statehood. With the assassination of King Abdullah of Transjordan and a series of coups in Syria, Israel lost the potential partnership of two of its neighbors. In the intervening years, three wars were fought between Israel and Syria: 1948, 1967, 1973. These don't include the wars in Lebanon, a country largely controlled by Syria.

Various armistice agreements have been reached, including a disengagement agreement brokered by Henry Kissinger in 1974. Peace negotiations were held during the 1990s, with all issues largely resolved. But each time when it came to signing on the bottom line, either Ehud Barak or Hafez al-Assad walked away.

As things stand, there are no diplomatic relations between Syria and Israel. Syria does not admit anyone with an Israeli passport or an Israeli visa stamp. Nor does Israel generally admit Syrians—and that would prove to be a critical issue for us down the road.

I was eager to find an entry point for bringing together these sworn enemies in the service of finally doing some tangible good. Now I thought I had found it. It would mean engaging in a lot of talk before we got to any action. And when the time for action finally came, it would be with a different set of partners than I had expected. But all that talk was necessary for strategizing, confidence-building, and laying the groundwork for the real stuff to follow.

The goal was to seed good relations in the southwest region and, from there, to expand to the whole of Syria. The tools would be the delivery of massive amounts of aid directly into Syria and media campaigns that would debunk Syrian's and Israeli's misperceptions of each other.

All did not go smoothly. Much of what we planned never materialized. We had to break through personal and political barriers. Foreign interventions, elections, breakdowns in trust, broken promises about financing—all interfered with building the bridges that could pave the way for future stability.

Many of the Tanenbaum peacemakers were clergy. Gal, Shadi, and Ghassan are laypeople. But like Tanenbaum's peacemakers, their courage and activism drew heavily on their identities as Jews or Sunni Muslims. And like Tanenbaum's peacemakers, they initially felt isolated and under threat.

In preparation for the Brussels briefings described above, I met with the Syrian Emergency Task Force and the Syrian Action Committee in Washington. I had been hoping they would join

MFA—and they did. But when I floated the idea of their CEOs joining Shadi, Gal, and me on a panel organized by EFD, they demurred. One senior staffer expressed concern about being on a panel with Israelis and Jews because of potential "blowback."

Yet, during our meetings, I heard words I never expected to hear from Syrians: "God bless the Israelis" and "one of our most valuable allies are the Jews."

Although neither SAC nor SETF could publicly align themselves with anything having to do with Israel, they felt that the time would come. Bassam Barabandi, the defected Syrian diplomat whom I met in late 2014, saw outreach to Israel as a win-win. He disclosed that there was active discussion among Syrian elites and intellectuals about engaging with Israel. Even the Islamic Front was open to Israeli involvement. Bassam understood Israel's concerns and the ways in which the Syrian war could spill across its borders: al-Qaeda, chemical weapons, Hezbollah, the Golan Heights. Hezbollah, he disclosed, planned to go to the Golan Heights disguised as the Free Syrian Army so they could conduct operations against Israel. That proved to be prophetic four years later.

"Syria needs to feel that Jews and Israelis are with us," Bassam declared. On his wish list from Israel was a no-fly zone in Syrian airspace to protect civilians from unrelenting bombardment. "We need something people can see in three to four months."

My hope was that the briefings being organized by EFD in Brussels for September would provide concrete results for Syrian war victims while demonstrating Israeli and Jewish commitment to alleviating their suffering.

When I saw Bassam again in August, I expressed my disappointment that SETF would not participate in those briefings because of the Israeli presence in the inoffensive form of Gal Lusky. Bassam was sensitive to my frustration about the unwillingness of Syrian organizations to acknowledge the humanitarian efforts being undertaken by Israelis. "People are aware of it," he explained, but with the 2014 Gaza War in full throttle, "It's difficult to deal directly with Israel now." There's nothing we can do to alter the current crisis, he continued, "but we need to focus on the future…Syrians are in great need." He insisted that it had to start with help from the American Jewish community and that this would lay the groundwork for outreach to Israel.

In a *Washington Post* op-ed, Raed al Saleh, head of the Syrian civil defense group, White Helmets, describes its motto as: "to save one life is to save all humanity." Ironically, that motto originates in Jewish scripture.

All this convinced me—again—that humanitarian diplomacy is a powerful instrument for building bridges and making peace. We would learn that by working with local councils and grassroots partners, we could stabilize a region, break down preconceptions, and change hearts and minds. We also learned how fragile such détentes can be. And I ultimately learned the limits of bridge-building.

Less than two months after the launch of MFA, and only a few months before these discussions, a Turkish televangelist, Adnan Oktar, hosted two Israelis and a Syrian on his TV program. (Oktar was later arrested for leading a cult and accused of sexual slavery, sex with minors, fraud, and a host of other crimes. His guests were not implicated.) Rabbi Yaakov Margi, affiliated with the Shas party in Israel, was a member of the Knesset and later named "Outstanding Parliamentarian" for his work on behalf of education and social justice. Muhammad Adnan Hussain, a somewhat marginal Syrian opposition figure, chaired the Future Syrian Revolutionary Assembly. Also present was Mendi Safadi, a Druze member of Likud, and a liaison for Israel to Syrian dissidents.

It was remarkable that they were in the same studio together. Even more remarkable was what they said.

Hussain declared: "It has been shown clearly to the Syrian people that this killer and his oppressing regime has invented a

lie…about an eternal enemy [Israel] who threatens us. But it has
been discovered that the real enemy of this region is the criminal
pyramid of the Assad family, Hezbollah, and Iran. This generation
has come to believe that Israel isn't the enemy, but the enemy is
the one who destroyed the country, killed its children and women
and men, and made its people homeless."

Margi added: "We are seeking…with other brothers from
the liberal Syrian opposition, to come together and go forward
together strongly and bravely toward peace and democracy and
for a common life for both people."

Having been ignorant of Oktar's predations at the time, I
took these sentiments to heart. And I would hear them echoed by
others in the years ahead.

One part of MFA's multipart mission is to plant the seeds for
future stability in the region through humanitarian diplomacy.
According to a 2015 white paper by the Geneva Platform on
Peacebuilding, the security landscape in many regions is fluid,
buffeted by conflict, instability, and proliferation of non-state
militias and foreign fighters. This volatile brew leads to chronic
violence as each faction fights over the state. The white paper
goes on to describe new types of armed actors with shifting affil-
iations and the impact of violence on women, children, and the
elderly. It also cites "the willingness of individual peacemakers to
take risks for peace—sometimes involving significant personal
danger…and novel ways of tackling new and old problems." This
would prove very true for our nascent team. And we would have
our ups and downs, complete with recriminations, betrayals, and
deep schisms.

Diplomacy at the government level can be slow, enervating,
and ineffective. Negotiations can seem fruitless. Talk can feel
endless. Even when agreements are finally reached and treaties signed, their successful implementation often depends on
preparing the people who must live with them. Witness the cold

peace between Egypt and Israel and Jordan and Israel. Engaging people is done through informal diplomacy that takes place at the grassroots level or at a level between the grassroots and officialdom. It's the buy-in from the people that confers legitimacy on accords decided at the government level.

Diplomats have their own jargon, so I need to briefly explain the terms that define the work on which our trio—now a quartet—had embarked.

Track 1 is formal government-to-government diplomacy.

Track 1.5 is government-to-civil society diplomacy.

Track 2 is informal people-to-people diplomacy, in which non-government actors—citizen-diplomats—find solutions to conflict or prepare the ground for the implementation of the formal work that goes on at the Track 1 level.

In Nir Bom's experience, humanitarian work helped create the bridges that were beginning to be used for diplomatic purposes at senior levels. What was most interesting was the humanitarian corridor into southern Syria. Injured Syrians were being transported in and out of that area. But the same corridor was also being used for high-level diplomatic meetings.

The process we were proposing would, inevitably, deal with sensitive issues. Nir's advice was that the civil society track should be public and the government track private. Of course, given the collapse of government in Syria, there could be no Track 1 process. Nor had the mostly secret diplomacy coming out of Madrid in 1991 yielded results in all the years since. The first Gulf War, in which Syria joined the US-led coalition against Iraq's invasion of Kuwait, along with the fall of the Soviet Union, created the impetus for Syria to come to the table. But, as previously discussed, the ruling Alawite minority saw any peace treaty with Israel as a death warrant.

Track 1 negotiations notwithstanding, Shadi recalled: "During the time I was living in Syria, I never noticed any change in the message of hate toward Israel. On the contrary, the influence of Iran in Syria was getting stronger. Hamas had its headquarters in Damascus and Hezbollah was getting steady [arms] shipments through Syria. And the bashing of other Arab countries trying to get normal relations with Israel never stopped." Clearly, any progress would have to be informal.

Following our work with EFD in Brussels, it was agreed that our core group would include only Syrians and Israelis. Gal put together her "hit" list for the Israeli delegation. They included influentials who were close to government. Most had served as high-ranking officials in the military, ministries, intelligence services, as well as industry. She also brought her husband, Yisrael Hasson, into the process.

Yisrael, a Syrian Jew who was born in Damascus and fled to Israel at age seven, had been Israel's envoy to Arab countries under five prime ministers. Formerly deputy director of Shabak (the acronym for Israel's Security Agency) and a member of the Knesset, he was now chair of the Israel Antiquities Authority. A man of immense charm and great achievement, he was our direct link to Prime Minister Bibi Netanyahu and our assurance that our activities had the informal sanction of the government. My husband and I instantly adored this lanky, warm, teddy bear of a man. The feeling seemed to be mutual. In planning one of our meetings, Gal confided that Yisrael said, if I wasn't present, he was staying home. He would prove to be an important link to our Syrian partners.

On the Syrian side, things were more complicated. "We now have a different situation in Syria," explained Shadi. "The regime is under full control of Iran" with limited ability to maneuver. The opposition is made up of different players with different agendas. According to Shadi's nuanced analysis, the Islamic radicals, such as ISIS, have no interest in any relationship with Israel. But groups such as al-Nusra are willing to deal with Israel on a tactical level in order to maintain quiet borders.

As previously mentioned, al-Nusra's active cooperation with locals in southwest Syria enabled Syrians in need of medical treatment to reach the border fence with Israel. However, there were no direct dealings between al-Nusra and the IDF. On the contrary, an IDF colonel made it clear to me that if al-Nusra approached the border, the IDF would open fire.

Islamic groups, such as the Muslim Brotherhood, are willing to deal with Israel, but only as a tactic. The moderate groups are splintered. The nationalist Arab groups don't want to deal with Israel. But some nationalistic Syrian groups see a tactical advantage in working with Israel in order to strengthen their own positions. Kurdish groups see Israel as a natural ally and would welcome working with them. (This would become relevant in 2018 and 2019, after regime forces, with the backing of Russia and Iran, launched a deadly offensive in southwest Syria.) Other moderates see mutual economic and security benefits in partnerships between Syria and Israel. We agreed that this was the group to target in our humanitarian diplomacy and saw this as an opportunity "to change the narrative from mutual destruction to mutual benefit."

Shadi averred that Syrian opposition and military leaders on the ground were willing to engage with Israel. But the presence of radical elements inside Syria made any *public* contact very risky during this volatile time. Like Nir, he determined that we needed a dual approach. The Track 2 process could be public, and the Syrian delegation should include Christians and Druze, with a majority being Sunni.

The situation with the Druze was complicated. There are Israeli Druze and Syrian Druze. When Israel conquered the Golan Heights in the 1967 War, a number of Druze villages were nestled along the border. Some chose Israeli citizenship. But the Druze population inside Syria tended to side with the Assad government. Like the Christians, they feared that the downfall of Assad would result in a state dominated by Sunnis or the Muslim Brotherhood, in which the Druze would be persecuted.

The clandestine Track 1.5 process was meant to be made up of people who have influence on the ground in Syria and the government of Israel. The idea was to work with a small group that could exert influence on their respective constituencies and buffer the public track against the incoming fire it would take. Some of the groundwork had been laid by Kamal Al-Labwani, one of the few Syrians willing to visit Israel and speak publicly.

Dr. Labwani, a physician, had been a leading opposition figure, twice imprisoned by the regime. He eventually fled to Jordan and was later granted political asylum by Sweden. Since then, his base of operations was Turkey, working for the Syrian National Council, from which he eventually withdrew to function independently.

In 2014, Labwani proposed a public initiative for cooperation and peace with Israel. In the wake of the failure of the Geneva peace talks, sponsored by the US, Russia, and the UN, he saw Israel as the military power that could break the logjam in the Syrian civil war. On the military level, he envisioned Israel as a factor in enforcing a no-fly zone in southern Syria. Because of its anti-aircraft systems, Israel could shoot down, within sixty seconds of takeoff, any Syrian jet flying in the one hundred-kilometer area between Damascus and the Golan Heights—without violating Syrian airspace. On a diplomatic level, the plan called for Israel to remove its objection to ousting Assad and agreeing to the provisioning of arms to opposition forces by the Western allies.

Labwani saw substantial benefits to both sides: For Israel, Hezbollah would be thwarted in building outposts in Syria from which to attack Israel. At the same time, a victorious opposition would take war with Israel off the table and begin the work toward a peace agreement. For Syria, the plan would prevent that country from sliding into extremism—which would also be a threat to Israel. Labwani anticipated, by years, the core principles of the Arab Council on Regional Integration and the benefits to the entire region for a warm peace with Israel. He saw Syria as the lynchpin that would make that possible.

But when it came to the Golan Heights, Labwani was inconsistent. In an *Al-Arab* interview, he advocated "selling" the Golan Heights to Israel. On Orient News TV, he later reversed himself, saying that a peace agreement with Israel would be conditioned on a return of the Golan Heights, which Israel had *de facto* annexed in 1981. Labwani's plan engendered both strong support and vociferous hostility among the Syrian opposition. Finally, his praise for Islamists impacted his credibility.

At about the same time, a group with which Nir was dealing, the National Syrian Group (Syrian Sunni Pulse) sent a communique to AIPAC. The letter echoed much of what we had been hearing from Ghassan and the other Syrians with whom we'd come in contact. The letter extended a hand of peace to Israel and proposed working together to stop the suffering of the Syrian people.

With such sentiments as a backdrop, we were inspired to go forward with a daring experiment. Our odd partnership gave us a powerful sense of purpose. We felt like the Three Musketeers, who like the three inseparables—Athos, Porthos, and Aramis—battled against the injustices and abuses of the Ancièn Régime. In our case, the regime was Syria.

Gal and Shadi were closely bonded because of their shared history. Together, they had undertaken daring humanitarian operations in Syria in which each had risked their life. It took a great deal of trust for a Syrian and an Israeli to attempt such ventures. Being a Johnny-come-lately to the Syrian crisis, I wasn't a part of that history and didn't wish to intrude on their relationship.

Therefore, I relied on Shadi to communicate questions to Gal and for updates on meetings.

Ghassan and Yisrael had a one-on-one meeting in Brussels which lasted seven hours. They reached an agreement to meet again in two weeks with five Syrians and five Israelis. The focus would be on lobbying Israel to enforce a safe zone along the Golan Heights. They decided to hold off on the public track until they worked out the strategy for the clandestine track. Yisrael opined: "This is an exceptional moment. We cannot fail and the potential is huge." Yisrael, as a Syrian Jew who spoke fluent Arabic and held a high position in Israel, became our point of contact with Ghassan. They spoke regularly, and Yisrael was the person dispatched to smooth things over when we hit bumps in the road. I eventually developed my own bond with Ghassan, affectionately greeting him with *habib albi* while he reciprocated with *habibi albi* (love of my heart).

Ghassan offered to match whatever funds the Israeli Ministries put up to cover the costs of the high-level meetings. This would later become a bone of contention.

At this stage, our tight group of Syrians and Israelis just wanted to focus on how to make the talks successful. Ghassan was feeling impatient about getting started, but we were stuck because Israel was now in the middle of an election.

Shadi and I were about to make our first joint trip to Israel, where Gal had scheduled a series of government and civil society meetings for us as well as university lectures for Shadi. I tapped another set of contacts. As it turned out, we would be in Israel for the election itself and in The Israel Project's election headquarters when Bibi was re-elected prime minister in 2015.

"I think our time in Israel will make everything very clear on how to proceed since there are different parties involved and a high level of security concern regarding what we are doing," said Shadi. "A lot of bad actors will try to disrupt it from Iran to Syria to Hamas...not to mention some Israelis. We should always look at the big picture, making this process successful, as it will be a game changer." Any Syrians working with Israelis could easily be discredited as traitors by those who had an interest in maintaining the status quo.

The Truman Institute provided Shadi with his official invitation letter and urged him to use his Bulgarian passport to avoid security problems when entering Israel. The Institute housed Shadi in the Dan Jerusalem, a beautiful hotel on Mt. Scopus. In its earlier incarnation as a Hyatt, the hotel had been the site of the 2001 assassination of Israel's minister of tourism, Rehavam Ze'evi, by the Popular Front for the Liberation of Palestine. When Shadi heard this on his first day there, he was unnerved. As a Syrian in Israel for the first time, he felt vulnerable. Shadi was my guide for all things Syrian, but I felt very protective of him in Israel. At the same time, I was intensely curious about his perceptions of this enemy country and wanted to see it through his eyes.

Fearing for his life, Shadi was using his pseudonym, Amin Ahmed, and forbade the taking of photos or the presence of any press at his Truman lecture. (As it happens, *Ha-aretz* and two Arab media outlets had somehow gotten into the room, and—surprise!—wrote positive stories.) He also limited the outreach that Truman could do in promoting his groundbreaking lecture. Otherwise, said Naama Shpeter, then Truman's executive director, she could easily have filled her 600-person auditorium rather than limiting the audience to a smaller room with a capacity of 200.

The enthusiastic audience of Hebrew University students and faculty perched on windowsills and filled every available crevice, far exceeding the legal capacity of the room. Other than the heckler described in the opening of Chapter 3, the attendees were entranced by this brawny Syrian, the story of his narrow escape from his home country, and his unlikely partnership with Gal—a local heroine—and other Israelis.

Shadi did similar lectures at the Universities of Herzliya and Tel Aviv. Our five-day schedule was crammed with more than two dozen meetings, lectures, interviews, and panels. At all our meetings, we advanced the idea of Israel serving as a staging area for humanitarian aid.

Following our maiden voyage in Brussels with the EU and EC, Gal, Shadi, and I did briefings for the UK Parliament and Canadian Parliament. And the MFA staff worked with the US Congress and government agencies.

In each of these briefings, we became closer. What had been a duo became a trio. In each of these capitals, after days of intense advocacy, we spent our free time together, roaming the streets of Brussels or Ottawa or London or Jerusalem, decompressing over a meal and helping each other pick souvenirs for our spouses. We met each other's families and eagerly anticipated, along with Gal and Yisrael, the arrival of their adopted son, Tom.

I cherished our selfless connection—as a Syrian, an Israeli, and an American—our unlikely ease with each other, and the deep affection we felt toward each other. The way in which we coalesced as a family gave me hope for a new spirit of cooperation, in which our differences receded in importance.

Our agenda was consistent: raise awareness of the crisis, advocate for raising the number of refugee admissions, debunk the misinformation and disinformation about Syrian refugees (discussed later), encourage funding for NGOs operating on the ground, and consider using Israel as a staging area for the delivery of outbound international humanitarian aid. It was now time to get the government of Israel on board with implementing the last agenda item.

At the Ministry of Foreign Affairs, nine officials met with us. "We're hearing a lot of things for the first time today. This is unique," said the senior officer there. She said Gal "has an open door at the Ministry and can come back with any ideas for agenda and participants." But it was our ability to offer Ghassan as a partner that most intrigued the Ministry of Foreign Affairs. Ghassan, a well-connected, billionaire entrepreneur from a powerful Syrian tribe, owned a media empire that gave him widespread influence through its power to control the message. They knew who he was and saw him as a valuable window into Syria. With his deep contacts, he could provide real-time information about the situation on the ground—especially as it concerned the Sunni majority.

I had been told by a political advisor to Ambassador Ron Prosor, then Israel's Permanent Representative to the UN, that 500,000 NIS (approximately $125,000) had been set aside for cultivating relationships with Syrian community leaders and delivering humanitarian aid. We were providing the perfect channel to use those funds. But that discussion was shut down by the senior official, who indicated that she would deal with that separately.

We met with Amos Yadin, who was short-listed to become minister of defense if Isaac Herzog won the election. Yadin was hugely enthused about the idea of Israel serving as a staging area for international outbound aid. He said this would be easy to do with Egypt and Jordan, but Lebanon would be impossible because it is controlled by Hezbollah. He felt even direct aid into Syria would work.

Herzog was soundly defeated by Bibi. But since Bibi was fully aware of our nascent people-to-people project, that didn't impede our ability to go forward.

Shadi and I met with Dan Meridor, who had formerly served as minister of justice, minister of finance, deputy prime minister, and a member of the Knesset. He was currently president of the Israel Council on Foreign Affairs. In thinking through our two-pronged diplomatic initiative, he expressed concern about what Israel could do without endangering Syrians and wondered how to engage in a Track 1.5 process without a governmental partner on the Syrian side. He advised that we start informally with a free trade zone—an idea completely consistent with Ghassan's vision of creating mutually beneficial business partnerships between Syrians and Israelis. Sunnis were good prospects.

In addressing Track 2, he suggested that we include INSS at Tel Aviv University, a think tank that works with former generals and high-level officials. However, they didn't seem very open to our proposals, pointing out that, under Assad, the Golan was quiet. If Israel were to get formally engaged, they feared they would be dragged into a war with him.

We encountered further skepticism when we met with Adi Ashkenazi at the Ministry for Regional Affairs. When we raised the issue of Israel serving as a staging area for outbound aid, he said, "I don't believe in it. It's a big dream. It's not realistic." He expressed concern about appearing to support al-Nusra and pressed us on the dilemma of working with enemy groups without giving them power. "Are we working with groups that will want to destroy Israel?" His reservations notwithstanding, he assured us that the Israeli government would fund the first Track 1.5 meeting once we had built a plan.

The president of Israel, Reuven Rivlin, fully embraced what we were doing, but was under the impression that Israel was already serving as a staging area. Gal felt that he didn't understand what I was saying and tried to explain it in Hebrew. I never did find out whether he got it.

Shadi also met with Ehud Olmert, the former prime minister and mayor of Jerusalem. Olmert was happy to help with the Track 1.5 process. But there was no way to do so. He had been convicted in May 2014 of accepting bribes to promote a real estate deal and was about to start a term in prison.

Apart from our many official meetings, there were three standout moments in this, Shadi's first encounter with Israel.

The first was a Shabbat dinner at the Jerusalem home of Mem Bernstein. Mem—the widow of Zalman Bernstein, co-founder of Sanford Bernstein, and a deeply committed philanthropist and activist in her own right—had invited a number of JFN members who were in town for the start of our annual conference. She graciously included Shadi. It was his first Shabbat dinner—a Syrian Sunni Muslim, sharing in this sacred ritual with a roomful of Jews. We went around the table so everyone could share a bit about themselves. Shadi got extra time because his story was so gripping. I constantly worried about Shadi feeling welcome in this land that he had been taught to fear and hate. But the warmth of that Shabbat meal was an apt way to ease him in.

Because Israel shuts down on Shabbat, Shadi and I, along with my husband and son, traveled to the north to spend the day with Gal and Yisrael. Before meeting for dinner, we went to the civilian part of the Golan Heights. From that elevation, Shadi glimpsed the southwest corner of his homeland for the first time. Arrayed before him were Mt. Hermon, the United Nations buffer zone between Syria and Israeli-occupied territories; and Quneitra, where battles had been raging at the time of the Polonsky Academy opening in 2013. "I don't understand all this fighting over a piece of land," he murmured as his eyes scanned the country he had escaped and where he had a target on his back.

But the most moving episode was Shadi's encounter with Shimon Peres. It was meant to be a brief ceremonial meeting. But Shadi ended up spending two hours with the Israeli statesman to whom, in gratitude, he had sent a ninetieth birthday video, along with a Syrian flag, two years before.

The climax of our visit was a panel on the Syrian crisis that we organized for the JFN Conference. Brigadier General Yossi Kuperwasser, former director-general of the Ministry of Strategic Affairs and chief of the research division of IDF Military Intelligence, discussed Israeli government policy and emphasized the humanitarian considerations that supersede all others. Gal spoke about the daring work of IFA. Lt. Col. Elon Glassberg, a doctor and military trauma specialist, managed the field hospital where Syrians in need of medical care were being treated in Israel. He spoke movingly about the risks that were undertaken by the soldiers under his command to save Syrians.

Shadi gave the Syrian perspective and expressed his appreciation of what Israel was doing to aid his fellow Syrians. With that, the packed room erupted in a standing ovation.

After a busy week in Israel, our takeaways were: the assurance that funding was in place for the Israeli side of Track 1.5; great support for Track 1.5/2 at all levels in Israel; most government actors with whom we met were willing to consider opening the country as a staging area for international outbound humanitarian aid. But this idea remained undeveloped at that time.

During that sojourn in Israel, a subtle shift emerged in the relationship between Shadi and Gal. Shadi felt as if he was being co-opted for IFA's fundraising purposes rather than our joint project. I was gradually becoming an intermediary as communications began to break down between the two of them.

Then there was a problem that was MFA's alone. By engaging with Israel in this process, was MFA carrying Israel's water? A number of Protestant church bodies—such as the Evangelical Lutheran Church and Episcopal Church—were part of the MFA network. Because they tended to be highly critical of Israel, there was concern that they would be uneasy being identified with MFA. But they stuck with MFA. It was the Syrian American Medical Association and American Relief Coalition for Syria that pulled out. We were told that an ARCS board member objected to affiliating with MFA because we include Jews and Israelis. All the other Syrian organizations that were in our network remained.

It's crucial to reinforce the point that people-to-people diplomacy is not about helping one side or the other. On the contrary, we were implementing the part of MFA's mission that called us to plant the seeds for future stability in the region. And as was later shown, our work helped to stabilize southwest Syria, including the area where the civil war began.

A month after our return, Shadi and I met with Ambassador Prosor. We discussed our briefings to the EU, UK, and US and the upcoming sessions in Canada. We sought his help in arranging briefings for other UN missions. But this was tricky because Russia would likely use that as an excuse to create obstacles for us. As we left, Prosor took me aside and said: "This is important." Prosor was correct. It was important. But in order to realize that importance, we had to first get through the mechanics of identifying participants and agreeing on a schema as we proceeded with our Track 1.5 process. Those encounters broke new ground. But they were sometimes fraught with conflict as agendas clashed and recriminations flew.

CHAPTER 7

LANDMINES ON THE ROAD TO ACTION

Navigating Conflicting Agendas

It was the end of August before we finally had our next Track 1.5 meeting. But it almost didn't happen. Ghassan was losing patience, and Shadi and Gal were in conflict. Gal complained that she wasn't getting the documentation she needed for her donors about the distribution and use of aid. Shadi complained that Gal was incommunicado when he needed to reach her. And because she gave some orders without consultation, Shadi felt that he was getting short shrift as a partner.

Then there was the larger problem of diverging Syrian and Israeli positions about the Track 1.5 process. The Syrian position was that Ghassan was a highly influential figure, much sought after by the UN and other governments in the region. Shadi had staked his reputation by bringing him into the process, certain that Ghassan would have access and influence throughout Syria. But he needed our group to deliver results. That meant working with Israelis who were in a position to make decisions.

Like Shadi, Gal had staked her reputation by engaging very high levels in the Israeli government.

In the meantime, Shadi was lobbying Ghassan to keep him on board—absent any firm budget for Track 1.5 or funding from the Israeli side.

We needed to figure out how to restore trust between Gal and Shadi and build on the initial positive feelings that Yisrael and Ghassan had for each other. A four-way phone call in late May seemed to heal the wounds for the time being.

Yisrael and I agreed that we needed decision-makers for the Track 1.5 process. But it was unclear what "decision-makers" meant in the context of the chaos in Syria. Per Yisrael, "either the Syrian side will need to upgrade or the Israeli side downgrade." We found ourselves on the horns of a dilemma: Should the heads of political parties in Israel be meeting with Syrians of lesser rank? But absent a functioning government in Syria, one could not make assumptions based on rank. The Syrian delegation could sway people fighting on the ground. Shadi turned the tables and reiterated that, in order to bring decision-makers, he needed to know what Israel could offer them.

Syria and Israel are different. Unlike Israel, Syria has no competing political parties. Syria is a tribal country. Israel is not. In Syria, there is no higher loyalty than the family. Both the Abouds and Martinis were among the leading families of Syria, and both hailed from the al-Na'ims, a far-flung tribe that spans the Gulf states—UAE, Oman, Qatar—Iraq, and Syria. As of 2017, its members were 15,000 strong in Syria, according to The Washington Institute for Near East Policy. One of the most powerful tribes in Syria, they are considered descendants of the Prophet.

That translates into influence. The definition of influence in the case of Syria would be those who can give commands. Who would be the Syrian counterpart to someone who leads a coalition in Israel? Gal demanded that the Syrian delegation include people from inside Syria.

I asked Shadi to give an example of such a person. He offered up his cousin, Dr. Mohammed Ammar Martini, head of Orient for Human Relief. Ammar had been involved in hostage negotiations and had experience dealing with radicals on the ground. During the last offensive in the north, commanders had come to his office to seek his advice about what to do. He operated 75 percent inside Syria and 25 percent in Turkey. Among the projects he managed was a mosaics factory for the disabled. At the same time, he was running a massive medical and education operation. Gal allowed that this was exactly the right person in the right place.

Gal and Yisrael agreed that Ghassan and Ammar were appropriate partners for the initial Track 1.5 meeting, which would be limited to four people on the Syrian side and Gal, Yisrael, and one high-level person on the Israeli side.

In that exploratory meeting, they began framing the priorities and identifying potential partnerships. *Trade:* Ghassan put forward the idea of Israelis and Syrians commonly branding and selling olive oil together. *Curriculum:* chipping away at prejudice by having Syrians and Israelis insert positive material about each other. *Media:* Israelis and Syrians doing balanced, multi-dimensional stories about each other. Orient Media, controlling as it does the main opposition media, was in a good position to deliver on that. Shadi pointed out that even Assad followers tuned in.

The initial agenda would focus on identifying the deliverables sought on both the Syrian and Israeli side. They would then identify and invite the people with the capacity to deliver to future sessions.

In the meantime, Shadi, Gal, and I were headed to Ottawa to do briefings for the Canadian parliament and various government agencies and ministries.

As the date for our Track 1.5 meeting approached, I asked Eran Lerman, Israeli scholar and former security advisor, to inquire whether the Track 1.5 funds were still in place on the Israeli side. Meanwhile, I was contacted by Asaf Shariv, Israel's former consul-general in New York, to arrange a meeting with him and Chemi Peres (Shimon Peres's son). Chemi and Asaf had started a fund, AMELIA (Middle East Long Term Investment and Assets), which was focused on capitalizing businesses that invest in the Middle East. He described it as translating "Start-Up Nation" into "Start-Up Region." I offered to make introductions in Oman and to Ghassan but also enlisted them to track down the 500,000 NIS that were supposedly being held for our work.

In the end, there was no funding from the State of Israel. I had now been let down by two governments. But just as Jordan had to tread a fine line politically in order to avert a revolt in its streets, so did Israel.

In 2011—the year the Arab Spring was in full swing and the first non-violent demonstrations erupted in Syria—Israel was dealing with its own civil rebellion. The burgeoning Israeli tech sector had generated huge wealth for a few families, who according to the *New York Times*, controlled 30 percent of the economy. The cost of housing and other necessities had spiraled up. Ordinary Israelis took to the streets and built tent cities to protest social inequality—a paradox for a country that had its modern roots in socialist Zionism and the kibbutz movement.

By encouraging NGOs, such as ours, the government took three risks. One was the risk of being dragged into an unwanted war with Syria. The second was creating a perception that Israel was supporting the rebels, which would delegitimize them in the eyes of their comrades. The third was resentment among its own populace for taking care of Syrian enemies before dealing with its own needy citizens.

In the end, the Israeli delegation was depending on an offer my husband had made to match Ghassan's funding until government funding kicked in. Never mind. We all felt the call of history: our process was the first time that Syrians and Israelis were meeting without intermediaries. And the advantage of our bottom-up process was that we didn't have the constraints within which official bodies had to operate.

Finally, the day came: August 27, 2015. The Syrian and Israeli delegations arrived in Brussels—each side staying in separate hotels so as not to risk being seen together. Our meetings took place at a third, neutral location. The air was electric with anticipation as we went around the table introducing ourselves.

On the Syrian side, there was a journalist who was born on the Golan Heights but grew up in Damascus. Her father, a prominent general, was said to be the third most powerful person in Syria. She was joined by her husband, a half Palestinian and half Syrian Arab broadcast professional, who was originally from Safed in Israel. He now worked for Orient TV but had previously worked for Al Jazeera and had served in the Syrian army. Both of them were new to our group, and the Israelis were concerned.

Dr. Mohammed Ammar Martini was already known to us. He had a big hospital in Idlib, where he had treated those who were wounded in the fighting. After the manager and other staff were arrested and killed by the regime—followed by a similar attempt on Ammar's life—he fled to Turkey. Since then, he had been the director of Orient for Human Relief, which, he reported, had provided more than two million medical services, 40,000 surgeries, and twenty-six dental clinics to Syrian war victims. This, in addition to the schools he was running inside and outside Syria.

Finally, there was Ghassan: "We are here because we believe there is a chance now to plan peace."

On the Israeli side, we had Gal, Yisrael, and a recently elected member of the Knesset (MK), who was newly retired from the military. "If he is convinced by this meeting," confided Yisrael, "he can move many people." Shadi and I straddled both sides.

Yisrael spoke movingly about his belief that our process would bring our people to a point they'd never been before. He said that he and Gal had checked with the Knesset and a wide range of Israelis. Some of the people they had approached were now ministers. He pointed out that, in Israel, civil society is an important force. They had found total receptivity to building a process from the bottom up, with civil society on both sides.

Yisrael pointed to me and said, "Georgette is an important part of the process because she sometimes sees things in a different way."

He then turned to the Syrians and said, "Syrians have the greater risk and much to lose...Since Syrians are taking the risks, they should guide us on when to take the next step. Israel must be very conscious of the security situation."

Ghassan greatly appreciated Yisrael's sensitivity to the risks his delegation was taking and felt him to be a real partner. He went on to say that "Syrians are experiencing something like the Holocaust. They're ready to open their minds. In the past, when Israel engaged in peace processes, it was...under the table, with dictators. They couldn't do real partnerships...Or, they made partnerships with minorities, such as Maronites in Lebanon, which destroyed them." The latter referred to Israel's 2000 pullout from the safety zone in south Lebanon. In the wake of the pullout, everyone in that area was viewed as a traitor by the Lebanese.

"In 2010," he continued, "a meeting like this would not have been possible." Because Israel was demonized in the minds of Syrians, they didn't see the humanity of the other side. But in comparing death tolls, Syrians now saw things differently. "Syrians see that when a prisoner comes out of an Israeli prison, he is fit. In Syria, he doesn't come out." But Ghassan wanted the prime minister to speak out about Syria and acknowledge the suffering of its people.

The MK explained that there are two levels in Israel—civil society, which is very engaged in humanitarian aid; and government, which is very focused on security. He urged that the bottom-up process is much more powerful than starting with government. He argued that civil society must be convinced of the possibility of change in the Middle East. "Everyone is focused on the risks and not the chance," he said. The place to begin is in the humanitarian sphere. Then press the government to take action." The proof of this was the response of the youth movement two years before, which Gal had mobilized to help the Syrian people via Operation Human Warmth, described in Chapter 4. When the prime minister saw 300,000 youths turn up to help, he came forward to condemn Assad.

"We are enemies, but we are human, and we can transform this conflict into a normal conflict between neighbors," said the MK.

Perhaps he didn't have the term in his vocabulary, but he was talking about humanitarian diplomacy.

Ghassan and the MK both understood the importance of breaking down stereotypes. To that end, Ghassan introduced the idea of sending one of his TV crews to Israel to do a multi-part series on "The Other Face of the Enemy." Given that Orient was the most popular channel in Syria, the idea was to introduce his people to the many facets of Israel beyond the Palestinian conflict and to prepare them to accept the idea of Israelis as partners.

Another potential area of partnership was trade and commerce, including a virtual free trade zone in the Golan Heights. Other partnerships: security, education, youth. And, of course, the biggest of all—humanitarian aid.

The issue of financing came up again. Each side would cover its own expenses, with MFA being responsible for coordinating the meetings. That was workable for Track 1.5, but not Track 2, where the logistics are more complex and expensive. Having already hired staff, I was put in a difficult and unacceptable position. Somehow—I can't recall how in the flurry of activity—the finances, with no help from Israel, got resolved, and we were off to Berlin, three months later, for our next Track 1.5 session.

The same core group came. But this time we were joined by an important Israeli industrialist, who in his time as a major general in the military had been involved in negotiations with Syrians.

In the interim since our last meeting, a new kind of intifada had taken root—random stabbings of Israelis by Palestinian youths. Also, in September 2015, Russia had launched its first airstrikes in Homs province in Syria in order to secure the western part of the country for the regime. Simultaneously, Russia was in talks with Israel.

The Israeli-Russian talks dealt only with how to avoid inadvertently shooting down each other's planes in the fog of the battles in Syria. Israel's policy was to stay out of the fight, except for bombing Hezbollah munitions and shooting down Syrian planes that entered its airspace (something that Syrians celebrated). But Russian jets were bombing the area near the Israel border, leading to the erroneous perception that Israel was supporting Russia—thus necessitating the very coordination that was creating that perception.

After the Brussels meetings, everyone with whom the Syrian journalists spoke was eager to start the Track 2 talks. But the Russian aggression in supporting Assad in Syria—and, by association, Israel's engagement with Russia—raised doubts among Syrians about whether Israelis could be a real partner in the talks. All the current negative press about Israel was coloring perceptions. Because of its perceived support for Russia, there was a view that Israel was opposed to Sunnis and that Syrians were pulling out. The Syrians on the ground, whom we wanted to engage in

Track 2, were now distrustful. They had too much to lose, and the timing wasn't right to risk their lives. Because of these developments, we could not launch Track 2.

Both delegations had their concerns. The Syrians were less concerned with who was sitting at the table than with the Israeli audience, who Syrians believed all shared the same suspect mentality. As for the Israelis, they had to convince their constituents that Ghassan represented a crucial population in Syria.

Ghassan's great value was his position within the Sunni population that can mobilize moderates and al-Nusra (but not ISIS) across Syria. Many of these, Ghassan believed, were pragmatists—businesspeople like himself—who were looking for relations with Israelis. In fact, he had written an article in English and Arabic advocating for relations with Israel, which got 250,000 hits—none of them negative. "People want to live together and be friendly with Israelis, not because they like you, but because they hate everyone else!"

The Israelis wondered how many Syrians are non-radical Sunnis, and the Syrians observed that it was difficult for Israelis to differentiate between moderate Sunnis and extremist Sunni organizations. That's because Israel had always worked with the minorities in Syria—and those minorities needed to scapegoat Israel in order to stay in power. We were meeting with a segment of the Syrian population that was at war with another segment of the population. That segment didn't want Israel to be an ally of their enemies.

Shadi explained that most civilians and fighters were non-radical. To the extent that they aligned with radicals, it was for safety in the void left by the government.

For their part, the Israelis wanted to see stability, stop the bloodshed, and help create a new Syria with a moderate, secular, rational regime. We were told that all the decision-makers in

Israel were aware of our Track 1.5 process. Yisrael said, "If you want to create a leader, we are here to help you."

In viewing Syria, the superpowers saw only two options: ISIS or Assad. The Syrians said that, if given a choice between Assad and ISIS, they would choose ISIS because ISIS doesn't have aircraft and barrel bombs. "Are you really saying that, among 25 million people, one can't find a leader other than ISIS or Assad?" asked Ghassan, disbelievingly. We agreed that we would create top-secret road maps that would present a third option: the moderate option. Ghassan was at the forefront of that contingent.

But was this the time?

Like Track 2, the planned Orient TV series had been deferred, as was an equivalent series about Syrians for Israeli audiences. A time of high tension did not seem like the moment in which to have Syrians in Israel asking questions about the country. But media are a vital tool in promoting understanding between people. So we agreed to go forward with the media project, starting with a joint Syrian-Israeli humanitarian aid project in Europe. But partnership in that project fell apart because of a dispute between Gal and Shadi over the allocation of grant funds between IFA and Orient.

In any case, visas needed to be issued for the project to go forward, and those hadn't yet been obtained.

So the group made another decision: Start with a top-secret road map for each side. After answering three questions, they would compare their road maps, reconcile them, and jointly present them to the Americans.

What is your plan for the future of Syria? Will there be one Syria? Several Syrias? Ghassan averred that Syrians would no longer accept Damascus as the center of Syrian life. It could serve as the seat of a decentralized federation, but under this vision, Damascus would serve the localities rather than the localities serving Damascus. The idea he put forth anticipated a charter city concept that he would later develop and which is more fully explained in Chapter 10.

Why do you believe you have the political power to make this vision happen? The consensus was that fighting terrorism was an interest both the West and the Middle East shared and that this could drive support for a new Syria. As such, a joint Syrian/Israeli road map could be very convincing to the superpowers.

How are you going to treat those who disagree with you—minorities? There was no further discussion of this at that or future meetings.

We agreed to hold the next Track 1.5 session on the Golan Heights—which would be hugely symbolic—focusing on security and bringing together Syria's Southern Front military leaders. One of the Syrians had met in Amman with the commanders of the forty militias of the Southern Front who were responsible for operations in the area around Damascus to the Jordanian border and east and west of the Israeli border. He had spoken to them openly about working with Israel. In order to manage expectations, he advised them not to expect weapons from Israel because that was subject to permission from the US. The Israelis were concerned about connections to jihadi organizations, such as ISIS, Martyrs of Yarmouk, and Jabhat al-Nusra. The Southern Front commanders, on the other hand, were concerned that cooperation with Israel would damage their support from others who were supplying them with weapons. But most were enthused. They had trust in Israel because of its treatment of Syrians in need of medical care. Moreover, they saw Israel as an intelligence source and as a means of enforcing a cease-fire along the border. They were ready to meet but wanted the relationship to be kept secret.

The Syrians were looking for Israel to enforce the neglected disengagement agreement signed between Israel and Syria in 1974. This would mean expanding Israel's base of operations so that the south could be a no-fly zone, off-limits to all but the

Israeli Air Force. The Syrians assured us that all the fighters in that area were Syrian—unlike other regions where there were foreign fighters. The Southern Front was in a state of war with ISIS and all those who cooperate with ISIS, as well as groups that were mostly Palestinian and Jordanian. In the north, military operations were carried out with al-Nusra.

The risk to Israel was that they would be moving from non-involvement to taking a side. Israel could not get involved until they saw the big picture. If this cooperation could contribute to future stability on Israel's northern border, and there was a critical mass that could deliver it, then Israel was in. But first, our group had to come up with something that could be sold to Israeli officials. And they would need to provide visas for the Syrians to come to the Golan Heights.

We were now on the road to our fifth Track 1.5 meeting, and the visa issue loomed large.

At the end of November, two out of the four ministers who needed to sign off on the visas were with Bibi in Paris, so no approvals. At the end of December, still no approvals. Credibility with the Syrians was getting seriously frayed. The Syrian road map had been ready for some time, but their delegation saw no point in sending it to the Israeli side if they couldn't even get their own government to issue visas for the next meeting.

We were at a standstill. For the Syrians, the visas were the dealbreaker. For the Israelis, it was the delay in Track 2. For the Syrians, the visas were a confidence-building measure that indicated commitment from the authorities in Israel. Gal and Yisrael continued to work on the visas and got security clearances from Shabak. The Ministry of Foreign Affairs had been updated and everyone was on board. But, in the end, the visas were denied by another intelligence service. No one knows the real reason.

The Syrian perception was that the visa rejection was because of Israel's deal with Russia. One theory was that the authorities didn't want to embarrass Bibi, who was speaking with Putin. But Gal and Yisrael didn't understand how hosting a clandestine Track 1.5 meeting could possibly embarrass the prime minister.

There was another theory. Yossi Kuperwasser had organized a public conference with media coverage to which he was bringing a defected Syrian minister of defense. Shadi had also been invited to speak at that event. That conference was canceled by the government, and Gal came to the conclusion that our visa denial had been an error. Somehow, our clandestine Track 1.5 meeting had gotten confounded with Kuperwasser's conference, and the denial had been intended for his Syrian guest.

A third theory was that there was concern about one of our Syrian delegates. The Israelis sensed they might not be who they claimed. For two years, that delegate had been denied access to our meetings. We later learned that the delegate had gone to an Arab media outlet, *Al-Arabi Al-Jadid* in 2018 to reveal our secret meetings, naming names, and providing photographs—one of which was featured on the cover of the publication.

Regardless of the reason, the Syrians read the rejection as a lack of commitment by the Israeli government. Without it, they felt at risk—especially those with only Syrian passports. Any Syrians who were involved in our process could be discredited among some groups and would be in danger. They needed assurance that Israel—the superpower in the region—was behind them, even if they couldn't be so publicly. This would allow Ghassan to approach the Emirates and other Gulf countries, knowing that he had an open channel with Israel to back him. The Syrians felt they were being asked to move public opinion in Israel without any assurance that there would be any results. Ghassan remained committed and willing to continue meeting. But he needed to have a commitment from the Israeli government.

The Syrians were having a crisis of confidence. Were they working with the right people if we couldn't even get them a visa?

Ghassan wondered where we would go from here and preferred to meet with all the key players in Israel, rather than one at a time in Track 1.5 meetings.

But we would have to continue to meet in Europe.

It was now mid-January 2016, and we were at a dead end. I turned to Ron Prosor to see if he could help. He was committed to getting the visa issue resolved at the highest levels. Yisrael was meeting with Bibi, but that meeting was postponed to the end of March. Ultimately, Yisrael was referred to the chief of staff who said we had to coordinate everything with the IDF.

Ghassan canceled the media project—no visas—and said there was no point in continuing to meet. Gal said the camera crew visas were a poor excuse to stop the dialogue. "We are ready to meet any time," she stated unequivocally.

Yisrael had been updating Ghassan every couple of weeks and had met with him twice in Brussels. Now it was the Israelis who needed to be assured of Ghassan's steadfastness.

Gal lamented the situation but tried to put it in perspective: "Visas will be issued one day. That shouldn't be a condition to proceed…while Syrians are suffering and killed. We have tons of other things to promote and do together in order to help change hearts and minds." She insisted that the Syrians needed to be unconditionally committed to our process, even though "we will win some and lose some."

The Syrian side, via Shadi, affirmed their commitment to the process and agreed, in principle, to continue meeting. They acknowledged that IFA was trying its best to mobilize Israeli officials to support our process, but sensed reluctance from the government. They took the absence of visas and matching funds as indications that the official side of Track 1.5 was missing. As such, they didn't see how the Track 2 process could proceed.

But I couldn't stand by and wait any longer for developments. I proposed an agenda that would allow us to move forward on several fronts while we waited for the visa situation to be resolved. I pointed out that, although we didn't have an official government presence, we did have people who were close to the government and could be helpful in moving the government. My big frustration was that both the Syrians and the Israelis averred that they were committed to this process, but Gal and Shadi weren't communicating with each other. They were communicating only through me. I insisted they each needed to consult with their own teams and give me a firm answer about whether we were going to confirm a meeting date—"yes or no?"

Gal replied that her team was ready to go back to the table.

Yisrael reported that visas were no longer a condition for Ghassan and his delegation to continue our process. Because of recent food deliveries from Israel into Syria, Ghassan reportedly told Yisrael that this could be the right moment for the two sides to "step forward" and "recognize" each other. Orient TV had aired a forty-five-minute interview with Shadi; MFA spokesperson and Oscar-awarded actor, F. Murray Abraham; and me in Washington, DC, following a briefing we had done on the Syrian crisis for both houses of Congress. It was the first time we had spoken publicly of the Syrian/Israeli engagement to an Arab audience.

The date for the next Track 1.5 conclave was set: October 7–8 in Madrid.

We had unfinished business from our last two Track 1.5 meetings: the road map, the media project, humanitarian aid, and education.

In August, there was a flurry of activity in planning the "Other Face of the Enemy" media project, agenda-setting—and the Syrian road map arrived.

In September, I received an email from Nir Boms, which would both solve our problems and blow up our process.

Nir asked whether I would meet with IDF Major General Yoav "Poly" Mordechai, who was coming to New York for the

UN General Assembly session that month. Mordechai was head of the Coordinator of Government Activities in the Territories (COGAT), a unit in the Israeli Ministry of Defense that engages in coordinating civilian issues between the Government of Israel, the Israel Defense Forces, international organizations, diplomats, and the Palestinian Authority.

Poly Mordechai arrived at my apartment at the appointed time, flanked by his aides, Colonel Mansour Hatib, a Druze security officer, and Lt. Colonel Yoav Bisritski, of COGAT. Our meeting was the last one scheduled before the general and his team returned to Israel.

With his chiseled features and gentle eyes, Poly didn't fit my image of a person in charge of managing relations with the volatile Palestinian Territories. Nor did his empathy for supposed enemies. Poly told me that he had been charged with building a small, new unit to facilitate expanded humanitarian aid deliveries of food and medical supplies to Syrians. He wanted to set up an efficient process and work directly with NGOs rather than through "middle-men" to ensure that aid would reach the intended recipients. To that end, he needed connections with leaders in the south of Syria and was seeking introductions to both Syrian and Jewish NGOs. The name of the initiative was "Operation Good Neighbor," and it was now official government policy. There was no more need to operate below the radar.

Poly guaranteed that anyone—Syrians included—coming to Israel to coordinate aid would get a visa and that there would be no customs duties for items passing through Israel for aid to Syria. He also assured me that crossing points would be no problem. He could open the border wherever needed to deliver aid directly into Syria. This new development made the delivery of aid through Israel faster, cheaper, and more reliable.

I couldn't believe it was finally happening! Israel could now become a staging area for the outbound delivery of international humanitarian aid. And our Syrian colleagues could, at last, get visas! Years of advocacy for that staging area and months of trying to get visas had just been settled in one conversation. I will never forget the date: September 21, 2016. It marked a critical turning point in our mission.

Poly and his delegation had spent the week meeting with UN agencies and NGOs in order to seek partners for "Operation Good Neighbor." They came up dry. Poly asked, "Why not support Syria through Israel?" Of course, Israel was politically toxic, and it's not surprising that no one wanted to take the risk. When he turned to USAID and the UN, he was told that the Golan border was not a formally recognized international border, and the dispute with Syria was not yet resolved. Poly thought, "What are you talking about? People are killed in villages 100 meters from this border. Let's discuss later whether this is an international border or not. Now we need emergency humanitarian support!"

Within five minutes, because of MFA's vast network of organizations, including a number of Syrian NGOs, I had Poly on the phone with Shadi and Dr. Yahya Basha, a prominent Syrian physician and Muslim interfaith activist in Detroit. After the meeting, we connected with SAMS, Orient, ARCS, and Rahma Relief Foundation—all Syrian NGOs—as well as IRC. Not all the connections succeeded but—here's the man-bites-dog story—Syrian organizations were the first to jump on board to take advantage of the new channel that was opening over the Golan Heights.

I asked Poly whether he could come to Madrid in October for our next Track 1.5 meeting. He couldn't, but he was eager to meet Ghassan.

I reported this game-changing meeting to Gal and Yisrael, and we arrived in Madrid with more optimism than we'd felt in a long time.

This time, we all stayed in the same hotel. Our same core group was there—with two additions. My husband and Gal and

Yisrael's baby boy, Tom. I felt immense joy at seeing the Syrian and Israeli delegates laughing together and playing with the baby. The mood was light, and we shared the easy comfort of a family reunion. We started with a meal—Jews and Arabs love to eat—and much animated chat. The Jews (except for me) all spoke Arabic, which made it easy to relax with each other.

The first day of our meetings focused on geopolitical changes since the last meeting—specifically the Russian intervention and the Druze of Israel and Syria—the obstacles and opportunities that these presented for Track 1.5, the media project, and the road map.

Russian bombing and the upcoming US elections were greatly complicating our work, even though there was not yet any change of power on the ground in Syria. Russia clearly had the upper hand because the US was not going to do anything before the 2016 elections in the next month. Everyone was holding their breath to see who would become the next US president—just as the earlier Israeli elections had put us in suspended animation. The Israelis felt they couldn't do anything because their country could not stand up to Russia without the US. Nor could it influence Russian actions. We concluded that the only way forward for us was to proceed with the education, media, and humanitarian aid projects we had identified.

Al-Nusra was still controlling the south, and there was a lot of movement by Iran and Hezbollah. Assad was almost absent. In September 2016, the al-Nusra Front, in its fight against the regime, actively bombed the Syrian Druze village of Khadr near the Syrian border, where the pro-regime Hezbollah had a strong presence. News reports claimed that Israeli Defense Minister Avigdor Lieberman was providing unprecedented support for the bombing campaign in order to secure previously bombed Syrian positions, which the terror group was now holding. The Israeli

Druze community was enraged and ready to cross the border to fight alongside their Syrian Druze brethren.

Akram Hasson, a Druze MK, furiously attacked this policy and accused Israel of aiding a terror group. Gal responded with an equally furious letter published in *Ha'aretz* in September. "There are two kinds of Druze...There are our blood brothers, the Druze to whom we owe an immense debt and whom we embrace as our own children; and there are your dearest Druze of Majdal Shams and three other villages at the Golan Heights who are not Israeli citizens as they have chosen Assad...The Syrian Druze, whom you now defend...are hosting....Hezbollah in Khadr... [conducting] on Assad's behalf...despicable killings of women and children."

The previous year, there had been two Israeli Druze attacks on IDF ambulances carrying wounded Syrians to Israel for medical treatment. The Israeli Druze were incensed about Syrian al-Nusra advances on Druze areas in Syrian Golan. Mistakenly believing that the ambulances were carrying jihadi fighters into Israel for care, mobs engulfed and stoned the ambulances, resulting in deaths and critical injuries of the patients and their IDF escorts.

With those attacks still fresh in her mind, Gal's letter continued to excoriate MK Hasson: "Have you raised your voice at your Druze brothers from Majdal when they chased after an Israeli military ambulance on behalf of Hezbollah...Did you protest the lynching of two severely wounded Syrians who were on their way to an Israeli hospital by more than a hundred of your brothers? Were you taken aback when one of them was murdered with sticks and rocks on the road after the military medical team was unable to withstand the Majdal Shams mob...? The Syrian Druze—your brothers in Syria, are murderers of women and children, who feed and arm Hezbollah."

Gal's closing salvo was: "If we were to sit back and do nothing in light of the suffering of the Syrian people by Assad's atrocities, we would have been guilty of the sin of indifference and silence. And if we choose, as we did, to deliver humanitarian aid...we are judged by you...and the likes of you."

After the blow-up over the Syrian Druze, the IDF announced its intention to protect Khadr. This didn't sit well with the Syrian delegates, because it suggested direct Israeli support for Hezbollah—now detested by the Sunnis—rather than the Druze. The Syrian side concluded that Hezbollah and the Shiites were trying to find vulnerabilities in Israel and were elevating the Druze issue in order to weaken Israel.

This was a revelation to the Israeli MK in our core group. "This discussion is very important to better understand why you [Syrians] are so sensitive to the Hezbollah-Druze relationship." Clearly, IDF Chief of Staff Gadi Eizenkot hadn't understood the impact of his announcement from a Syrian perspective, and the MK pledged to meet with Eizenkot to clarify the meaning.

This was a matter that needed to be managed with the utmost delicacy because thousands of Druze serve in the Israeli army— including the Lt. Colonel who had accompanied Poly Mordechai to his fateful meeting with me.

We then turned our attention to the "Caesar Bill" wending its way through the US Congress. The bill was inspired by the Syrian photographer who had documented the torture in Syrian prisons and brought them to the US when he defected. The gruesome photos, first exhibited at the National Holocaust Museum in Washington, DC, were also exhibited at UN headquarters in New York. The bill sought to impose fresh sanctions on individuals and entities that assist the Assad regime and its agencies—including Russia and Iran.

The Obama White House was trying to stop the bill because it threatened the Iran deal it had concluded in 2013. There was a perception among Syrians that the Obama doctrine was to empower Iran. One of our colleagues maintained that, during the Iran negotiations, Iran was ready to walk out if the US attacked Syria.

Our delegations wanted to do something to promote the Caesar Bill as well as mount more exhibitions of the photos. Gal thought Israel should host exhibits in its three major museums and the Knesset in order to influence decision-makers.

The Iran nuclear deal was no longer a consideration. Donald Trump had unilaterally withdrawn from it, despite Iran's compliance with its terms, precipitating a diplomatic crisis for all the other signatories. But with the US no longer constrained by the deal, the Caesar Civilian Protection Act of 2019 was successfully incorporated into the National Defense Authorization Act of 2020 with bipartisan support.

Given the changing geopolitical landscape, we had to reevaluate the road maps we had discussed in Berlin and concluded we now needed a different kind of road map. This one would focus on perception. Syria and Israel were still enemies, but it was time for them to start looking at each other differently. Phase I of the new road map would focus on the human side of the enemy and on mutually shared issues—history, values, periods of successful coexistence. We would then need to create an infrastructure to broadcast to Israeli audiences what is happening in Syria. This could include the Orient website, Syrian-Israeli Facebook dialogues, and the TV series that we'd been discussing for months and which was now being fleshed out.

But humanitarian aid was where Poly's announcement was enabling our biggest breakthrough. With a grant that I had endorsed with JDC, IFA had tested the delivery of two containers from Israel to Syria—one with food and the other with medical supplies. We now had to divide the labor in scaling up.

Some Syrian organizations—such as Orient—were comfortable working directly with the Israelis and were ready to ship forty-foot cargo containers of aid to Haifa and Ashdod. From there, the IDF would pick up the containers and transship them to the Golan Heights. Other organizations could not visibly work with Israelis. We agreed that Orient would be the main coordinator of aid, and for those other organizations, Orient would be the cover and take the flack.

Orient also committed to refurbishing a hospital just inside the Syrian border. For this Ammar would need to survey needs from a network of doctors in southwest Syria. Orient would then send equipment and funds for paying salaries. Ammar also offered fully equipped ambulances to pass through the border. How, I wondered, could we prevent the Druze from attacking the ambulances?

Then there was the matter of education: Half of Syrian children had been out of school for years, and many schools had been bombed. Orient had created a mobile curriculum on iPad tablets that would enable children to learn from anywhere they were. But Ghassan and Gal had bigger dreams. What about building a school near the border? What about providing lunches for the students? What about creating a joint curriculum for Israelis, Arab Israelis, and Syrians?

"Syrians have concluded that they are living on lies and realizing that Syrian history is not correct. The question is not just about school but Syrian perception entirely. We will have no illusions about what we were taught in school," offered one of the Syrian delegates. Another pointed out the contradictions between school lessons and real life: "You can teach one thing, and in the afternoon, he will see something else."

We agreed that our next steps were to get two containers into Syria through the Golan channel in Israel, get Syrian journalists into Israel, and start the flow of Orient's tablets into southern Syria.

Much of what we planned didn't happen, and Madrid would be the last time that we would meet together. But relationships were forged. Important ideas emerged. Projects that didn't get done at the time were picked up in a different form later. Our partnership shattered. But that's when we finally moved from talk to action.

Some of the 907 passengers on board the *St. Louis* arriving in Belgium after being refused entry into Cuba and the U.S. Antwerp, Belgium, June 17, 1939.

WW2 anti-tank barriers along the river in Budapest. Retreating Germans and Hungarian forces destroyed the Chain Bridge as Soviet forces took the city, February 1944.

Memorial on the banks of the Danube to the Jews of Budapest killed during the Holocaust.

Bennett as a child with her parents, Sidonie and Ignatz Beitscher in Nice, ca. 1950.

Rabbi Marc Tanenbaum with Vietnamese refugees, 1978.

International Rescue Committee Report that inspired Bennett's engagement with the Syrian crisis, 2013.

Syrian refugees arrive near Lesbos in a rubber boat, 2015.

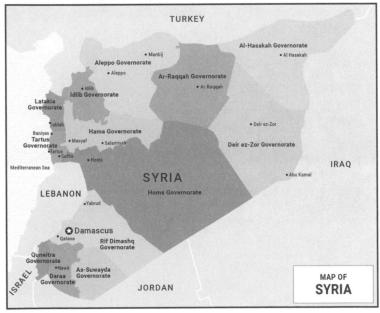

Map of Syria.

Bennett at Zaatari refugee camp in Jordan with camp officials and colleagues, David Ford, Sarah Snyder, and Douglas Leonard, 2015.

Bennett with Jordanian Lieutenant in Zaatari, 2015.

The "Champs Élysée" main street in Zaatari, 2015.

Bennett with Syrian refugee family in their caravan in Zaatari, 2015.

The destruction of Aleppo in the Syrian Civil War, 2016.

National Press Club and Nathan Mitchell Photography

MFA Joint Congressional Briefing on Syrian crisis in May 2016 with (l. to r.) Bennett, Representative David Cicilline (D-RI); actor F. Murray Abraham, and Shadi Martini, MFA, May 2016.

F. Murray Abraham speaking at MFA Congressional Briefing, Capitol Building, Washington, DC, May 2016.

F. Murray Abraham with children volunteers, Park Avenue Armory, New York City, at the MFA Faith & Heart packing event for Syrian war victims, June 2016.

Bennett and Shadi Martini in London, June 2016. Taken for an article by Ruth Gledhill for *Christian Today,* published September 14, 2016.

"Selfie" of Bennett, Shadi Martini, MFA; Adib Chouiki, Rahma Worldwide for Aid and Development; and Dr. Yahya Basha in Jaffa, Israel, 2017.

Israel Defense Forces soldier opening MFA cargo container of humanitarian aid to be delivered inside southwest Syria via the Golan Heights, 2017.

View of Quneitra and UN observation post in southwest Syria from Israel side of Golan Heights. The roads below show the route of MFA deliveries into southwest Syria.

Meeting at the residence of Cardinal Timothy Dolan, New York Archdiocese, 2017. From l. to r.: Bennett; General Mordechai "Poly" Mordechai, IDF; Cardinal Dolan, Lt. Colonel Sharon Biton, IDF; Bishop William (Francis) Murphy, New York Archdiocese; Vicky Downy, New York Archdiocese; (unidentified).

Bennett with Pope Francis at the Vatican, 2017.

World Refugee Day event hosted at the Metropolitan Club in New York City by Marcy Syms on behalf of MFA. From l. to r: Bennett and husband Leonard Polonsky, Mandy Patinkin, Kathryn Grody, and F. Murray Abraham, June 2018.

MFA Press Photo—Humanitarian Aid delivery in southwest Syria, September 2018.

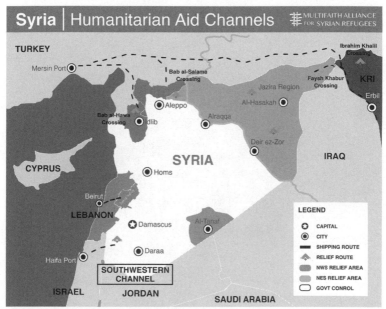

MFA Humanitarian Relief Shipment Routes.

Refugee trucks leaving from southern Idlib Province at the end of 2019 when the Russians and regime took over that region.

MFA Press Photo—Al-Hamama Camp, February 3, 2020. MFA sent ready-to-eat meals and water purification and hygiene kits to the people who fled the Russian and regime attacks in southern Idlib. They fled so quickly that MFA had to provide cooked meals because they had no cooking materials.

MFA's ready-to-eat meals, water purification, and hygiene kits being distributed in the Darkush Area, February 2020.

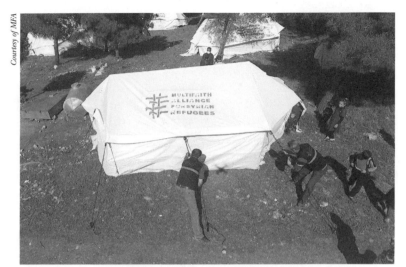

MFA Emergency Tent Program: Camp 4 near Maryamin Village in Idlib Governate, April 13, 2020.

Al-Hamama Camp in Northwest Syria with MFA/Orient Tents, 2020.

CHAPTER 8

A NEW BEGINNING

The Fluid Border Between Enemies Is Breached

Shadi, Ammar, and I are standing at the border fence on the narrow, pitted road between Syria and Israel—a stone's throw from the abandoned UN observation post on the Syrian side. UN peacekeepers had, for decades, been deployed there along the demilitarized area of separation between Syria and Israel. In 2014, because of several abductions by al-Nusra and continuing threats to their safety, 1,100 UN troops were evacuated to Israel, as regime forces and rebels fought for control of the area near the border.

We've been brought to this military area by Colonel Sharon Biton, IDF's Head of the Operation Division for COGAT, who had replaced Colonel Hatib and served under Poly's command. We are there to survey a dilapidated building directly across from the UN Disengagement Observer Force (UNDOF) post. That's where Orient is planning to renovate and expand a hospital on the Syrian side. The IDF is to provide safe passage for doctors and supply all the water, fuel, and electricity for the hospital. MFA is to source and ship the medical equipment, medical supplies, and medication that will help service an area surrounded by regime forces.

It was now late November 2016. Visas had been issued for Ammar and Shadi. The IDF made special arrangements to meet them at Ben Gurion Airport to ensure that, as Syrians, they wouldn't be suspect when entering Israel. Our itinerary had been arranged by Poly's staff, and I wrote to Gal to let her know that we would be arriving on December 6. At the time, Gal was, literally, fighting fires that had been raging out of control across Israel, especially in Haifa. After we arrived, we again tried to reach her to arrange a time to get together and settled on a dinner at the end of our stay. That dinner marked the final splintering of our partnership.

In the meantime, external events were shifting our priorities. Donald Trump had been elected president of the United States. One of his first official acts was to impose a travel ban from Muslim countries as well as reduce—illegally, in his first year (when he was bound by the quotas established with Congress in the last year of the Obama Presidency)—refugee resettlement numbers. Displaced Syrians were nearly excluded from entry. The refugee pipeline into the US was thrown into turmoil and, in a rightward drift, countries all over Europe and the Middle East were closing their borders. As mentioned in the last chapter, Trump would later withdraw from the Iran deal, but this would not translate into any appetite to confront Iran in Syria.

In this environment, advocating for increased refugee admissions was an exercise in futility. MFA made a strategic pivot to providing aid in place instead of resettlement. We differed from other humanitarian organizations in that Israel would be our conduit for getting aid into a part of Syria that was almost entirely surrounded by regime-held territory. The regime didn't permit aid to reach areas it didn't control. That meant southwest Syria was difficult to access—but not from the Golan Heights. It could also be reached through Jordan. But our partners told us that Jordan made things very hard, and a lot of the aid was diverted to store shelves.

During a 2018 meeting at the White House, Ghassan urged support for providing aid to the Syrian people through the Israeli border. He was told to go through Jordan instead. But Ghassan insisted that his work with Israelis was a way for Syrians to help themselves, rather than relying on Jordan. He pointed out that Jordan takes 30 or 40 percent commission on transferring humanitarian aid. But he also cited a political reason: He viewed cooperation between Syrians and Israelis as a grassroots process for peace in which the Syrian people needed to deal with Israel without any intermediaries. Only through direct contact did he think progress toward peace could be made. This, in contrast to the endless prior negotiations that never came to closure. To my knowledge, his entreaty fell on deaf ears, although in 2018 he received assurances from the CIA that they supported him—whatever that meant.

At our Madrid meeting, we had agreed that IFA would handle all logistics for Orient in Israel. Our first two cargo containers, packed with food, were already en route to Haifa, but these didn't come from Orient. They came from another Syrian NGO, Rahma Worldwide Aid and Development Foundation. Nevertheless, this first foray into Israel with Dr. Ammar was essential for setting the stage for other activities.

Shadi and I wanted to make Ammar comfortable, so on our first evening in Tel Aviv, we took him to an Arab restaurant in Jaffa. Breaking pita over the traditional array of Arab salads and meats, we filled up on the foods that spoke of home to my Syrian colleagues. At the end of the meal, Shadi and Ammar selected their preferred tobacco flavors and contentedly vaped the bubbling *narghiles* that were available.

Early the next day, we were to leave for a day-long site visit to the Golan Heights, from where we could scan southwest Syria, where our first deliveries of aid would soon arrive. This time, we weren't on Mt. Bental, with its café and scenic overlooks. Our vista encompassed Iron Dome anti-missile batteries, border fences, and military barracks. For my two Syrian associates, this must have felt like being in the belly of the beast.

The reception they received was anything but beast-like, though. Shadi and Ammar were instantly welcomed as trusted colleagues. They were brought into the inner sanctum of IDF operations in the Northern Command. There we met with the heroic Eyal Dror, commander of an Operation Good Neighbor unit on the Golan Heights, and Aviv Kochavi, who would in a couple of years become the Chief-of-Staff of the IDF. General Kochavi was entranced with the bridge-building vision we shared and offered complete logistical support. Ammar couldn't believe what he was hearing and was raring to get started.

Unfortunately, things had reached a breaking point with Gal. At our Madrid meeting, Orient had spontaneously proposed two additional projects inside Syria—education tablets and a hospital. Gal felt that she should be Orient's sole representative for those projects, as well as their humanitarian aid shipments. She interpreted her mandate as covering all of Orient's activities in Israel and felt territorial about that role. Orient vehemently disagreed. IFA's insistence on playing a role in the hospital and the schools was the dealbreaker for Orient because IFA had no experience running such institutions inside Syria.

For her part, Gal felt betrayed because she thought we were bypassing IFA after all her work making high-level connections in Israel. We assured her that there was a major role for IFA. But unfortunately, it all fell apart.

THOU SHALT NOT STAND IDLY BY

In the end, Orient focused exclusively on the hospital and not on shipping cargo containers of aid via the Golan channel. Rahma Worldwide Aid and Development became our lead partner for distributing aid throughout that region.

Our planned dinner took place just before we left Israel. Yisrael showed up without Gal and said he was bringing a message from her. The message was: "See what happens if you try to do this without me." He averred that the IDF couldn't do anything in Syria without Gal. It just wouldn't work.

We were all stunned. Ammar, who was elated after his heartening encounters with the IDF team and commanders, instantly deflated. It was more than deflation. He took this as a threat to his life. After all, the message was coming from a former deputy director of Shabak—one who was close to the government. And Gal had close relationships with the IDF. Ammar was risking his life by putting his trust in the IDF. "We won't go into a venture where someone has a grudge against us...What if I get stuck inside the border," Ammar speculated, "and the IDF won't extract me?" Although we'd done nothing to hurt Gal, she was Israeli and we were foreigners. Ammar feared that she could make the kind of trouble that could get him killed.

Sharon reached out to Gal, who was shocked that her message had been interpreted as a threat. She had never intended to threaten Ammar personally or professionally. She simply meant that our operations would not succeed without her. The fact that Yisrael had been a senior security official was irrelevant. He was simply the messenger. But the misunderstandings sown by this episode illustrate how vulnerable Syrians felt when first starting to work with Israelis.

Ours had been a completely reciprocal partnership. Gal had succeeded in bringing important people to the table. She spent months preparing for Shadi's first trip to Israel in which we met with key ministers as well as current and former presidents. She was strategic in identifying the six areas of Syrian-Israeli partnership that guided many of our discussions. She worked mightily to obtain visas. But in the end, none of this delivered the results that Ghassan—our most important Syrian partner—needed.

Shadi and I had also done IFA a great deal of good. Shadi had provided the connection to Ghassan. As a Syrian, he had taken huge risks in acceding to Gal's requests to go on radio or make videos to promote their work. I had advocated for IFA and helped raise significant money for IFA. I had also funded—personally and through grants I obtained—IFA's participation in our Track 1.5 process. While Gal had provided important platforms for us in Israel and Canada, we had provided equally important platforms in England, the EU, and the US.

There's so much more we could have done together. But our exceptional relationship devolved into a turf war. All of us shared a deep, visceral commitment to alleviating Syrian suffering and, with the best of intentions, we brought people together to form unprecedented partnerships. As long as institutional interests were aligned, all went well. But when interests diverged, perhaps our rupture was inevitable. With genuine fondness and respect, we'd shared a history and built something bold together—and then agreed to go our separate ways.

It took more than a month, but things calmed down and Ghassan was ready to go forward with building the hospital and launching the education project. Orient offered to pay a salary for some teachers and provide the tablets with the e-learning curriculum. The curriculum would be filtered to exclude all political material.

In what must surely be a first, Ammar turned to Sharon and said, "I'd like you to look over the curriculum on these tablets and let us know if there's anything that concerns you." The Israelis had made no demand to review the curriculum for incitement or anything else. But they took Ammar up on his offer and found no problems.

But, like so many other plans, the education project didn't get off the ground at that time. The media project would later be resurrected in a different and more daring form.

* * *

Ghassan was willing to proceed with another Track 1.5 meeting, but we were now working with another cast of characters—one that was in a stronger position to make things happen.

Our new Track 1.5 group met in Zurich. This time, the Israeli delegation was made up of Poly, Sharon, and a representative from the prime minister's office. Ghassan, Ammar, and Shadi were on the Syrian side. Each side put its agenda on the table.

For Ghassan, this was about more than simply delivering food and medical supplies. He was looking to lead the way to a new Syria, one with Israel as a partner.

For the Israelis, the first priority was humanitarian aid. The next was security. To achieve both, they wanted no intermediaries in the Golan. Eliminating intermediaries would solve the problem of diverted aid, and we would be able to document that all our deliveries went to their intended recipients. Our target area covered 600,000 people, including IDPs, in the forty or so Syrian villages along the border. Both sides agreed to ship containers through Israel. To that end, Israel had started building warehouses.

Orient would refurbish and expand the hospital near the UN Observation Post and focus initially on medical supplies. The hospital was urgent because Hezbollah was starting to move south into our intended delivery area.

Poly, formerly a spokesperson for the IDF, would work with Israeli media on a series about Syria. Ghassan was ready to send his team to Israel as soon as Poly was ready.

Then there was the hot potato—a safe zone. Israel did not want to take part in the Syrian civil war. Protecting a safe zone on Syrian land would ensnare it in that war. Sharon had met with American teams to enlist support for the creation of a safe zone, without which Israel could not undertake this responsibility. Ghassan felt that Jordan should also be a part of such an undertaking.

Our next trip to Israel occurred a few days after our Zurich gathering. This time, Shadi and I were accompanied by Adib Chouiki, vice president of Rahma Worldwide Aid and Development Foundation, and Dr. Yahya Basha. Basha was contributing two echocardiogram machines and a CT scan for our deliveries into Syria. No problem with visas.

Yahya Basha was a name that came up almost everywhere I turned in the Syrian American community. He was the embodiment of what Syrian immigrants meant to America. Basha was born in Hama to a poor family left without resources in the wake of the early death of his father and grandfather. Witnessing the suffering of two generations of his own family left him deeply sensitive to the suffering of others.

Hoping to be an eye surgeon, he came to the US from Damascus in 1972, with his Syrian medical training, to do an ophthalmology internship in Detroit but ended up in radiology instead. He had to overcome barriers of language, culture, and religion, and for his first four or five years in Detroit, he was insecure and fearful—anxious that he wouldn't fit in or succeed.

Eventually, he built one of the largest imaging businesses in the area. Basha Diagnostics now operates in four states, has 4,700 referring doctors and a staff of seventy to eighty employees. But this behemoth is a business with a heart, and Basha provided free car rides to refugees to bring them in for diagnostic testing.

In 1973, he started to attend a mostly Lebanese Islamic Center in Dearborn where he was able to meet other Syrians. Finally, group of Syrians got together and established their own Islam

Center, of which Dr. Basha was a founder and major supporter. He eventually rotated through leadership roles in key Syrian and Muslim organizations—Islamic Society of North America, Syrian American Council, Syrian Emergency Task Force, Syrian American Medical Society. He also worked closely with the Detroit chapter of the American Jewish Committee, and later with the Muslim Jewish Advisory Council and ADL. In 1982, after Hafez al-Assad crushed the city of his birth, Basha brought his entire family to the US. At that point, he vowed to devote himself to giving oppressed Syrians a voice and helping them live a decent life.

Given the fear of resettling Syrians in the US, I wonder whether people are aware of how long Syrians have been part of the immigrant tapestry of America. Most arrived after the 1960s when the Immigration Act of 1965 abolished quotas on Syrians. Like the majority of the 90,000 Syrians now living in the US, Basha was more highly educated, more prosperous, and more high-skilled than the US norm. Like his, the average income of Syrians in America is higher than any other foreign-born group. Like many of the thousands of Syrian physicians in the US, he was also very philanthropic. At a time in which anti-immigrant, anti-refugee, and anti-Muslim rhetoric were driving public policy, Basha gave the lie to all the misinformation that was extant.

Dr. Basha had been to Israel before. But it was the first time for Adib Chouiki. The risky decision to work with Israelis was driven by the difficulties of dealing with Jordan: closed borders, delays, the 35 percent fee, the *baksheesh* that would follow, and the frustration of wading through its bureaucracy. In weighing whether or not to work with Israel, the board reasoned that Rahma is a non-political humanitarian aid organization. Therefore, if Israel is offering to open its border, this was a "no-brainer." That said, Rahma was concerned about the reaction of the Syrian American community, including the potential loss of donors. They did lose a couple, but most accepted the partnership and gave Rahma the green light to carry on.

When Adib landed at Ben Gurion Airport, a military officer was waiting to escort him. "It was surreal, really. Being brainwashed in Syria, I didn't know what to expect," recalled Adib. "But all I saw was the urge to provide help. How can we make things easier for you?" Even his own family doubted this undertaking. "The Israelis have an agenda," they warned. "Whatever agenda they have is not relevant to me. I did not see bad agendas," replied Adib. "It's a humanitarian agenda."

The next day, we again set off for the Golan with Sharon. This time, we followed a truck that was carrying one of our cargo containers—one whose contents would be spirited across the border after nightfall. We arrived at the military post on Little Mt. Hermon, where we were greeted by Eyal Dror, his Uzi dangling from his shoulder. The wind was blowing hard. Right below us was Syria. Eyal, Adib, and Sharon moved past forbidding concrete bunkers, toward the edge of the crest, to survey the road along which our goods would travel.

Some time later, the head of Rahma, Imam Shadi Zaza, stood in the same place with Sharon. It was his first time in Israel, and he was terrified. Hours after he landed, he was sitting in Sharon's car, headed to the Golan Heights, with Sharon in full uniform. It was the first time in his life he saw Syria from that vantage point. He then asked Sharon to take him to Tiberias. Sharon was puzzled. Why Tiberias? Imam Zaza's grandfather used to tell him stories about how their family had owned Tiberias until the Israelis took it. "I still can't believe I'm in Israel, sitting in an Israeli Colonel's car," Zaza said to Sharon. "I was taught all my life to hate you." When in 2020, Sharon's nineteen-year-old paratrooper son was deathly ill, Imam Zaza wrote Sharon to say that he was praying for his son. "Imagine," Sharon said to me, "a Muslim Imam prayin for an Israeli soldier to get well!"

Shadi motioned Dr. Basha over to the truck, grinning broadly, with pride and anticipation. "Come on, Dr. Basha. Let's see our products." This, while Adib was giving one of the IDF soldiers directions in Arabic, and another IDF soldier took souvenir photos of Shadi and Basha. Adib was given the honor of unsealing the cargo container, but the doors were stuck. Sharon and Eyal, in full IDF uniform, came to the rescue and the door gave way. "Mazel tov," I yelled out. It was a jubilant moment for all of us. Syrians relaxing with Israeli soldiers with guns—that weren't pointed at them. Israelis encountering Syrians who weren't pledged to kill them. The exultation of presumed enemies discovering their common humanity.

But there was a price: A WhatsApp group in Horan "got very hot," recalled Adib. They knew that Rahma was sending aid into Syria through the Israeli border and accused Adib of being a traitor.

Mirabile dictu, the next visa to be issued was for Ghassan! He went to Israel two months later and would finally meet with the decision-makers who could help advance his broader agenda. One of those was Defense Minister Avigdor Lieberman, who in 2012 had told *Ha'aretz*: "Israel is willing to provide wounded Syrians all humanitarian aid at any minute it is requested." He and Ghassan had dinner with Poly and Sharon. At some point, Sharon understood it was time to leave the Syrian and Israeli titans alone. Ghassan took three giant cigars out of his pocket and he, Poly, and Avigdor went to the roof terrace of the King David Hotel. There, looking out over the Al-Aqsa Mosque, they convivially puffed on their cigars for two hours and got down to the *tachlis*. It was the beginning of an ongoing relationship between kindred spirits. Other meetings would include the head of Mossad and Intelligence. With the relationships he was building in Israel, Ghassan was laying the groundwork to potentially become the next leader of Syria—the moderate alternative that had been intensely debated at our earlier Track 1.5 meetings.

The Israelis refrained from going public because they were concerned about risking the lives of Syrians who received aid through the IDF. When Ghassan visited hospitals in the south of Syria through the Golan gate, he met some army officers who were responsible for supplying aid and advised them to release the videos of their activities on behalf of Syrians. He told them and Poly that they were making a big mistake by holding back and pushed hard for media coverage. Finally, he took matters into his own hands and decided to go public rather than hide his outreach to Israel. That year, in a historic first, Orient ran a forty-five-minute piece featuring Shadi, a Syrian refugee in the US; Dr. Ammar, a Syrian refugee in Dubai; and Fadi Al Asmai, a Syrian reporter in besieged Quneitra, to reveal their humanitarian partnership with Israel.

Dr. Ammar described the dire humanitarian situation in southern Syria and the crucial role Israel was playing in operating Orient's hospitals near the border—water, fuel, access, and supplies. He stressed his duty as a doctor to provide help inside Syria from whatever country offers access. By way of background, Ammar told of his meetings with officials and NGOs in Israel.

Shadi bravely shared his experience inside Israel and how different it was from everything he had been taught. He was surprised to find so many Arabic speakers and stunned by the diversity of opinions and the freedom to express them.

Fadi discussed the calamitous situation in the south, due to the Regime blocking all aid. The locals wanted help—especially medical aid. They didn't care if it was coming through Israel, because it certainly wasn't coming from other neighboring countries.

Al Jazeera picked up the story and bashed the three Syrians as traitors. When the network posted the story on its Facebook page, the overwhelming majority of responses bashed Al Jazeera for bashing the Syrians for working with Israel. A sampling of th posts from Syrian listeners reveals their contempt for the hypocrisy of the critics:

- *We're happy with the Israeli aid. At least Israel makes real raids on the Regime from time to time.*

- *So now helping Syrians and saving their lives is a crime? Especially after our Arab countries closed their borders to our wounded?*

- *Where's the problem? Why don't you come and give us aid instead of selling us dreams and illusions at our expense?*

These responses were consistent with Adib's monitoring of social media. He found that a vast majority of responses to Rahma's work with Israel garnered positive posts.

One year after our initial meeting, General Poly was back in New York for the September UN General Assembly meetings, which, this time, included Sharon. What a difference that year made!

MFA was working with Syrian, Mormon, Catholic, and secular partners in sending aid. The IDF, along with our contacts on the ground in Syria, provided us with shopping lists of needed items. We would then source those items among our donors—such as Catholic Medical Mission Board, Kirk Humanitarian, Rahma, Save the Syrian Children, Church of Latter-Day Saints, Afya Foundation, Smith Medical, National Police Aid Convoys, Delivering Good—and ship the cargo containers to Haifa or Ashdod. These containers were filled with ambulances, food, clothing, sanitary kits, medication, flour—whatever was needed. These deliveries would also support three medical facilities and a bakery that produced 15,000 pitas a day.

Per Adib, "The greatest success story is building the bakery in Quneitra." The twenty-by-ten-meter building was imported through Israel, and all the equipment was donated by Israelis. The flour was donated by the Mormons in the US.

The cloak and dagger transfer of aid into Syria always took place under cover of night. It was an operation done with military precision. The cargo containers would be brought to a cleared space at the border by the IDF. Once delivered, the military officers backed away. Eyal would alert Adib as to when the goods could be picked up. It was a twenty-minute drive on a dirt road from the camp in Quneitra to the border fence. The road was excavated on the Syrian side so that big trucks could drive through. When the Rahma team arrived at the excavated area, the Israelis opened the fence. Five or six Syrians were permitted to enter the Israeli side to take the goods and upload them to Syrian trucks with a forklift. Once they had the goods, the Israelis would again close the gates. Technically, the IDF officers and the Rahma team had no actual contact.

One day, IDF soldiers were placing medical equipment into the Orient hospital in Quneitra. A few al-Nusra fighters rode up on bikes and a pick-up truck with a machine gun mounted on the back. They had received a tip that Israelis were installing intel equipment in the hospital. When they arrived, they found themselves face-to-face with Israeli soldiers. Separated by three to five meters, the IDF and al-Nusra were in a stand-off, pointing guns at each other.

With their lives threatened, the IDF could have easily opened fire. Wisely, they instead took two steps back, allowing the other side to enter the hospital and see that there was only medical equipment there. Happily, al-Nusra was mollified, the IDF was restrained, and the humanitarian operation kept going.

Three to five nights a week, Israeli soldiers would come to the border fence. They simultaneously had to perform three tasks: protect each other from danger coming from Syria; protect themselves from weather that was always either too hot or too cold; and act as mules, carrying tons of flour, books, medical supplies, and gasoline. Imagine what must have been going through the minds of these eighteen-, nineteen-, and twenty-year-old youths. They were trained to view Syria as enemy territory, and here they were risking their lives to funnel in humanitarian aid.

And yes, the weather was a factor. One day, heavy snow blocked the roads and the goods couldn't get to the waiting Syrians. A call to Sharon was made by the Northern Command. The IDF bought mules in Israel and gave them to the Syrians. The mules carried the goods to the villages, where they were distributed and then came back the next night—and for many nights thereafter—saving the lives of countless Syrians.

In this way—and any other way that worked—our partnership delivered aid that added up to more than $120 million over a two-year period. The IDF spent tens of millions of shekels funding their end of the operation. Our aid would penetrate deep into southwest Syria, beyond Daara, and assist a population of more than 1.5 million—far beyond the initial target area.

This was the first time that Israel had opened its border for humanitarian purposes. "People in the villages knew from where the aid was coming," recalled Adib. "Every time we go, they say, 'Thank you, Israel. We'll never forget this.'"

We had a story to tell, and I arranged a meeting for General Poly with the *New York Times* editorial board, among others. The *Times* wanted access to the border to see Operation Good Neighbor in action. Given the paper's perceived bias against Israel, the IDF wanted them to do a story before being given access to the border. But the *Times* had already done a front-page story about our work in July. Still worried about the risk to Syrians, the information Poly provided was off the record. We also had a meeting with Mary Kissel of the *Wall Street Journal* editorial board. When Kissel fortuitously left the *Journal* to become a top aide to Secretary of State Mike Pompeo, I was able to lobby her on behalf of more productive policies toward Syria.

That week, I also arranged for General Poly and his delegation to meet with Dr. Basha, who had flown to New York and brought along Omar Hossino of the Syrian American Council to speak with the Israelis. There he spoke of the commitment of Syrian Americans to the future and prosperity of Syria and laid out the work being done to garner both political and financial support from Syrian Americans, the administration, and Congress—both Democrats and Republicans. Among their other efforts, Dr. Basha and his brother, Ishmael, were lobbying hard to resettle Syrian refugees in Pontiac, Michigan—a dying city that was hemor-rhaging population and in urgent need of resourceful newcomers.

Omar emphasized the threat posed by Iran and Hezbollah in Syria and his unsuccessful efforts to get both the Obama and Trump administrations to take that threat seriously. At the most basic level, there had even been a reluctance to place certain Iranian-backed militias on the terrorist watch list. Was this all in service to the Iran nuclear deal? If so, this was one of a number of compromises made by President Obama to rescue that pivotal deal, which in any case was swiftly abrogated by Donald Trump. (As of this writing, President Joe Biden has stated his intention of reviving the deal.) Those compromises were, in ways both direct and indirect, made on the backs of the Syrian people, to little practical effect.

Because MFA is a multifaith organization, I also arranged meetings for Poly and Sharon with Bishop Andrew Dietsche of the Episcopal Diocese of New York and Timothy Cardinal Dolan of the Catholic Archdiocese of New York.

Episcopal Relief and Development was part of the MFA network. Its work for Syrian refugees is centered in the Zaatari and Arzaq camps in Jordan, where it prioritizes aid to young chil-dren and integrating children with disabilities into public schools. However, it also provided blankets and stoves, to help thousands of families in regime-held areas inside Syria survive harsh winters

Much of the aid ERD provides is done in conjunction with the Fellowship of Middle East Evangelical Churches, a consortium of Evangelical Protestant churches.

Dietsche offered to review our request to make use of the Golan channel with the Episcopal Bishop of Jerusalem. Because the Episcopal Church is part of the Anglican Communion and the Anglican Communion is in the forefront for calling for boycotts of Israel, I assumed that would be the kiss of death. The Protestant churches, with which ERD works, in general, tend to be highly critical of Israel. As I feared, nothing came of it.

Cardinal Dolan was enthusiastic about engaging parishes in the Archdiocese to adopt containers to fund. That never happened. I suspect this was because of a renewed escalation of tensions between Israelis and Palestinians. Because Christians are under threat in Arab countries, the Church must tread a fine line when it comes to Israel. It was much the same in the 1960s. At that time, my late husband was doing the back-channel work during Vatican Council II, which resulted in the landmark document, *Nostra Aetate*. The ratification of the document was delayed for years, largely because of warnings from Bishops in Arab countries that Christian lives would be in danger if the text was too conciliatory to Jews.

This history notwithstanding, a couple of months later, with introductions by His Eminence, I had two key meetings at the Vatican. One was with Cardinal Turkson, head of the Dicastery for Promoting Integral Human Development. With him was Msgr. Segundo Muñoz, the person responsible for humanitarian aid. Msgr. Muñoz said "Wow!" when he learned of the new Israeli channel and said he would reach out to Caritas International, Caritas Syria, and the Association of Volunteers in International Service (AVSI).

These organizations are among the main arms of the Catholic Church engaged in humanitarian aid. AVSI is focused on development activities and programs, mainly through education, while drawing from the social teachings of the Catholic Church. Their programs in the Middle East are based in Iraq. Caritas, "the helping hand" of the Catholic Church for the "poor, vulnerable, and excluded," works at the grassroots level in almost every country in the world. Emergency operations are coordinated from Rome.

Caritas Syria, headquartered in Aleppo, has six regional offices in that country and partners with Shiite and Sunni organizations to provide housing assistance, food and basic items, education, support for the elderly, and psycho-social support for children.

Muñoz mentioned three upcoming meetings with bishops, curia, and others and invited me to speak. Cardinal Turkson also offered to help in several important ways, such as making introductions to Drs. Biaggi and Czerny, under-secretaries who work directly with the Holy Father on refugee issues.

The second meeting was with His Eminence Cardinal Sandri, Prefect of the Congregation for the Oriental Churches. Sandri expressed great enthusiasm about the multifaith dimension of MFA's work and was particularly impressed with the new Israeli channel. He offered to connect MFA with the Apostolic Nuncio in Syria. At the same time, he planned, at their annual meeting, to inform all the Catholic organizations that provide aid in the Middle East of MFA's work in the hope that they would engage with us. His Eminence advised that the steering committee would meet in January to identify issues to be covered at their annual conclave, and he planned to present MFA's work at that time.

During our conversation, Cardinal Sandri referenced the difficulty of supplying three hospitals that the Catholic Church had built in Aleppo and Damascus. Wanting to be helpful, I suggested that MFA might be able to make connections to Syria organizations that deliver aid through Turkey. Because two these were in areas controlled by the regime, MFA had no access them directly. Nor, at the time, did we have operations in the north that would have allowed us to access Aleppo. We had no way of knowing that this would soon change. By the time we started operating in the north, Aleppo was under regime control.

My initial purpose for being in Rome was to address the "Migrants and Refugees in a Globalized World: Responsibility and Responses of Universities" conference, organized by the International Federation of Catholic Universities. The conference ended with an audience with Pope Francis.

In his remarks, the Pontiff highlighted the role of Catholic universities in harmonizing science and theology. Now, he said, was the time for studies of forced migration and identifying practical solutions. As always, he decried the xenophobic reactions to migrants "in countries of ancient Christian Tradition." He invited Catholic universities to educate their own students, some of whom would become future leaders, and to apply standards of justice, global responsibility, and cultural diversity to their understanding of forced migration. Perhaps he wasn't aware that we were a multifaith group. But that didn't matter. His message was universal.

Group audiences with the Pope take place in a large hall with brocade walls, richly painted ceilings, and marble floors. The Pontiff, dressed in white robes, is seated on a throne-like chair, flanked by two aides in black robes with fuchsia sashes. Rows of seats are set up, auditorium style, facing the front. The Pope delivers his remarks and then stands. Row by row, we're called to stand on a line in the center aisle, where we are ushered to the Pope, one at a time, to get our brief face time and photo op with him.

The normal sixty-second elevator pitch would be far too long ꭓ this setting. Thirty seconds is more like it. As I approached, ꭓcalled my late husband's many visits to the Vatican and his ꭓ more private meetings with prior Popes. I looked up at the ornate ceiling and thought to myself: "Hey, Marc—can you believe I'm here!" At the same time, I couldn't help feeling sorry for Pope Francis, who had to remain standing until each of us had filed through—and to remain alert, while listening intently to the dozens of people who seized their moment to have his ear. I used my brief one-on-one time with the Pope to cite my meetings with Cardinals Dolan, Sandri, and Turkson and share MFA's hope of finding ways to work more closely with the Vatican.

Meanwhile, the Orient TV series was still waiting to be born. A new reporter/producer had been assigned, who was busy coordinating with Nir, Shadi, and me. However, by the fall of 2017, Israel was again on the verge of war with Palestinians and the Israelis could not focus on the long-planned series. Nor could they properly follow up on Ghassan's trip to Israel. Ghassan felt he was being "hung out to dry."

Despite that, he had made a bold decision to speak at a semi-public event at which he shared a program with Poly at the West Side JCC in New York City. This was the first time that a high-ranking IDF General and a prominent Syrian leader had shared a platform. The March 2018 program was billed as: "Private Briefing on Geopolitical Situation and Humanitarian Diplomacy Between Syria and Israel." Out of concern for Ghassan's safety, the program attendance was by invitation only. The invitations included philanthropists, Orient Media, Dr. Basha, Vicki Downey from the New York Archdiocese, and select others.

In my introduction, I drew heavily from an insightful analysis by Nir Boms about the current state of play in Syria. Geopolitically, the Syrian War seemed to be nearing an end and there was a new status quo in the country. Tens of thousands of displaced Syrians had returned home. Syrian contractors were clearing the way for new roads. Russian cranes were building a new port terminal. Iran was constructing a modern medical city near Damascus. Russian and Iranian forces had become entrenched.

On the humanitarian front, Israel's policy had evolved from passive onlooker to good neighbor. Whereas aid had initially been given unofficially only by Israel's civil society sector, assistance was now sanctioned by the government and given in coordination with the Syrian side. This started with medical aid in Israeli hospitals, where more than 5,000 Syrians had been treated. It culminated in the Good Neighbor program, in which more than $100 million (soon to be $120 million) in aid had been delivered in coordination with MFA and Syrian partners. Operation Good Neighbor opened channels of communication between Syrians and Israelis and created a modicum of self-sufficiency in southwest Syria.

From these bridges sprang the hope that humanitarian aid would, in a calmer future, translate into regional cooperative ventures.

And that brought us to this moment in 2018 with Poly and Ghassan, who were at the point of the spear of this grand vision.

For Poly, there wasn't much risk in making this appearance. But for Ghassan Aboud—a self-made Syrian billionaire with international businesses, a media empire, and a humanitarian aid operation—there were many potential losses, including the loss of his business and even his life.

As the moderator, I asked Ghassan about his great act of courage in reaching out to Israelis. Having been raised like every other Syrian, I wondered what personal transformation he had undergone. He replied that all Syrians "would like to be sitting here to talk to you. I am not different." He said there was no "hard history" between Syrians and Israelis. He also made a point that I've not often heard—and certainly not from an Arab. "I don't know how many Syrian people Israel killed: 1,000? 10,000? People say that it's 20,000." (The actual combined number was under 5,000 for the wars of 1967, 1973, and the 1982 Lebanon invasion, according to a *Los Angeles Times* article published in March 1991.) Regardless, Ghassan pointed out, Assad killed 20,000 in just *one month,* dwarfing the number of deaths at the hands of Israelis during all the wars that Syria had initiated.

He reaffirmed his conviction that peace between Israelis and Syrians would not come through governments, but from the bottom up through civil society groups. And through business. Ghassan had a vision of Israeli companies working with Syrian entrepreneurs to rebuild Syria—starting with co-branded olive oil. Poly concurred: "It's very important that we have peace with Jordan and a peace with Egypt. But it's more important that we build a peace…between people."

Poly, in turn, talked about the Israeli government's motivation in starting Operation Good Neighbor. The IDF had already been providing critical medical aid to Syrians who found their way to the border. As Sharon observed, IDF was doing things that are not part of an army's natural DNA.

"Each time those little children would cross into Israel with their moms, many of them without shoes, they would arrive at the crack of dawn on the Israeli side. We always waited for them with food and beverages. Israeli soldiers would escort them to an Israeli hospital. On the way back, they had to wait until dark. We would take them to one of the kibbutzim near the border where they would stay for a couple of hours and get food. No one would go back home without new shoes, new toys, new clothing and small package of sugar and rice. Israeli soldiers sat on the floor drawing pictures with Syrian kids and moms." One child drew a big heart with an Israeli flag in the middle. That drawing was hung in the IDF Northern Command offices.

Eventually, Poly realized that Israel could build on these inter- actions. After that, the IDF started to think about expanding its activities. They realized that the villages along the border often lacked electricity, water, and baby products. So, Poly tappe the IDF budget to buy baby products and send them across border. He never expected that Syrian organizations—like Orient and Rahma—would become prime partners in this outreach.

Some suspect, as did the militiamen who encountered Israelis equipping the Orient hospital in Quneitra, that this entire humanitarian operation was a foil for intelligence gathering. Sharon vehemently disputed that: "I was conducting a civilian humanitarian operation. I was not an intelligence officer. We didn't even share the same contacts inside Syria. Intel is a completely separate operation. I truly, truly, truly believe that by doing what we've done, we are not the same people Assad and his regime are telling them we are. Maybe one day there's a hope for peace."

Poly echoed that sentiment. "What we started in Syria is to show…that Israel is not the big devil…like what they heard in their education." When products were first sent from Israel, the labels were removed out of concern that they wouldn't be used. But in later deliveries, the labels were in Hebrew. "Today it's normal. Today there are villages asking us to send more products…It's a process to start to build trust," Poly explained.

Shadi pointed out the benefits of bringing Israeli branded products into Syria: "Israelis don't send flour with insects inside—the UN does, the World Food Program does…All the aid coming through Israel is good quality—like the medical aid."

The World Food Program has been criticized for fostering corruption. Local politicians have been known to steal food to bribe voters or to sell the aid on the black market, damaging local agriculture. But that's less the fault of the World Food Program than a problem that is inherent in the UN Charter, which requires its aid agencies to work through sovereign governments—which are often corrupt. An independent evaluation that coincided with the onset of the Syrian crisis found that WFP generally achieved its humanitarian objectives, but only 42 percent of the evaluations ound that it did so in a timely and efficient manner. Chronic erfunding—which forced a near shutdown of food aid to

Syria—often stymies its work, as do logistics and the need to serve widely dispersed populations.

We were very aware that any pharmaceuticals coming through Israel had to have a distant use-by date, lest Israelis be accused of trying to kill Syrians with expired medication. Perhaps that, too, added to the quality of the aid that was sent.

For Poly, the good news was that many of the Syrians coming to Israel for medical treatment weren't just coming to the border fence from villages in the south. Syrians were coming directly from Damascus. Some were flying into Ben Gurion Airport. Among these was the Syrian boy whose treatment at Save A Child's Heart in Israel had been orchestrated by Shadi in the earliest days of the conflict.

Poly saw this as the basis for building a relationship. For the past forty years, the border between Israel and Syria had been quiet. But it was then in full control of the regime. Poly said Israelis now understood that they had to open a new relationship, based on humanitarian and economic partnerships, with the Sunni majority. He expressed his hope that Sunni leaders could become a force in Syrian politics. For now, however, two major powers—Russia and Iran—were propping up the Alawite minority rule. The Alawites, with their allies, were crushing and disenfranchising the Sunni opposition and rendering them largely powerless.

As for the contentious issue of the Golan Heights, Ghassan's solution was to turn it into a free trade zone for tourists so that both Syria and Israel would benefit.

Poly concluded by acknowledging Ghassan's commitment and expressing the hope that he might one day be the one to redress the balance of power in Syria and bring moderate Sunn' to the fore. Above all, he praised Ghassan for his courage in gc public with his fearless actions.

In my view, we had accomplished a great deal—far beyond just delivering massive amounts of aid. Because people were receiving services and medical care, the extremists were denied a meaningful foothold in the region. By working through local councils in Quneitra and Daraa provinces and contributing to a rudimentary economy via the medical facilities and the bakery we supported, we helped stabilize the entire southwest of Syria.

In short, we had changed hearts and minds, built bridges of trust, and nurtured formerly unthinkable partnerships.

The Center for a New American Security studied our work and co-authored a *Foreign Policy* article with Shadi in May 2018 entitled: "The One Place in Syria That Works." In that article, they explained why southwest Syria was an island of stability.

There were a number of factors that contributed to that stability—such as the de-escalation zone established the previous year by Jordan, the US, and Russia—but our work was a critical factor.

MFA had consistently delivered aid—$120 million worth—through an unprecedented partnership between Israel and Syrian NGOs. This lifeline empowered NGOs and civic organizations and stymied recruitment efforts by extremist organizations.

By going through the Israel-Syria border and working with Syrian NGOs on the ground, we were able to penetrate a region with a population of 1.5 million people. (As noted earlier, southwest Syria was surrounded by regime-held areas, making it difficult to access from anywhere but the Golan Heights.) The aid we delivered planted seeds of self-sufficiency and enabled a measure of normal life. Because locally elected councils were the conduits for our assistance, it also contributed to propping up Syrian civil authority at a time of near-total collapse.

"The Only Place in Syria that Works," summarized these posi- results and also made the important point that this was "a -driven process," which ensured that aid was distributed efficiently "and in a way that it does not end up in the hands of extremist actors."

In short, the distribution of humanitarian aid was an exercise in soft power, which is a highly impactful tool of diplomacy. Without it, the parties end up relying on weapons, which ultimately extends and deepens deadly conflicts.

There was a great deal to learn from our experiment in southwest Syria, and in 2019 our staff spent a lot of time on the Hill conveying those lessons to Congress and other US government agencies. At the invitation of Mary Kissel, I wrote a think piece for her to share with Secretary of State Mike Pompeo, making the case for humanitarian diplomacy and enumerating some of the lessons we had learned.

Values-driven Policy — As with the Israel case, values-driven policy is powerful. The US has the highest rate of religiosity in the developed world. As such, it has strong Abrahamic values on which to draw including the Golden Rule: the obligation to care for the poor and the stranger; to provide sanctuary; and to "do justice, love mercy, and walk humbly with thy God." Appealing to these values, in a country that prides itself on its piety, is a muscular basis for secular policy.

Changing Hearts and Minds — Syrians who had been raised from birth to hate Israelis and Jews were suddenly confronted with an enemy that was there to help them, not kill them. This triggered a realization that it wasn't the Israeli enemy who was driving them off their land and killing them, but their own government. Many Syrians asked themselves, "If that was a lie, what else that we've been taught was a lie?" Eventually, the Syrians who were working in partnership with Israelis went public on Arab media, acknowledging the help Israel was giving them in their hour of greatest need. The response was mostly positive.

There are many parts of the world in which America is hate but none more than the Middle East. If humanitarian policy change Syrian attitudes toward Israelis, it can change hearts and minds toward Americans.

Security — Southwest Syria is a strategically important area in which Israel and Iran are competing for control. Notably, in the two years that "Operation Good Neighbor" stayed in place, it remained stable and largely inoculated against radicalization. The unprecedented partnership between Israel and Syrian NGOs also provided Israel with trusting relationships in the region on its northern border. All this immediately collapsed when humanitarian diplomacy stopped. Now, Hezbollah is firmly entrenched on Israel's border and Iran's sphere of influence is reinforced. It is in US security interests to provide aid, education, and hope to displaced populations, which are otherwise vulnerable to hate and radicalization.

Bottom line: At a time when borders are closed and refugee resettlement is largely shut down, it is strategically important to increase aid in order to maintain stability, reinforce civil society, provide basic needs, and enhance US interests through enhanced intelligence opportunities and anti-radicalization measures.

The Trump administration targeted stabilization funding and other foreign aid for drastic cuts. It was clear to me that this was an irrational policy in the case of Syria and I argued forcefully against it in *The National Interest* issue of November 2017.

During congressional hearings about the cuts, Senator Dick Durbin asked then-Secretary of State Rex Tillerson about the effects of reducing the budget for migration and refugee assistance on Jordan, a US ally. Tillerson averred that US troops and diplomatic resources were restoring conditions that would allow the refugees to return home and cited successes in Iraq, which he ᵃsured the committee could be replicated in Syria. In so doing, ᵉver, he ignored certain fundamental differences between ᵃ situations and was promoting a policy that was based on significant misunderstandings. As such, the lives of real people were being severely impacted.

The idea that Syrian refugees could return home was wildly unrealistic. Every refugee response agency prioritizes returning refugees to their home country. But with Syria, there is, for most, literally no home in which to return. In Aleppo alone, at least 30 percent of homes are destroyed or uninhabitable. In addition, the regime has an active program for disenfranchising returning refugees, which is described in more detail below. More to the point, according to IRC president David Miliband, today's conflicts last an average of thirty-seven years. Victims can remain displaced for decades. Tillerson's assurance that Syrian refugees could return home sometime soon was thus naïve at best and cynical at worst.

Unlike in Iran, it was not ISIS that drove Syrians out of their country. It was the brutal tactics of the Assad regime, which have been amply described in earlier parts of this book. By the time ISIS was formed in April 2013, according to the UN High Commission for Refugees (UNHCR), 529,000 registered refugees (with tens of thousands more unregistered) had already fled Syria. ISIS did not take root in Syria until 2015. By then, nearly ten times the number of registered refugees had fled. Therefore, defeating ISIS does not solve the problem that caused Syrians to flee. Nor does it create conditions conducive to bringing them home.

In his testimony, Secretary Tillerson described his strategy: "We are talking to other countries and asking them to do more, to step in to fill some of the needs that Jordan has in refugee camps. Same in Turkey." There were three fallacies in his reasoning:

First: fewer than 10 percent of registered Syrian refugees are in camps. More than 90 percent, the majority of whom are women and children, are urban refugees. We don't know how many hundreds of thousands or millions are unregistered and belo the radar. The millions of urban refugees put a huge strain their host countries' infrastructure. If those countries—esp the ones that share a border with Syria—are to remain stable, they need more support from the US, not less.

Second: others are not stepping up to the plate. The US is the single largest donor nation, having provided nearly $6.5 billion to the region since the start of the crisis. But it's also the wealthiest. The EU had already mobilized €9.4 billion by then, with an additional 33 percent of that amount pledged for 2017. Even tiny Kuwait had, by 2016, donated $360 million (proportional to their size) to UNHCR for the Syrian crisis and Iraq—making it the sixth-largest global donor, per capita.

Third: Tillerson noted the need to assist refugee camps in Turkey. But Turkey was not preparing Syrians to return home. Syrians speak Arabic, while schools in Turkey teach only in Turkish. As a result, some refugee parents were refusing to send their children to school, since Turkish would be of no use if they returned to Syria. In addition, Turkey was not granting exit permits to highly educated Syrians, who it saw as a means of stemming its own brain drain and as useful assets for its economy. (There's a lesson here for the United States.) Simultaneously, Turkey used its Syrian refugees as pawns with which to extract concessions from the EU, by threatening to open the floodgates and send them to Europe.

Donald Trump reduced the cap on refugee resettlement in the United States from 110,000 to 45,000 when he came into office. By 2020, he further reduced it to 18,000, with only 193 Syrian refugees having been admitted. Given that the US is not resettling refugees, we should be allocating more funds, not less, to provide urgently needed aid to refugees in place. Cutting the budget for refugee assistance doesn't make sense at a time when the suffering is intensifying and borders are closed.

Such irrational policies were being driven by misinformation, ⁀nformation, and three great fears—fear of negative economic ⁀t, fear of terrorism, and Islamophobia. Facts need to displace myths in driving public policy. However, policy has been going in the opposite direction. And that makes the exercise of soft power via humanitarian diplomacy all the more important.

In the CNAS piece, the authors warned that: "The alternative to Operation Good Neighbor would be the rapid collapse of the opposition communities, either to be ruled by extremist actors or to Assad's forces, spearheaded by Iran." In September of 2018, that's exactly what happened in southwest Syria when Operation Good Neighbor and MFA's Golan channel had to be shut down. But that didn't stop our work. We simply rerouted our deliveries to northwest and northeast Syria, via Turkey and Iraq. In the process, we vastly expanded our network of in-kind donors as well as partners on the ground.

CHAPTER 9

MAINTAINING MOMENTUM

As One Door Closes, Another Opens

In mid-2018, the Assad regime, with the backing of Russia and Iran—and the compliance of Israel—launched a major offensive to retake one of the last rebel strongholds in southwest Syria. The offensive was in clear violation of a ceasefire that had been negotiated between the US, Russia, and Jordan. Russia, which had been charged with enforcing Syria's observance of the ceasefire, was instead supporting the Syrian Army's attacks with massive air cover. The US, for its part, made no moves to enforce the ceasefire.

At the same time, Israel made a deal with Russia in which they agreed to accept the incursion that was bringing the regime right back to its borders. The deal included shutting down the Golan channel for humanitarian aid operations. Russia took responsibility for the delivery of aid. (Not only did it fail to deliver aid, but it blocked the opening of cross-border channels in the UN Security Council.) In return, Russia was expected to keep Iran away from Israel's borders and not interfere with the Israeli bombing Hezbollah munitions inside Syria. It was a devil's bargain. But

184

with the regime back in control of southwest Syria, the 1974 Disengagement Agreement was again in force, and the INSS "old think" about a quiet border again became Israel's policy.

The southwest immediately descended into chaos, with infighting and assassinations. Aid and services suffered a complete breakdown. No heat, gas, flour, or electricity. We heard that the medical facilities we had supplied were destroyed. Rebels' heavy weapons were either voluntarily surrendered or their caches exposed by civilians. Reconciliation talks took place, but it was hard to believe that Assad would not exact revenge on those who had fought him, once the regime reasserted control. And they were correct. Russia had promised to protect the insurgents from arrest and interrogation, but military intelligence lost little time pressing for the names of local rebels. Many were arrested, tortured, and pressured to become collaborators.

Israel extracted intelligence officers and—at the request of Germany and with the intervention of Richard Harrington, a Jewish British MP—the White Helmets. But our partners were left to their fate. Feeling abandoned by Israel after risking their lives to work with them, some bitterly fled north. Others remained. It seemed all the trust and goodwill, so painstakingly built, had been destroyed. And the stability to which our efforts had contributed in the southwest felt like a mirage.

Tens of thousands of ordinary Syrians tried to flee the carnage. A large percent massed on the Israeli-controlled Golan Heights, but Israel was not admitting refugees. Jordan, which had recently experienced protests triggered both directly and indirectly by the influx of Syrian refugees, closed its borders. Most fled to the last opposition stronghold in the north.

Assad had largely won the military victory. But now he needed to govern and provide for the people. The few remaining are not under regime control were in much better shape—with ries, water, electricity, and services—than those that had fal

* * *

Ghassan returned to Israel in August, and General Poly coordinated a meeting for him with a senior political personality. There wasn't much of substance to discuss. Chitchat about the elections—and an apology from the official for the situation in southwest Syria. Ghassan then visited the Golan Heights, where he reviewed military maps and identified a location where Russian military police were stationed. Ghassan warned his hosts that the area was flooded with soldiers disguised in regime uniforms who were actually Shia militias.

Ghassan was unsparing in his criticism: "It's terrible what you're doing. You took a promise from Russia that allows the Israeli Air Force to strike everywhere…But you're already doing that. Russia gave you nothing." In despair, he concluded, "I have no more cards to play. You took all my cards and destroyed everything."

Our work had been designed to plant seeds for the long term. In that plan, Israel could be a leader in stabilizing the region, backed by strong agreements with a Sunni majority on the ground in Syria. Instead, Ghassan predicted, "Assad will wait twenty years and Israel will have Shia militias at the border."

He was sure the agreement with Russia would not succeed. In one sense, he was right. Iran-backed Hezbollah took maximum advantage of the newly ceded region to set up posts near the border. In another sense, though, it did succeed, because Israel was able to bomb those posts and munitions with impunity, interrupting Iran's smuggling of arms into Syria. An Israeli intelligence officer confided that the bombings numbered in the thousands.

This setback was discouraging, and we were at a loss as to what do next. Under General Poly's wing, Ghassan also met with IDF ef of Staff General Gadi Eisenkot and Deputy Chief of Staff al Kochavi, as well as other senior Israeli officials. Kochavi encouraged Ghassan to wait until after the election and try a new approach. The following month, Ghassan, Poly, and I returned to Berlin to explore our alternatives.

For MFA's part, after the Golan channel was shut down, we rerouted our deliveries to the northeast and northwest of Syria via Turkey and Iraq. The plight of those Syrians was becoming more dire as international agreements broke down and they came under attack in the last remaining rebel stronghold. As of May 2020, there were 6.2 million people in that area, and two-thirds of them were in need of humanitarian assistance.

Rizwan Mahmoud Hassan, whom we assisted through the Joint Crisis Coordination Center, fled with his family in October 2019 to the Kurdish Region of Iraq (KRI), arriving in Bardarash Camp near the city of Duhok. "We have been on the road for two days," he attested. "We fled because of the bombing and air raids in Qamishli and because people are getting killed and injured." The camps were initially set up in response to the displacement crisis engendered by the rise of ISIS in Iraq and Syria in 2014. But Syrians, (primarily Kurds) have continued to flee there because of the terror engendered by Turkey's cross-border operation in northeast Syria in October 2019. The Kurdistan Regional Government reports that it costs about $1 billion annually to sustain aid for the more than one million displaced people living in the KRI.

Given our track record in the southwest, the US force stationed in the northeast was eager to work with us. In doing so, we would be replacing the IDF with the US Army. However, it turned out that the US military wasn't set up to deliver the amount of aid that we could bring in from the new donors we had added to our network—a list including Massimo Medical, GlobalMedic, Gymboree, Kids for Less, Kirk Humanitarian, Global Gateway, and Action Meteor. We instead worked with other local partners, such as People Demand Change, Bahar, Orient, Watan Rise, and Gift of the Givers.

People Demand Change was founded in 2013—the same year as MFA—by defected Syrian diplomat Bassam Barabandi. Working at the grassroots level, PDC's approach to humanitarian aid is to promote self-sufficiency and reduce the need for emergency supplies. This is entirely consistent with the work that MFA did in southwest Syria. But self-sufficiency was unrealistic under the cruel conditions in the north. Many were forced to sleep in the wild without food and water. Children were malnourished. Water-borne diseases swept through informal encampments as people drank from polluted rivers and streams.

We worked with PDC in the north by sending medical equipment and supplies, food, water purification, and hygiene kits. PDC distributed our medical supplies by partnering with Kurdish Red Crescent, for which we provided more than one hundred boxes of medical supplies. With branches throughout north and east Syria, KRC has ambulances and health facilities, which provide medical care, vaccinations, and free medicines. Our cargo containers, with donated supplies from GlobalMedic, provided aid for 5,600 people.

Bahar, a large organization founded by three Syrian doctors, was our partner in distributing urgently needed pre-natal pregnancy and lactation vitamins—nearly 120,000 bottles to be divided between northeast and northwest Syria. Half went to the Turkish-controlled area of Afrin. The other half was shipped to Erbil, Iraq, and then trucked to the Hasakah region, which is controlled by Kurdish forces.

Orient had been an MFA partner from the beginning of our humanitarian aid operations. In the north, we provided them with medical supplies and equipment, vitamins, hygiene kits, food, water purification, and children's diapers. Among those who received help through our partnership was Sarab Mohamed Saloom.

A mother of five, with a malnourished ten-month-old son, Sarab had fled from her town of Koeres east of Maret Al-Noman.

Resources, including formula and diapers, were scarce for her and her family. Sarab said that nearby villages had no diapers, which were only available in larger towns. And due to their high cost, she could not afford to buy them in any case. Now she had access through Orient.

Abo Azzam, who fled his hometown in the countryside of Hama, is another war victim who was aided by the MFA/Orient partnership. "We have been moving for months from one place to another after the Syrian regime and its allies bombed our town continuously," Abo said. "They forced us to leave our house and take only light baggage in fear of our lives." His case is not unusual. Many Syrians have been forced to relocate multiple times within Syria as the conflict continues for an eleventh year. "We are short of food and many daily necessities, including clean water, blankets, tents, and clothes," Abo explained. "Your assistance will help us a lot."

Watan Rise, based in Turkey, works in Idlib, Aleppo, and the refugee camps near the north. MFA shipped them food, water purification kits, hygiene kits, and school supplies. The latter are vitally important. A 2018 OCHA assessment of 226 camps in Aleppo and Idlib revealed that 73 percent had no education services at all. The lack of safety is also a critical barrier. Since the crisis started in 2011, there have been more than 762 reported attacks on educational facilities.

After receiving school supplies, brightly clad children in the IDP camp come joyfully tumbling out of their school tents, clutching their textbooks and notebooks. Some settle in front of the banner bearing the MFA logo and speak of their longings. Says one young boy: "I hope one day we can live like students abroad and study in a real building instead of a tent." A girl, Shihid, says, "I hope one day we can study like students in America and have school supplies." Nada adds, "And also notebooks, backpacks, and clothes." Another wishes "to have blankets and fuel for our heaters." All express their wish to live like Americans.

The connection to Watan Rise was made by Ahed Festuk. Ahed first joined MFA as a volunteer and rose to become MFA's Manager of Humanitarian Relief. When the Arab Spring erupted, she had been working for four years as an accountant for Cave, a retail chain in Aleppo. Inspired by the uprising in Egypt, she quit her job and became one of Syria's pioneer women demonstrators and a member of the ancillary staff of the Aleppo local councils.

Her path to protest began with a Lebanese grandmother who used to visit and regale the family with vivid descriptions of life in her country. She spoke about politics. She spoke about right and wrong. She spoke about freedom. Ahed realized that they could not speak about such things in Syria. "I loved Syria, but I wasn't proud to be part of it. We don't fight for our country because we love it. We fight for it just because we have to."

In school, she saw pictures of the Assads everywhere. She dutifully wore her military uniform, but the rigidity of the teachers suppressed her motivation. Once, after having drawn a mustache on a photo of President Assad in her textbook, she was punished for making fun of the Syrian leader. Another time, she was a few minutes late for class. Her teacher smacked her on the ear, causing Ahed to lose her hearing for two months.

So when Ahed saw Egyptians mass in Tahir Square in Cairo, she thought: "Oh my God, how lucky they are! As soon as I saw people were taking to the streets, I didn't even think about it." She immediately logged onto Facebook and joined a protest group. They called themselves "Flowers" and organized demonstrations. Initially, they encountered resistance from their fellow Aleppians, and the Flowers had to lobby hard to explain the urgency of the revolution. In the beginning, there were only thirty people in their group. But students saw what was happening in Homs and Daraa and their ranks swelled to 10,000. Before the Free Syria

Army came to Aleppo to protect the demonstrators, many were killed. As elsewhere in Syria, doctors were particularly targeted. Three doctors who were treating protestors were arrested, burned, tortured, killed, and dumped in a park.

When the bombing started in Aleppo in 2012, Ahed's terrified mother beseeched her husband to leave. "I can't live here anymore. You need to take us out." Her parents fled to Lebanon and later to Turkey. Ahed refused to go because she felt duty-bound to stay in Aleppo to treat the wounded. When the war erupted, she worked as a paramedic on the frontlines.

By this time, she was working in a hospital because she had been trained to administer first aid and was contracted to train hostile-environment and first aid responders inside Aleppo. She remained in Aleppo's rebel-held side until late November 2015. In the interim, Ahed lost many close friends—some were arrested, some were killed, some fled to Europe. Ahed felt alone and hopeless. "What am I doing here?" she wondered. In the depth of her despair, a friend approached her about a short documentary she was making. When the film was released, Ahed was invited to come to the US to speak publicly about her experience as a Syrian woman activist. While there, in 2016, she decided to seek asylum in America.

Among the organizations with which she worked in Syria was Watan Rise. Now, like her countryman Shadi Martini, Ahed continues her humanitarian activities from the outside.

Adjusting to the US was "super hard" for Ahed. A year after she arrived in the US, Aleppo was under siege. "It was very hard to be in a place where you have everything you need—electricity, a shower whenever you want, any kind of food you want—when my friends are hungry." She needed "to feel that I'm doing something here."

MFA's director of operations, Marlene Adler, happened to see Ahed speak at an event, and they started spending time together.

Ahed asked whether she knew of any organization where she could provide help. Marlene suggested MFA. "The work we're able to do makes me very happy and gives me the satisfaction of knowing that I'm helping my people." Ahed smiles and says, "The depression I used to feel is gone because I feel I'm doing something useful."

Gift of the Givers, an African humanitarian aid organization, is the largest of its kind on that continent. It has built and staffed hospitals in Syria, where the medical infrastructure has been nearly destroyed. Shadi and GlobalMedic connected MFA to Gift of the Givers. We provided medical supplies and equipment, hygiene kits, food, and water purification for their life-saving work.

Gift of the Givers is deeply embedded in the town of Darkush in northwest Syria, where they are training residents in how to deal with COVID-19. But they don't limit their support to medical aid or hygiene kits. With the prevalence of stories like the one below, Gift of the Givers asked MFA for school supplies, after we sent them to Watan Rise.

"My children never went to school, and I cannot afford to send them," said a mother living in a camp visited by Gift of the Givers. The mother's three boys are unable to read or write. "I can't afford the cost of pens or notebooks. I have no money or any support," said the mother. "They only help me. I cannot do anything for them."

Among others who received assistance through MFA's partnership with Gift of the Givers is Omar, a fifty-four-year-old man living in Adam Camp near Darkush. He and his family were forced to flee after their home in Latakia was bombed by the Syrian regime. "I had a small shop and a humble house. I was happily living with my wife and four children," Omar said. "All of a sudden, I lost my child, my home, I lost everything." In the bombing, Omar's thirteen-year-old son, Ramy, died. "I wish I would have died before putting my family in a tent where we lost our dignity," Omar said, bursting into tears. "Sometimes I feel embarrassed to look into my daughters' eyes when they stand in the queue for the toilet."

Then there is Rama, a fifteen-year-old girl from Ein Elbikara camp near Darkush. Displaced children in Ein Elbikara camp are unable to go to school because of its distance from their tents— especially in the cold winter months. Rama's dream of becoming a teacher was shattered eight years ago when she and her family were forced to flee their home. "I keep asking myself a lot of questions about my family's situation. Is it because we aren't rich—so other countries think we deserve to live like this?" Rama muses. "Or is it because we are not important, so the decision-makers think that we are valueless?.... I don't know how to answer myself and I don't know how to describe my feelings." Like Rama, life for many displaced Syrians is marked by a widespread feeling of abandonment and despair, and children often feel neglected in their camps.

Myriad other organizations are operating in the north which are worth mentioning though MFA has not worked with them. Molham Team Volunteering, founded in 2012, operates in the Aleppo countryside, Idlib, Jordan, Lebanon, and Turkey. It was founded by Syrian students to provide for the basic needs of Syrian refugees and their countrymen in northern Syria.

Shafak was founded in 2011 and officially established in 2013 as a grassroots organization by Syrians for displaced Syrians. It is based in Turkey and operates in Jordan and inside Syria.

Space of Hope was established in Aleppo in 2012 by a group of that city's expatriates to aid local community members.

Violet Organization was founded in Idlib in 2011 and initially focused its volunteer activities in Idlib. It has since expanded to other provinces in Syria and has set up three camps for Syrian refugees near the Turkish border. It has also teamed up with IF and Save the Children and is part of the eighteen-member Sy

NBO Alliance that includes the Syrian American Medical Society and Shafak.

All these organizations have several things in common. They were established early in the conflict to fill the void left by the slow international response. They are independent, locally-based, and have credibility at the grassroots level. Such local roots help ensure that aid is not diverted before it reaches its intended recipients.

In short, the shutdown of the Golan channel wasn't at all impeding MFA's operations in Syria. We were able to continue our humanitarian mission without missing a beat. Within a short time, we had delivered another $45 million worth of aid in the north on top of the $120 million worth we had brought into the south.

But we weren't ready to abandon our efforts to plant seeds for future coexistence in the region—a mission in which we had already invested so heavily. We were determined to revive and sustain the trailblazing partnerships we had nurtured between Syrians and Israelis and searched for ways to keep that connection alive, in the absence of a shared border. That search would take us back to Israel's Ministry of Foreign Affairs as well as the Israeli industrial sector. And Ghassan would outline a new vision for Syria's future.

CHAPTER 10

A NEW VISION OF SYRIA

An Unlikely Partnership Is Revived

We still believed in the importance of preserving the Syrian-Israeli partnerships we had fostered during the two years of Operation Good Neighbor. In Berlin, we explored ways to keep Israel engaged in humanitarian diplomacy with Syrians. One way to do that was through a reverse version of Operation Good Neighbor: Instead of Israel serving as a staging area for the outbound delivery of international humanitarian aid, Israel would send out its own products. Poly checked with Lieberman, who responded positively to the idea.

Nevertheless, we faced a number of obstacles, including the still-raw feelings of those in the southwest who felt abandoned by Israel in 2018. More problematic was the absence of a shared border in Syria's north. The proximity to Israel of Syrians in the south enabled a kind of habituation. But in north Syria, there had been no such direct experience with Israelis—except for those who had fled from the southwest. Absent that, any deliveries of aid coming from Israel would be fraught in the Arab world.

Our solution: send products that are unique to Israel and can't be obtained elsewhere. "Start-Up Nation" is known for its technology—including its medical technology. We identified several medical devices that fit the bill. Among these: WoundClot, a special gauze that stops severe bleeding from traumatic injuries; ReWalk Robotics, a wearable exoskeleton that enables paraplegics and those with spinal injuries to walk; and OrCam, a spin-off of Mobileye, one of Israel's most successful start-ups, which was acquired by Intel.

By now, Poly had retired from the military and was a businessperson working with OrCam. OrCam, named for "Or," the Hebrew word for "light," is a device that allows the blind and visually impaired to "see." It can also help children learn to read. Based on AI technology, the device can read text, do facial recognition, detect colors and currency denominations, and identify products. Thousands of Syrians were blinded or visually impaired in the violence of the civil war. And half of Syrian children were out of school. This device could make it possible for those with limited vision to function in everyday life and could help educate the lost generation of Syrian children.

We were extraordinarily excited about the possibilities—and careful to avoid a conflict of interest for Poly. OrCam created an Arabic version, renamed NoorCam ("noor" being the Arab word for light), and Orient geared up to train doctors and distribute the devices.

Because Orient supplies many hospitals in Idlib, they could assure distribution. And Orient media would provide publicity. But Israel still faced the same issue that had derailed its funding at the outset of our Track 1.5 process. How could the government fund the costs of goods to go to Syria before it takes care of its own citizens?

The devices were very expensive—even with the discount ꞏing offered by OrCam. The Gates Foundation is probably the only foundation large enough to cover the costs for the 10,000 devices we wanted to distribute. But when I reached out to the appropriate program officer, I was quickly, but kindly, rebuffed and told that such funding was outside the Gates funding areas. I was given no specifics.

We placed great hope in receiving government funding from Germany because this type of aid bypassed some of its geopolitical concerns. OrCam and MFA's Fund-a-Container program were vehicles through which Germany could provide aid without having to engage with either Turkey or Iran. Russia was trying to get German money to rebuild Syria. But if Germany was to get involved in reconstruction, it would not do so as long as Iran was a presence there. (Germany is not the only country: the US and its other allies have also refused to provide funds for reconstruction so long as Assad holds power.)

At the same time, Germany has a tense relationship with Turkey, and Erdogan had recently made an unsuccessful State visit to Germany. Saudi Arabia was a counterweight to Iran, but Angela Merkel would not sell the Saudis arms until the matter of the murdered journalist, Jamal Khashoggi, was addressed. Germany's relationship with Jordan was unambiguous and its support generous. Therefore, it was suggested that we provide Israeli goods to refugees in Jordan.

I didn't see how that would work because Israel cannot operate openly in Jordan, and several of our partners in aid had complained about the large commissions the government takes for goods that flow through its borders.

Attempts to get the OrCam project off the ground continued through 2019 with meetings in London, Bucharest, and Berlin. The German government, like many others, is guided by the priorities established in the UNHCR annual Regional Response Plan's scale of needs from one to six: food, shelter, health, protection, winterization, etc. OrCam was too much of a niche proje to be included among these priorities, and we were told it was highly unlikely that the government would fund a project outside this framework. Visual impairment was not among the UNHCR priorities, so as of this writing, this was another dead end. But a church group in Germany still appeared to be interested, and we hadn't given up.

Even if funding had been obtained, though, the ground had shifted dramatically during the time we were trying to get this project off the ground. The northeast and northwest were the last remaining rebel strongholds. But Idlib had come under attack, in violation of deconfliction agreements. More than 900,000 Syrians fled to closed borders in order to escape unrelenting aerial bombings—especially on medical facilities—and brutal attacks on civilians. It was winter and thousands were without food, shelter, and protection of any kind. Mothers were waking up to find their babies frozen to death. MFA focused its attention on building tent cities with Orient to provide at least a modicum of shelter for displaced Syrians.

Under these circumstances, there could be no orderly way to distribute the devices—admittedly a luxury at a time when people still needed the basics in order to live another day.

The situation was so desperate that Syrians in the north were ready to receive Israeli products—even those that were not unique. So we started searching for other goods that we could get to them. In 2020, we began a trial program with Tikkun Olam Makers (TOM), an Israeli NGO founded by Gidi Grinstein, an entrepreneur and founder of the Reut Group (where Asaf Hazani worked when we met in Chapter 4). TOM was building a vast database of open-source medical supplies and protective equipment for emergencies around the world. This was their first foray into Syria. But at this point, the Israeli government had no appetite for getting involved in the Syrian crisis beyond keeping Iran and Hezbollah out of the Golan.

While north Syria was under attack, we received a report from a researcher with close ties to the CIA, Turkey, and Emirati intelligence about conditions in the south. The report was written three months after the recapture of the south by regime forces, backed by Russia and Iran. A reconciliation deal had been struck with the Free Syria Army and other local fighters, with Russia as a guarantor. The deal was repeatedly violated by the regime, and Russia took no enforcement action. Some locals tried to make nice to the regime with banquets for senior security members in the hope of being protected or obtaining personal privileges.

The Southern Front included forty-four factions. Cash was used to get the fighters to accept the new status quo. Being trapped in the region, many quickly swung to the regime side in the futile hope of shielding themselves—especially in the face of having been let down by FSA commanders. Nevertheless, the regime proceeded to track those who had been trained at the Jordanian Jafr base or who had received any kind of support from Israel.

That said, the region was anything but stable. The counterweight to the regime were the ten or so influential tribes that inhabit that part of Syria. Although the tribal leaders submitted to the regime at the outbreak of the war, the tribes rejected the presence of the regime. For some, the enmity was deeply rooted: sons lost in the battles of Daraa; a relative turned dissident; injuries suffered during regime military campaigns.

According to Akil Hussein, a Chatham House analyst, 60–70 percent of Syrians belong to a clan or tribe. (Clans are subsets of tribes.) This is true of virtually all Middle Eastern countries, and of developing or preindustrial societies all over the world. In the absence of a strong national state, social order is maintained through these decentralized extended-family networks. Clan and tribal leaders can be highly influential on the community or military level.

Hussein describes a strong tribal presence in northeast Syria, including the self-administered Kurdish area. These are divided between regime loyalists and opponents. The Arab tribes, such as the al-Sanadids, which joined the Kurds, established a strong force. In the south, contrary to the intelligence report we received, Hussein opines that attempts to build a similar force had failed as of 2018.

Because of their power, the regime is attempting to win over the tribes in the south, where the main center of the large al-Naim tribe is based. Many stay silent because of infiltrators who monitor their movements. However, there are others who command military factions. If the tribes were to merge, the report concludes that a force of a mere 3,000 fighters could retake the south for the opposition. This in turn could lead to reopening the Golan channel.

In short, the tribes are deeply split. But Ghassan believed in the ability of the tribes in the south to retake that region.

In light of the intelligence report, we began to reconsider Jordan. Ghassan posited that any action in the south must benefit Jordan economically. He pointed out that Jordan is motivated to rebuild Syria because the billions of tons of concrete that would pass through Jordan would generate vast sums for the kingdom.

Poly felt that if the situation changed on the ground in the southwest, Ghassan's idea of creating a buffer zone with local police and councils to support local villages could become a reality. Either way, he believed that a showdown with Hezbollah was imminent. Sunnis want Hezbollah out of Syria.

Ghassan was ready to provide major media support if Israel were to go to war with the nemesis of both Israel and Sunni Syrians. That didn't make sense to me. If Hezbollah leaves Syria—where it is broadly despised—and returns to Lebanon in full force—where it is broadly admired—this would intensify Hezbollah's focus on Israel. True, explained Poly, but a major supply route for smuggling arms to Hezbollah would be cut off, thereby weakening it.

By early 2019, Israel was again facing paralysis-by-election. Bibi was under investigation—and later indicted—for corruption. The government's main focus was on the Shia threat, and it continued to make strikes on Iran-Hezbollah positions inside Syria. Meanwhile, President Donald Trump had just announced the pullout of US troops from northeast Syria, throwing America's allies into turmoil. In the void left by the US, Ghassan reported that influencers in the Gulf were seeking a stronger relationship with Russia. At the same time, infighting had broken out between Russia and Iran in Syria. And in January 2020, General Qasem Suleimani, the architect of Iran's ground war in Syria, was assassinated by a US drone strike near Baghdad International Airport.

The assassination of General Suleimani brought the US and Iran to the brink of war and was almost universally criticized. It rattled America's other allies and further chipped away at trust in the US. But Bibi Netanyahu was supportive. Suddenly, I saw an opportunity to connect some dots in messaging and humanitarian diplomacy, in which the US would come out looking good (for a change), which I shared with Mary Kissel at the State Department.

Southwest Syria had become destabilized since the Iran/Russian-backed offensive of September 2018. This was bad for Israel, and for the region. It wasn't in the US' interest to cede southwest Syria to Iran. With Suleimani gone, Iran's operations in Syria would likely be in disarray, providing an opening to create a sphere of influence in southwest Syria via Israel.

Most media coverage of the killing focused on its impact in Iraq. In fact, Suleimani was responsible for hundreds of thousands of deaths in Syria. By shifting the focus to Syria, the president's actions could be seen in a more favorable light.

MFA's goal never wavered: After the great success of Operation Good Neighbor, we were intent on getting the Golan channel reopened. Using our knowledge of the situation on the ground, we reached out to our contacts in the Ministry of Foreign Affairs to convince them that this was the right moment to act.

Russia had promised the rebels protection for surrendering southwest Syria. They had also promised aid and services to replace the goods that had flowed through the Golan channel. They didn't deliver on either. When the Atlantic Council mapped the aid provided by Russia's Center for Reconciliation of Conflicting Sides in Syria (CRCSS), they found that one-third of missions were concentrated in areas recaptured by the Syrian government. Most missions, across Syria, were one-offs or very limited. That was true throughout southern Syria. Because the same entity—Russia—that provided aid to these communities was also a major factor in their violent surrender, this breached the principles of impartiality and neutrality that govern human-itarian aid. Even worse, in 2020, Russia was pushing for all UN humanitarian aid to be controlled by the regime in Damascus—a guarantee that the distribution of aid would be corrupted by politics and cronyism.

MFA's sources on the ground told us that the current Russian presence in the area is confined to very few military posts with minimal personnel. Seemingly, the Russians have abdicated their role as a mediator between the Regime and the opposition in the southwest.

The rebels in the southwest, who had gone underground, were beginning to resurface. As part of the reconciliation agreement, they had surrendered their heavy weapons to the Russians, but still had their personal AK-47s and a large store of ammunition.

The economic and humanitarian situation in the southwest was dire. The locals were contrasting how much better off they were when the Golan channel was open. A new insurgency had begun with identifying collaborators and regime intelligence personnel and was being carried out with assassinations and bombings. The insurgents claimed to have the ability to retake the whole region, and to do so quickly. But they were asking for the backing of a regional power—that is, Israel—so that they could take out the Iranians and the regime presence. In order to do so, they needed a resumption of the humanitarian aid that we had previously supplied through the Golan channel. This seemed like an ideal time to resume Operation Good Neighbor and the humanitarian diplomacy that had been aborted at the end of 2018.

For the third time in a row, Israel was in election paralysis in which there was no clear majority to enable the formation of a government. As such, Israel was about to miss a prime opportunity to get Hezbollah off its border and reestablish valuable partnerships with Sunnis.

It was a lost opportunity for the US as well. By intervening, the administration could have taken credit for creating a situation in which humanitarian aid deliveries, via the Golan Channel, could resume, thereby re-stabilizing southwest Syria and saving lives with aid. It could also take credit for increasing Israeli's safety by helping to re-stabilize southwest Syria via humanitarian diplomacy. In any case, it was not in the US' interest to yield southwest Syria to its archenemy, Iran.

Finally, after three elections, and three failures to form a government, in April 2020, Benny Gantz and Bibi Netanyahu agreed to a power-sharing arrangement. But now Israel was in the throes of a lockdown triggered by the COVID-19 pandemic. And this, alone, was enough to divert attention from the reopening of the Golan channel that we were advocating.

Nevertheless, Ghassan was still very much a person of interest for Israel as a future leader of Syria. Midst the dramatic realignments taking place in the Middle East, he was pragmatic, courageous, open-minded, and well connected from the Gulf States to the CIA. He had a vision of a new model for an accepted, legitimate government in Syria: a federation and charter cities.

Partnerships with Israel were central to his vision, and this was consistent with MFA's commitment to future regional stability.

Ghassan drew a direct line from the centralization of government and population to the Arab Spring. By focusing development on major cities, like Damascus, those outside the center were being systematically marginalized. "Syria cannot return to dictatorship and a centralized economy," he wrote in 2018—a time in which the Assad-Iranian alliance controlled only 40 percent of the country. In the civil war, he saw new opportunities for the establishment of local specialized development areas linked to autonomous Charter Cities in Idlib/Aleppo and Daraa/Quneitra.

Aleppo fell entirely under regime control at the end of 2016. But with a population of 4 million people distributed among fifteen cities in Idlib province, a seaport, and an airport, Ghassan saw a critical mass for creating an autonomous region—one with a multi-season agricultural environment. The area was tribal, and tribal buy-in was important because they could serve as mediators between government and individuals in the new model. In Ghassan's vision, armed militias would be transformed into local police. But the success of this concept needed more than buy-in from the tribes; it needed the buy-in of the US, Turkey, and Israel.

The second autonomous area Ghassan identified was Daraa and Quneitra, where MFA had been delivering aid throughout Operation Good Neighbor. Here Ghassan envisioned large-scale economic projects that would employ a large youth population in agriculture and manufacturing for export to Europe. This, after undergoing remediation for the years of education that had been lost.

He saw a critical role and key incentives for Israel. Helping to build an organized security force to keep Hezbollah at bay, without needing to intervene militarily in Syria or Lebanon. Investing capital in a small area around the Golan, which would allow Israel to maintain some economic and political influence in south Syria. Building office parks and manufacturing facilities for Israeli companies that would open Arab markets to them while supporting Syrian businesses with products branded in the name of the region. Helping to build small and medium-size workshops, which could provide needed labor for the Israeli economy.

The presence of Charter Cities in both the north and the south would put financial pressure on Iran, the regime, and Hezbollah, thus weakening their presence in Syria. But this model required a strong state sponsor—such as the US or Turkey—that would prevent Iranian and Russian intervention. At the same time, the Charter Cities would provide passage to the sea through their territories and create an economic boon for Jordan in the south.

This was Ghassan's formula for building hope, maintaining stability, and keeping extremists at bay. But the focus of the US was on northeast Syria, where its troops had been stationed and working in partnership with the Kurds. Israel's appetite for any engagement with the Syrian crisis beyond the shared border was put on the back-burner for the time being.

In 2019, Ghassan reiterated his faith in Charter Cities as the way forward for a new Syria with freedom of religion, expression, and movement, along with free trade, personal safety, and economic security.

For him, the time was right—but perhaps the time had passed.

That year, the chaos in the south and the attacks on the north, with Turkey entering the fray, had changed the political geography.

There was no significant change of control in northwest Syria because the Turkish incursion and movement of Russian and regime troops was much farther to the east. It was in the northeast that the US acceded to Turkish demands to create a thirty-two kilometer-deep and 300 kilometer-long "safe zone" along the border, inside Syria. In so doing, the US gave up the tremendous leverage it had in Syria. By driving ISIS out of its "caliphate," the US and its allies had established a zone of control over nearly one-third of Syria's territory. That zone was home to Syria's key natural resources—oil fields, arable land, water, and electrical production. Assad, Iran, and Russia were eager to get their hands on these resources. Had the US chosen to do so, it could have exerted great influence on the conflict. Instead, the US abandoned the region—and the Kurds, after they had done most of the heavy lifting in ridding Syria of the ISIS caliphate. This drove the Kurds south. Out of desperation, they invited Russia and the regime to northeast Syria in order to repel their mortal enemy, Turkey.

Now there were joint Turkish-Russian patrols from Tal Abyad to Ras al-Ain. Once Russia started bombing Idlib, the joint patrols turned into adversarial battles. In the meantime, a small contingent of US troops returned to control the oil fields. US policy narrowed to a reliance on increasingly restrictive sanctions focused on any US or non-US person doing business with the Syrian government or government-controlled construction projects. The screws were tightened by the broadly supported and applauded "Caesar" bill that was passed by Congress in 2019. This meant a hold-up on any reconstruction efforts until the regime ceased its human rights abuses. The unintended consequence could also impede human-itarian aid because of the difficulty of determining whether the contracting entities may be acting on behalf of the Syrian govern-ment or its allies. So the policy of "slow bleed" continues, and the hapless Syrian people remain the main victims.

Fortunately, MFA operates in the crevices, having nothing to do with the government. The critical crossings through which MFA was delivering aid—such as Faysh Khabur in northern Iraq—remained open. We continued to send medical supplies, meals, and vitamins that, in 2019, reached 90 IDP camps, 13,500 families, with 65,000 emergency meals, 20,000 water filtration kits, 120,000 bottles of prenatal vitamins, and hundreds of tents to house thousands of people.

Helala, a widow and the mother of two disabled children, now lives in an MFA tent camp. While struggling with a heart condition, she has repeatedly fled bombings. The first time was an airstrike in which her husband and cousins were killed. The second displacement took her and her remaining family to the countryside of Jisr al-Shughur for safety. "We didn't have shelter. We didn't have the resources to rent a place," she said. "Now, we have this tent, thank God."

We just kept on doing what we were doing in the north to the extent that geopolitics allowed. But we didn't give up on returning to the south. The bakery in Quneitra hadn't been destroyed—and that was a glimmer of hope. After the Syrian government took over, Adib contacted the regime saying that the bakery—which had been equipped by Israel and supplied by Americans—was a gift from the Syrian community in America to the Syrian people.

And Adib confided in me that, should the Golan channel re-open, Rahma was ready to work with us again in bringing aid to southwest Syria. Shadi and I lobbied hard to re-open the Golan channel. But with the 1974 Disengagement Agreement in place, we were repeatedly rebuffed.

Nevertheless, the Ministry of Foreign Affairs was open to helping MFA in northeast Syria, where it had solid contacts with the Kurds—and even Lebanon, where so many Syrians were living in misery. We identified several promising areas in which Israel could continue to play a role. One of these was the revival of the education partnership that had originated in our Track 1.5 process.

As of this writing, three out of the six areas of partnership have been mobilized: humanitarian aid, education, and commerce. With the help of Israel's Ministry of Foreign Affairs, MFA received seed funding to multiply the curriculum tablets created by Orient and distribute them widely among the Syrian children who were, for years, deprived of school. The Ghassan Aboud Group is making connections with myriad Israeli companies to distribute their products in the UAE. We are also exploring a revival of the Track 1.5 process itself with new participants. And, coming full circle, we're discussing webinars in which Israeli trauma specialists and other areas vital to displaced Syrians. Finally, we've initiated a partnership with Watergen, an Israeli tech company that has developed a device for turning air into water. Our pilot program was targeted for Hasakeh province, a water-starved area in northeast Syria.

* * *

Since 2016, as the previous chapters make clear, MFA has focused primarily on bringing aid to displaced Syrians. But MFA's early years prioritized advocacy for increased resettlement, successful integration of newcomers, and countering misinformation about Syrian refugees. We never stopped doing any of those things. But three external factors caused MFA to pivot away from its initial focus on resettlement: the election of Donald Trump and his "America First" ethos; the rise of right-wing nationalist governments in Europe, which closed their borders to refugees; and the COVID-19 pandemic, which gave governments a reason to both reject further inflows of refugees and oust many of those who were already in their countries.

But aid in place is just one part of the solution for Syrian refugees. The fact remains that most Syrian refugees will never be able to return home, and they cannot be allowed to languish in limbo. In my journey across this vast landscape of human suffering, I learned many lessons about the myriad ways in which geopolitics influence policy.

CHAPTER 11

NOWHERE TO GO

The Stubborn Geopolitics
of a Humanitarian Crisis

This story ends largely where it began—with intractable suffering and displacement.

Since late 2019, nearly 950,000 have fled northwest Syria in the face of clashes between Russia, Turkey, and the regime. Another 400,000 may potentially join them. More than 80 percent are women and children. In the northeast, 70,000 remain displaced as a result of the Turkish offensive against the Kurds.

But the regime has also played a role in ongoing atrocities in the north. In its February 2020 update, "Search for Life," the White Helmets, the Syrian Civil Defense organization, documented the following over the prior nine-month period: Internationally prohibited cluster bombs used against 322 locations. Nearly 12,000 additional civilian sites targeted with other weapons. Attacks on main roads used by displaced people to flee villages and towns that are under assault. ISIS, although deprived of its territorial caliphate, continues to launch attacks in the East Euphrates area.

And in those areas retaken by the regime, people still get shot at checkpoints, and humanitarian aid is waning. David Miliband concisely summed things up in mid-2020: "The situation resembles a frozen conflict rather than an emergent peace."

The refugees are not welcome at home or in their host countries.

When the displaced return, many are considered enemies of the state by the regime. Miliband recounts anecdotal evidence that: "The government has levied a wide range of criminal charges against returning refugees, meaning that many of them risk imprisonment and torture if they try to return." The Syrian government has also invoked Law 10 to appropriate and redevelop land that once belonged to displaced families—especially Sunnis. As a result, those refugees have no home to which to return.

Law 10 requires that, if a property owner does not appear on official documents, he or she has one year to provide proof of ownership after being notified that their property is designated for reconstruction. For IDPs and refugees, who have fled for their lives without papers and other vital possessions, it's almost impossible to provide that kind of proof remotely. According to the Washington Institute for Mideast Policy, Law 10 provides a convenient and "legitimate" way to alter the demography of Syria by rebalancing its ethnic mix.

For those who do return, it's usually due to tensions with the host communities.

Lebanon

Half of the Syrian population that is displaced remains outside the country, although some—primarily from Lebanon—have spontaneously and voluntarily returned, mostly to Syria's Daraa and Aleppo governorates. There is a push by the Lebanese government for Syrians to return to their home country. IRC has been denied access to provide services to Syrian refugees in some towns and villages because their municipalities regard humanitarian aid as an incentive for refugees to remain in Lebanon.

The tensions in Lebanon echo those in Jordan, as described in Chapter 3.

Turkey & Greece

Turkey also wants to rid itself of Syrian refugees. Yet, the 3.5–4 million Syrians it hosts have been a convenient pawn for President Recep Tayyip Erdogan to extort concessions from Europe. Europe was traumatized in 2015 when a flood of refugees and migrants poured onto its shores through Turkey. Most of those going to Europe were young men—unlike the typical Syrian refugee demographic of women and children. The maleness of the exodus was spurred by four factors: fear of conscription, targeting by the regime, the vulnerability of women to gender violence en route, and the strength to undertake a perilous journey. Female-headed households and those too poor to afford the journey were left behind. These optics raised alarm bells in Europe and the US. Caught unprepared, the ensuing chaos catalyzed right-wing governments and provided easy scapegoats for terrorist incidents and economic downturns.

In order to take off the pressure, the EU made a deal with Erdogan to pay Turkey to keep the refugees within its own borders. When Turkey invaded Syria and went into battle with Russia in 2019 and 2020, it called on its NATO allies for assistance. Absent that help, Erdogan threatened to open the floodgates, letting loose tens of thousands of refugees on Europe. Not only did he threaten to open the Turkish border with Greece, but also the Turkish border with Syria, where hundreds of thousands of would-be refugees were trapped.

By weaponizing the plight of the desperate refugees, Erdogan was warning that Idlib's problem would become Europe's problem. Europe was caught between two NATO allies with conflicting agendas—Turkey wanted to send the refugees in, and Greece wanted to keep them out. But Turkey had had enough of carrying the refugee burden for a seemingly somnolent Europe—with some justification. The EU's member countries owe it to Turkey to resettle more of the refugees it is hosting.

Meanwhile, in Greece, one of MFA's partner organizations, IsraAid, was co-managing the International School of Peace near Moria, a severely overcrowded refugee camp housing 20,000 people. ISOP was the product of the Israeli Hashomer Hatzair Life Movement and its sister Arab-Israeli youth movement "Ajyal." Together, they had been operating an educational center for refugees on the Isle of Lesbos for more than 250 refugee children and youth from Syria, Afghanistan, Iran, and the Congo. The faculty was an unlikely fusion of Israelis, Syrians, Iranians, Iraqis, Greeks, Afghans, and Congolese.

In March 2020, ISOP contacted us with the appalling news that their building had been burned down in Lesbos.

Arson was suspected. It wasn't motivated by anti-Semitism or anti-Zionism, as I had assumed, but by Greek extremists who wanted to hurt refugees. A few months later, Camp Moria burned down. But this time, it was the frustrated refugees themselves who did it.

Na'ama Moshinsky, co-CEO of Hashomer Hatzair Life Movement, reported: "In recent weeks, tensions have increased... following the struggles between the Greek authorities and its citizens as a result of the opening of enclosed camps in the islands and the opening of borders by Erdogan and the arrival of many refugees to the country." The subtitle of a March 2020 report from Human Rights Watch graphically describes the consequences: "Detained, Assaulted, Stripped, Summarily Deported."

Imagine this: You're a refugee, fleeing terror, who has been repeatedly displaced. You've found some respite in Turkey but hope to eventually make your way to the EU, to which Greece

is the gateway. Turkey is finally willing to let you go. Helpful
Turkish police actually take you to the Pazarkule border gate,
which enables you to cross safely overland instead of risking
death at sea in a fragile dinghy. The Turks even point you to the
exact spot where you can cross. If that looks risky, they direct
you to a place where you can wade across the Evros River. You're
almost home free!

But when you cross into Greece, you're greeted by a motley
cadre of armed men—some in Greek police uniforms, some in
civilian clothes, some dressed in black with their faces covered
by balaclavas. They're carrying guns, truncheons, and tasers.
After all you've endured, you're now detained, beaten, stripped,
robbed of your food, documents, mobile phones, and clothes.
Even if you're an old woman or a young child, you aren't spared.
And after all that, you're forcibly shoved back across the border to
Turkey. You think the EU Charter of Fundamental Rights—which
guarantees protection from forcible return where there is a risk
of persecution or serious harm—is there to save you. But you have
no recourse, and no one will let you file an asylum claim. You
return in ignominy, with even less dignity and fewer possessions
than when you left.

February 2020 was the first time, since 2016, that Turkey had
unilaterally opened the border. With that, the deal between the
EU and Turkey—which had kept millions of frantic refugees from
crossing into Bulgaria and Greece—collapsed. Once again, a
flood of Syrian Boat People embarked on flimsy rubber dinghies
to reach safety in Greece and find asylum in Europe—a Europe
with no unified strategy for dealing with them or, per Miliband,
for reacting to Turkey's use of refugees for leverage.

At the same time, the first case of the coronavirus that trig-
gered a worldwide pandemic in 2020 was documented in Lesbos.
Iran became the epicenter for the novel COVID-19 virus. From
Iran, it spread to Iraq. From there, Syria, Lebanon, and Jordan

were threatened, and that threat had become real by summer 2020. Similar to the spread of polio among refugees described in Chapter 2, substandard and crowded living conditions, along with the absence of adequate medical care, accelerated the spread of the pandemic throughout the region. Shortages in masks and other protective gear left refugees completely vulnerable. Hand-washing with soap, an effective measure for reducing contagion, is a luxury when you're living in the open. Our shipments of aid were delayed by short-staffed customs offices. But with our partner, GlobalMedic, we sent Personal Protective Equipment to first responders, sanitizing material to hospitals, and 200,000 bars of soap. Gift of the Givers started making masks. We also provided more than 20,000 water purification kits and in excess of 65,000 emergency meals.

Europe

There were hundreds of thousands of Syrians in Europe now. Germany alone had admitted 770,000 Syrian refugees. There, of all places, the government was grappling with an old problem that had taken a strange new twist: Anti-Semitism. Along with the refugees, it had imported the virulent anti-Semitic hatred with which Syrians are routinely indoctrinated. This has instilled deep fear among many Jews. Given the surging anti-Semitism in Europe, they're afraid that Syrians will become one more group of Muslims attacking Jews. This is the very fear encountered by my colleagues at HIAS when they tried to mobilize the Jewish community on behalf of Syrian refugees. I didn't encounter any resistance in my own dealings with Jews. But it's easy to under-stand their concern about bringing more Jew-haters to the US and Europe when there has already been such a surge in anti-Se-mitic vandalism and violence.

My answer to that is my own experience working with Syrians and Israelis. When they came into contact with each other and saw each other as human beings, the stereotypes and preconceptions melted away. The proof is in what we accomplished in southwest Syria and are continuing to do in the northwest and northeast.

Providing life-saving aid is a noble intent. But good intentions alone don't cut it. In reality, humanitarian activism takes place within a geopolitical context that must be carefully navigated via the pivotal role of trust.

The United States

First, there is the loss of trust in the US. In light of President Obama's seeming encouragement of the Arab Spring, insurgent Syrians expected to get major support from the US. It didn't happen. Then there was President Obama's ineffective enforcement of the red line he had drawn for chemical weapons. Instead of a military intervention, the US and Russia entered into an agreement to remove and destroy Syria's chemical stockpiles. Although the weapons Syria disclosed were eliminated under international supervision and Assad signed on to the Chemical Weapons Convention, it was clear from future chemical attacks on civilians that Obama had been tricked. From his point of view, he had found a way to divest Syria of its chemical stockpiles without risking any American lives or damaging the Iran nuclear deal. Commendable. But in the process, he had handed Syria to Russia—at the time, a marginalized, has-been power. Thanks to Obama, Russia has become a key player in the Middle East and Europe and a further reason that Syrians feel betrayed by the US.

Then along came Trump, whose administration, in yet another betrayal of a beleaguered people, shelved the Syria budgets for both the State Department and the US Agency for International Development. In talks with Erdogan, Trump offered to get out of Syria if Turkey would finish the cleanup of ISIS. We know how that ended. Turkey attacked, the Kurds fled, and the ISIS prisoners they were holding escaped. That's because Turkey's real focus was the Kurds, not ISIS. In the end, Trump unilaterally whittled away the US presence, gave up US leverage to Turkey without getting anything in return, and left valuable allies high and dry.

Luke Mogelson, in a 2020 *New Yorker* article, sums it up succinctly and powerfully: "One could argue that Obama's painstakingly considered inaction enabled more violence and misery than any of Trump's carelessly impulsive actions. At the same time, Trump's repudiation of American responsibility…has reduced parts of the country to wasteland."

One might sum up US policy as using Syria as a tool to drain resources from Iran and Russia.

"Trust is the most important thing in the Middle East," warns Shadi. "Once it's gone, it's very hard to regain."

Russia

Trust in Russia has also been lost, if indeed, it ever existed. "No one believes that the Russians can deliver safety from the vengeance of the Assad regime," observes Shadi. In that case, there's mistrust because of Russia's failure to act. When it did act, Russia was an obstacle to getting aid to non-regime held parts of Syria. Cross-border aid required a UN Security Council resolution invoking Chapter 7—a resolution repeatedly vetoed by Russia in order to consolidate control in the regime it is so heavily invested in propping up. When it was finally passed, it expired after a few years. The next time it was invoked, the number of cross-border openings was reduced from four to two and then to one.

But Chapter 7 is not the only resolution blocked by Russia. In the absence of any Security Council resolution to protect Syrian civilians, the White Helmets accused the UN in their "Search for Life report" of "participation and support for" the war crimes being committed in Syria. But how can any such resolution pass when one of the perpetrators of those crimes—Russia—is sitting on the Security Council?

The emotional impact on its people of Russia's collapse as a major power with an expansive empire cannot be underestimated. For Russia, the zone of influence it has acquired in Syria—largely due to US inaction—is one more step toward restoring Mother Russia to its former glory. On a more practical level, its foothold in Syria is a means of containing extremists and keeping them from penetrating Russia's borders. But Syria is a very expensive prize for a country with a weak economy and social unrest. Therefore, there is a real fear that extremists could incite insurgencies against Putin's autocratic government.

The Russian Orthodox Church is a power center in its own right and has largely operated in lockstep with Putin. In post-Communist Russia, Orthodoxy and Russian identity are closely intertwined. Putin frequently invokes Christian Orthodoxy in advancing his agenda and uses it to reinforce the view of Russia as a bulwark against the West and its decadence. But there have been recent rifts between Putin and the Church. In 2019, when pro-democracy protesters took to the streets in Russia, Orthodox Christians were a significant presence in their ranks. Ironically, for a once "godless" Marxist country, many of them invoked their religious beliefs as the reason for their dissent. Even more important, clergy have begun to push for the incorporation of Christian values into Russia's geopolitics.

Russia's brutal bombings of civilians in Syria violates every tenet of Christianity. Putin's stranglehold on power is abetted by the Church. Therefore, the Orthodox Church should pressure the government to prioritize morality over raw power. **Stop** vetoing the invocation of Chapter 7 of the UN Charter to deliver humanitarian aid into all parts of Syria, not just the areas controlled by the regime. **Encourage** Israel to reopen the Golan channel for delivery of aid. **Protect** all such channels from attack. Stop blocking condemnations of Assad's actions in the UN, and hold him accountable for his war crimes. Of course, Russia is committing the same war crimes in Syria. But perhaps Russia can be granted some kind of immunity, relief from sanctions, or trade benefits in exchange for its cooperation in holding Assad liable for more than a decade of horror. Such deals are made in local criminal justice systems all the time.

Iran

Trust is needed even in dealing with COVID-19 outbreaks among displaced populations. In an April 2020 interview in *The New Yorker*, David Miliband stated: "The first ingredient of effective health response is not a health facility. It's trust. If there's not trust among the local population about the messages that are being given about how to stay well, then your health facilities are going to get overwhelmed." IRC addresses this need by employing local staff. And MFA does the same by working through local partners. But how does a hungry mother, trudging along a cratered road with few belongings, trust any authority after having been betrayed by so many?

Ironically, the COVID-19 pandemic may be the straw that breaks any remaining trust in their government among the people of Iran. And that could be the factor that breaks Iran's stranglehold on Syria. Nir Boms, in a paper for The Washington Institute for Near East Policy, makes a startling argument.

As mentioned earlier, Iran became the epicenter of the virus in the Middle East. This was largely due to its cynical continuation of travel to and from China, well after the pandemic had spread. There was already widespread discontent among its people. Taxes had been raised to compensate for the crippling sanctions imposed in response to Iran's bad behavior in the region. Gasoline prices had tripled. Despite the suffering of its people, Iran was funneling resources into supporting proxy wars in Yemen and Syria, triggering slogans like, "We wish to live in Iran rather than die in Syria." Countrywide protests were met with violent clampdowns.

Then came the assassination of Qasem Suleimani and Iran's retaliatory—and mistaken—shooting down of a Ukrainian passenger plane, which had many Iranians on board. The government equivocated before finally coming clean. Layered on top of all this came the coronavirus outbreak. The government downplayed its severity, dithered in its response, kept shrines open, and failed to protect its people. Perhaps there is poetic justice in the fact that the virus spread through the leadership that showed such callous disregard for the lives of its own people.

Not only did Iran disregard its own people, but also those of the region. The same Mahan Air planes that continued to fly from Iran to China were used to transport weapons to the Quds forces and other Iranian proxies in Syria, thereby spreading the plague through the Iranian-backed militias permeating Syria. Various Israeli news outlets related that Hezbollah had brought COVID-19 into Lebanon from Iran, as well. In a twist of fate, Hezbollah Secretary-General Hassan Nasrallah was, himself, reported to have tested positive for COVID-19, along with others in the Hezbollah leadership.

In light of this history, Boms argues that the Iranian revolution no longer serves the interests of the younger generation. That generation now constitutes the majority of the population, and this may, at last, presage the end of a regime that is the nemesis of Syria, the US, Israel, and the Sunni world.

Intersections

Assad is first and foremost a butcher of his own people. But without Russia and Iran, there is no Assad. The question is how Russia and Iran can incentivize Assad to change his behavior. Or to how to incentivize Russia and Iran to get out of Syria and allow a moderate, democratic leader—Ghassan Aboud being one such example—to come forward and unite the country. All the main parties to the war—Russia, Iran, Saudi Arabia, Turkey—have at one time or another expressed a willingness for (and, in some cases, have insisted on) Assad's replacement. Now that all the parties have experienced the economic drain of the ongoing war, this should be revived as a negotiating point.

Although dependent on both Russia and Iran, the Assad regime feels more aligned with the former. Iran's sectarian, religious agenda is at odds with the Ba'ath party's secular roots. The same is true of the Gulf States, which fear an Islamist government in control of Syria. Given that Assad is more comfortable with Russia than Iran, if Russia were to threaten to withdraw political support, Assad would have to change his behavior. On the other hand, Russia doesn't have the funds to rebuild Syria and has nothing more to offer Assad. Nor will western countries invest in rebuilding the country so long as Iran is a presence there. This could make Assad more open to making a deal with the West.

Russia, the US, the Gulf States, and Israel have a common interest: they want to push Iran out of Syria, where it is pursuing its own agenda. According to John Bolton, former Ambassador to the UN (and National Security Advisor to Donald Trump), Russia wants to consolidate the Syrian state in order to prevent chaos and seeks the complete withdrawal of Iran. However, Russia has not been in a position to pressure Assad to oust Iran because he is counting on Iran to quash the Syrian Opposition in Idlib.

Russia doesn't want to give up Syria, and Saudi Arabia has invested considerable effort into building closer ties to Russia. The Saudis could provide Russia with a financial lifeline, which would give them some leverage. Because Saudi Arabia is the archenemy of Iran, the Saudi-Russian relationship could foster a realignment.

For Iran, Syria is the final puzzle piece in its ambition to extend Shia influence from the Arabian Sea to the Mediterranean. Iran shares no borders with Lebanon, the stronghold for its proxy, Hezbollah. It needs Syria to maintain open supply lines to its proxies. With its neighbor, Iraq, already within its sphere of influence, Syria is the only country blocking Iran's access to the Mediterranean. Iraq is both a strategic partner of the US and an ally of Iran. It also shares a border with Syria. Accordingly, there could be opportunities for Iraq to serve as a broker between two hostile countries.

Iran's interests are local. As such, they diverge from those of Russia. Russia wants to elevate its status as an international player and use Syria as a potential bargaining chip to resolve the Ukraine issue. Then there's the delicate question of Russia's relationship with Israel, which requires a balancing act with Iran, a country that is sworn to destroy Israel.

The 2015 Joint Comprehensive Plan of Action—a.k.a. the nuclear deal—with Iran was a signal that Iran was opening up. A more moderate leadership emerged and there was hope for an economic reintegration with Europe. The deal created a template for future discussions aimed at curtailing Iran's missile tests and withdrawing Iran's support for terrorist groups. The trade-off Iran sought in signing the deal was the lifting of sanctions. When President Trump unilaterally walked away from the deal, Iran's moderate leadership was discredited, and the US lost much of its leverage over Iran's behavior. But the additional sanctions imposed by the US bit hard and provided a new kind of leverage for incentivizing Iran to loosen its takeover of Syria. Europe, which is more open to Iran than the US, could use its economic power to lean on Iran to influence Assad and reduce Syrian suffering. Because Russia started drawing down its troops in 2016 and has largely abdicated its role in southwest Syria, this is the right time to take action. President Biden's openness to reentering the JCPOA is another opportunity to exert leverage.

Jordan & Israel

In my initial outreach to Jordan, I learned that the source of help couldn't be too Jewish. Nor, because of the Palestinian street, could there be a *public* engagement with Israel, lest one be dubbed a "collaborator." Protests and resentment drove some of Jordan's decisions about when to close its borders.

Israel, for its part, couldn't aid an enemy people at the expense of its own needy population. Israel wanted to avoid getting dragged into another war with Syria. At the same time, its priority was to keep Iran and Hezbollah off its border and to cultivate a moderate neighbor to its north. As events unfolded, humanitarian diplomacy sometimes helped and sometimes got in the way.

During Operation Good Neighbor, southwest Syria remained comparatively calm. Both the regime and Russia were reluctant to provoke Israel. Now, Israel should resume humanitarian aid operations on its northern border, and a safe zone should be established to protect the civilians on the Syrian side of the border. Israel will not take responsibility for a safe zone on its own but has, in the past, expressed willingness to do so in partnership with other countries. Jordan would be a logical partner by dint of geography and a shared interest in maintaining peace in Syria's south. But this would require overcoming—or overriding—the Jordanian street's aversion to Israel.

For the international community, Israel was politically toxic. In the European Parliament, there were countries for which Israel could do no right and other countries that waxed enthusiastic about the kind of engagement we were promoting.

In the Arab world, the shared interests of the majority Sunni countries and Israel were opening up new opportunities for working together. In that sense, the time was ripe for humanitarian diplomacy. At the same time, with the contraction of

American involvement, some Arab groups and the Kurds were turning to Russia to fill the void.

For Syrians, Israel's war with Gaza, the 2016 "stabbing intifada's" knife attacks on Jews in Jerusalem, and the optics of its policies toward Palestinians hindered full participation by some of the parties we hoped to draw into our diplomatic process.

United States

Above all, it is critical to maintain an American presence in Syria. The relatively small troop deployment in northern Syria was costly in neither dollars nor lives. It gave the US control over Syria's critical resources and one-third of its landmass—thus providing both leverage and relative stability in the region. When the Trump administration made the unilateral, impulsive decision to withdraw US troops, military battles erupted between Russia and Turkey, and the Kurds were driven away, triggering another mass exodus and a new humanitarian crisis.

* * *

The Syrian people have been pawns on a regional chessboard. The powers that are moving the pieces must prioritize an orderly transition of power in Syria. They all, to some degree, bear responsibility for the suffering inflicted on civilians. Nevertheless, in the world of *realpolitik*, there must be a reward for pushing Assad aside and tempering their interests in Syria. Once he is gone and Iran has withdrawn, the West will be induced to help rebuild Syria. Israel could potentially play a role, contributing to new stability in the region.

As for MFA's work, we were impacted at every point by the geopolitical environment in which we operated. At key times, our work was stalled as we awaited the results of elections in both the US and Israel. With each of those elections, we had to adjust our priorities. Those priorities will likely shift again with new elections and the eventual abatement of the coronavirus pandemic.

The scale of the problems is unfathomable, and the scope of the agencies addressing them is vast. Given the scale of both the problems and the resources, I return to the question with which I began my journey: What can one person do that will have some meaningful impact?

I started my voyage of humanitarian activism by focusing on what was do-able and on finding a niche that didn't duplicate what the big boys were doing. That niche was to first mobilize a Jewish communal response to the crisis and then scale to a multi-faith response. I ultivated counterintuitive partnerships between enemies—Syrians and Israelis. And, when we got directly involved in the delivery of humanitarian aid, we focused on the NGO sector and operated in the crevices. We organized aid shipments from Canada, England, the Netherlands, Germany, and a host of American states—California, Idaho, Michigan, New York, Ohio, and Utah. We were able to mobilize massive donations of urgently needed goods from partners like Catholic Medical Mission Board and Kirk Humanitarian.

There were bumps in the road, dead ends, and failures. But behind them all was a grand vision of what was possible between two peoples in a chronic state of war. The false starts and ideas that died on the vine are there to be picked up when conditions allow. In the meantime, we got a lot done. We saved lives. We brought hope. We forged friendships. We proved that it's possible to rise above politics, mutual suspicion, and hate to alleviate terrible human suffering. I also learned the geopolitical limits of bridge-building and humanitarian activism.

As Miliband warned, "What starts in Syria does not end in Syria." The Syrian crisis has had a profound global impact. It has placed huge strains on host countries in the Middle East and Europe. The American response has shifted the balance of power in the Middle East toward Russia and Iran, while inadvertently altering relations among allies—most notably the Kurds, who were our staunchest partners in eliminating ISIS's physical caliphate. If we fail to implement humane and rational policies towards Syrian war victims, their crisis will become our crisis.

That means we must prepare for a time when conditions again allow for resettlement. In order to prepare the ground for that, we must first separate fact from fiction when it comes to refugees in general and Syrians in particular.

CHAPTER 12

SOMEWHERE TO GO

The Case for Resettlement

My father was just a young boy when he and his family escaped starvation in Syria and were welcomed to America. Since that time, his contribution to America was a way of saying thank you. He worked hard to feed his sisters and raise his sons, he put his sisters through college, he lost two sons in the regular army and marines.

I have relatives in Syria, but I'm not in contact with them because they have left their homes or been driven from their homes and they're hiding in the hills or wherever they can; or they've tried to escape the country. How they're surviving I have no idea; I've lost contact with them. Because it is difficult for Syrian refugees to be allowed into America, my relatives, whose doors are open to them, are helpless….

America has the most stringent security procedures in the world. But people have no reason to fear these refugees.

Most Syrians who come to this country…are hard-
working, serious people… I'm an example of that… My
uncles made themselves millionaires selling clothing,
door-to-door out of the trunk of their car. These are
only a few examples [of contributions] that Syrian
Americans—Muslim Americans—have made to this
country; and continue to make.

—Excerpts from interview with MFA spokesperson
F. MURRAY ABRAHAM on Orient TV, May 2020.

Oscar-winning actor F. Murray Abraham became MFA's spokesperson through a chance meeting on the street. He, along
with my husband and I, was honored in 2014 by Theater for a New
Audience (TFANA), a Shakespeare repertory company. Among
our invited guests was our friend Jonathan Schaefer, himself an
actor and writer. Some months later, Jonathan was walking down
the street in Greenwich Village when he spotted Murray and
struck up a conversation.

Knowing of my zeal for helping Syrian war victims, he phoned
me with some excitement and said, "Did you know that F. Murray
Abraham is Syrian?"

Syrian? How could anyone with names like "Murray" and
"Abraham" be anything but Jewish? How could someone who
played Shylock with such poignancy in Shakespeare's *The Merchant
of Venice* be anything but Jewish?

I said to Jonathan, "Please give me his email address. I need to
get in touch with him!"

It turned out that Murray was looking for a vehicle to help
his fellow Syrians in their time of extraordinary need. And MFA's
multifaith message moved him to the core. Ironically, Murray
had experienced anti-Semitism firsthand because of his name.
And when it became known that he was a Syrian Arab—albeit

an Orthodox Christian—he became the target of anti-Arab sentiment.

Murray was and is the tip of our spear in debunking the myths and disinformation that derail rational and humane policies toward displaced persons—especially Syrians. Murray regularly touts the work of MFA on behalf of his Syrian compatriots. When he was honored by the Ellis Island Foundation in 2016, I sat in the audience as he told his story and tied it to MFA's advocacy and humanitarian outreach. On a recent World Refugee Day, he recruited Mandy Patinkin and his wife, Kathryn Grody, to address a group of donors we had corralled for a fundraising dinner. All three made heartfelt pleas in support of resettling more Syrian refugees in the US and upping humanitarian aid for those who were trapped where they were. Murray made TV appearances and did magazine interviews for us. And at his eightieth birthday party, in an intimate Greenwich Village restaurant, he squired me from table to table to introduce me to his close friends, and them to MFA.

One of his most important appearances for MFA took place in May 2016. That's when he, Shadi, and I set off for Washington, DC, to address a joint, bipartisan, congressional hearing entitled: "They Have Faces and Names: Fresh Approaches to the Syrian Refugee Crisis." The hearing took place toward the end of the Obama administration, shortly after a surge of 10,000 more Syrian refugee admissions had been approved. Just under 2,000 were actually admitted. We were in the Capitol Building to argue for more.

Murray's impassioned remarks focused on his story as a Syrian Arab. His father fled with his family to the US to escape starvation in Syria. His father never spoke of life in Syria. But he frequently spoke about his unfaltering gratitude to the country that gave him refuge. That gratitude cost him two of Murray's brothers—Private Robert Abraham, US Army, and Private Jack Abraham,

US Marines—killed in service to his adopted country. Both are buried in a military cemetery in Texas.

In speaking for MFA, Murray offers himself as an example of what Syrians are and can become in America—which runs counter to the preconceptions that torpedoed refugee admissions in the Trump administration. Trump attempted to completely suspend admissions of Syrian refugees in 2017. Whereas the refugee quota in the last year of the Obama presidency was 110,000, Trump steadily reduced that number and finally slashed it to 18,000 by 2019. A disgrace for the wealthiest country in the world!

Pre-Trump, the US generally took in about half of UNHCR's worldwide call for refugee admissions. Even at that, only 1 in 500 are actually resettled. And 80 percent of those are resettled by developing countries that can least afford it.

Murray cited his relatives in El Paso, who are ready to take in their compatriots from Syria. He spoke of the Orthodox Church, which is ready to open its doors. But there have been few Syrian refugees for them to welcome—only about 700 in recent years.

On the scale of religiosity, the US ranks highest in the developed world. For better or for worse, religious piety has become a litmus test for elected offices. But one cannot lay claim to being a pious person if one ignores the basic tenets of our faiths: care for the poor, welcome the stranger, provide sanctuary, and take action in the face of human suffering. Somehow those obligations have been lost in sanctimonious justifications and hypocritical policies that deny all of those to displaced persons.

Part of the problem is the conflating of immigrants, illegal immigrants, and refugees. Immigrants voluntarily leave their home countries in search of better opportunities. Illegal immigrants generally leave for the same reason. Refugees and asylum seekers, however, are driven from their homes by persecution and violence.

The world has historically looked to the US as a model of humane refugee policies and has counted on it to carry its weight in resettling those who are permanently displaced. In fact, the US is bound by several treaties to provide asylum and resettle refugees: the 1951 Refugee Convention, the 1967 Protocol Relating to the Status of Refugees, and the Refugee Act of 1980.

Nevertheless, Murray points out, for all its wealth and all those treaties, Americans have historically been leery of welcoming refugees. Pew surveys going back decades reveal that, with the exception of ethnic Albanians in 1999, the majority of Americans disapproved of admitting refugees. This included Jews fleeing the Holocaust in the 1940s, Hungarians fleeing communism in 1956, Indochinese fleeing Vietnam in 1979, and Cubans fleeing the Castro regime in 1980. Fast-forward to the Syrian crisis: a 2015 Bloomberg poll showed that 53 percent of Americans rejected the resettlement of any Syrian refugees.

In response to the previous refugee crises, there was always a leader who was willing to buck public opinion. Legislation was introduced to enable the admission of refugees. Invariably, each of these groups made important contributions to America, as documented in this chapter.

By 2016—the year Donald Trump was elected—Bloomberg polls showed an increase—59 percent—of Americans in favor of admitting Syrian and other refugees from the Middle East. Of the 41 percent opposed, the vast majority were Republicans and Trump supporters. Unlike prior administrations, the pressure to admit refugees must now come from the bottom up. As Shelly Pitterman of UNHCR put it: "The leadership of states will need to be influenced by public opinion and religious leaders."

Opinions can be changed with the right messaging. In an international TENT Foundation survey conducted in 2015–16, respondents overwhelmingly reported a sense of responsibility. They want to help but don't know how. This comes back to the question of how a person of goodwill can identify a point of entry in the face of an overwhelming, paralyzing crisis. For me, resettlement remains a priority. But until policy changes make resettlement possible, I must continue to focus on providing aid in place for Syrian IDPs.

The more people know, the more positive they feel toward refugees. Knowledge of the conflict is crucial, as is understanding that refugees are not displaced because they want to be. Nearly half of respondents to the TENT survey were open to changing their opinions, especially after learning that most refugees hope to return home. Finally, people like to hear stories about the successful integration of refugees. That requires policies that enable the five pillars of successful integration: housing, work, language training, education, and trauma treatment. To that end, the Canadian model of private sponsorship has worked well. "A program embracing private sponsorships would help so much," affirms Murray.

We also have a lot to learn from public opinion surveys in Britain. A 2014 British Future survey found that approximately 25 percent of the country is liberal on immigration and 25 percent is anti-immigrant. This leaves 50 percent in the "anxious middle"— those who have humanitarian impulses but are fearful. With the right narrative and information, this 50 percent can be moved to shift their views.

Much of the frustration that led to the UK's Brexit vote in June 2016 was driven by anxiety about immigration policy. But according to British Future, being anti-immigration did not equate to slamming the door on refugees. According to a BBC poll, 41 percent of respondents said Britain should accept fewer refugees from Syria and Libya. But more than half (56 percent) were ready to accept refugees in their communities once they had arrived in the UK.

And with good reason. Take the example of Hassan Akkad. He fled Syria in 2016, trekked across Europe for eighty-seven days, and managed to get to London, where he has been living since. When COVID-19 hit England, his local hospital was in need of cleaners. He immediately signed on to help. When interviewed by a local news channel, he said: "I know I'm Syrian and I'm also a refugee, but I also consider myself a Londoner.... The way I thought about it is that this is the hospital to which my neighbors could go...and they probably are there, the ill ones. And it's the hospital that I would go to. So the hospital needed cleaners and I signed up. And I'm so proud to be cleaning and disinfecting my hospital. It's the least I can do."

That said, the resettlement process is inefficient. About 70 percent of applicants for asylum are turned down. But after appeals, 50 percent of all asylum seekers are admitted. Voluntary deportations cost £1,000; involuntary deportations cost £11,000. That means there's a lot of wasted time and money in this process. Both can be avoided by supporting education, jobs, and trauma counseling in the Levant itself so that there is less incentive to flee to Europe. In other words, aid in place.

"We cannot let our fears define us," Murray asserts. Yet, for the past few years, US policy has been driven by misinformation, disinformation, and three great fears: fear of negative economic impact, terrorism, and Muslims. In order to arrive at rational policies, the myths behind these fears need to be understood and addressed—and that's what Murray has been doing for MFA with his own story.

Taking in Syrian refugees does not impede economic growth; rather, it's a good investment. In Western European countries, where the population is aging and not reproducing at maintenance levels, the only source of growth is immigration. Refugees contribute a much-needed labor pool.

In the US, refugees arrive with few resources, but they quickly become self-sufficient. There are about 90,000 Syrian immigrants in the US. Most, like Dr. Basha, arrived after 1965 and are highly educated and successful. They are well-positioned to provide a social and economic support network for their newly arrived compatriots, especially within a private sponsorship framework. The International Rescue Committee has reported that 85 percent of the refugees that they resettle are employed within 180 days. Despite the upfront costs, outlays for refugee resettlement decrease over time, as refugees integrate.

When they arrive in the US, refugees are immediately eligible for three months of public benefits. The use of those benefits declines over time. By the time they've been in the US for eight years, refugees, on the whole, pay more in taxes than they receive in welfare benefits.

Refugees have a higher rate of entrepreneurship (13 percent) than other immigrant groups and the US-born population—making them job creators rather than job takers. The picture for Syrians is even more impressive. Witness Dr. Basha and his medical imaging empire. Murray speaks with pride about a cousin who worked his way through Texas A&M and became chief engineer for the first commercial satellite launched by Hughes Aircraft. "It's still up there!"

Yet the Center for Immigration Studies released a report in November 2015, "The High Cost of Resettling Middle Eastern Refugees," that ignored these positive data points. The report concluded that it costs taxpayers twelve times more to support each refugee in their first five years of resettlement in the US than what the UN estimates it costs to care for them in Middle Eastern countries. That leads to the simplistic conclusion that it's better for the US to pay for services in the Middle East. As Josh Hampson of the Niskanen Center points out, this ignores some of the hidden costs of supporting refugees in overseas camps. For example, there are costs associated with ramping up US security and infrastructure support for Lebanon and Jordan, as well as other host countries. Further, it ignores the matches from charities and government agencies that support basic needs. Refugees remain in camps for many more years than they remain dependent on aid in the US, where self-sufficiency is more quickly achieved.

The CIS report argues that it is more humane to resettle refugees in Jordan and Lebanon. But as I've shown in prior chapters, these countries are straining under the burden of human misery that they're ill-prepared to handle. Should these countries collapse, the refugee crisis will multiply.

With its vast space, large population, and highly developed infrastructure, the US is far more capable of absorbing refugees than these struggling countries in the Middle East.

Hampson concludes: "Given the conditions that refugees tend to be in if they are resettled in the Middle East, the costs associated with keeping them there are likely to not be offset by *any* benefit to the US economy. They will be pure costs."

Further buttressing the argument that refugees don't negatively impact the economy are the very countries bearing the greatest burden of the Syrian refugee crisis: Turkey, Lebanon, and Jordan. A report on a cash assistance program in Lebanon showed that for every $1 given to a Syrian refugee, $2.13 circulated in the local economy.

Even those countries are continuing to see economic growth. If permitted, refugees can be a resource to their host countries' economies. There's one additional factor to consider: leaving Syrian war victims to languish in camps deprives them of a path to citizenship, protection from deportation, or access to the job market to which all refugees are entitled under international law. That applies even more to the more than 90 percent who are unregistered and/or live on the fringes outside of camps. As reported in an earlier chapter, it fosters the conditions for the very thing we fear the most: radicalization and terrorism.

The fear of importing terrorism is a major obstacle. "The Syrian people are not to be feared," contends Murray. "They're fleeing from the same terrorists that we fear."

The US has one of the most—if not the most—stringent and comprehensive eighteen to twenty-four month vetting processes in the world. Syrian refugees are subject to enhanced scrutiny. Unlike Europe, this entire vetting process occurs *before* refugees set foot on US soil and involves layers of federal agencies. Those who are permitted to resettle are among the most vulnerable. No Syrian refugee resettled in the US has been associated with terrorist activity in any way.

In fact, the threat from resettled Syrian refugees is essentially nonexistent. Of the more than 750,000 refugees resettled in the US since 9/11, only three have been arrested for planning terrorist activities. None of them were Syrian. The Cato Institute, in a startling report, reveals that *the annual chance of an American being killed in a terrorist attack initiated by a refugee is 1 in 3.64 billion.* By contrast, the yearly odds of being murdered by someone other than a foreign-born terrorist—say one's American-born next-door neighbor—are nearly 253 times greater.

Nor have Syrian refugees been shown to pose a major security threat to neighboring host countries, despite concerns about radicalization. However, as explained in Chapter 3, extremist groups take advantage of the dearth of aid and holes in security to recruit displaced persons, whose despair and damaged dignity leave them vulnerable to radicalization.

At the root of our fear of imported terrorists embedded among resettled refugees is a fear of Muslims. Specifically, we fear that Syrian refugees, most of whom are Muslim, will not assimilate. We hear far-right groups warning that the US and Europe will be overrun by Muslims, changing the nature of laws and customs. Some argue that only Syrian Christians, like Murray's father, should be admitted.

It's an understandable concern, but the fear of a Muslim tsunami is misplaced.

Polls show that Muslim Americans are predominantly patriotic, share American values, and tend to be progressive rather than traditional. Muslim Americans are highly assimilated into American society.

According to the Cato Institute, Muslim Americans have more liberal views on social, religious, and political issues than Muslims elsewhere. Muslim immigrants in the United States are less likely to support terrorism, violence against civilians, and aspects of strict Islamic law. In fact, 82 percent of American Muslims indicate that they are concerned—and more likely to be "very concerned" than the general public in the US—about extremism in the name of Islam around the world.

Despite the hostility and discrimination that they face in the US, 92 percent of American Muslims are proud to be American. They are more racially diverse than the population as a whole. And they serve in the US armed forces, where nearly 6,000 self-identify as Muslim. (Because soldiers are not required to give their religious affiliation, the actual number of Muslims serving is likely higher.)

There are about 3 million Muslims living in the UK. But fewer Brits—28 percent—hold negative views of Muslims than people in other parts of Europe. In turn, most Muslims in the UK—73 percent—identify with the UK, stating that as their *only* national identity.

* * *

My husband, Leonard, is British, so we have a home in London. During one of our planned stays there, Murray showed that he was more than a spokesperson for MFA. He showed himself to be a deeply caring friend.

In 2016, Murray was starring in a play in London, *The Mentor*. He invited us to see him perform and go to dinner afterward. But Leonard had become very ill, and we had to cancel our trip. When the play ended its run on the West End, and Murray returned home to New York, he asked whether he could visit Leonard to perform some of the monologues from the play we had missed. Soon after, Murray arrived at our apartment, where we sat in the living room, as this passionate actor gave us a private performance. But the monologues he performed were not from *The Mentor*. Instead, he performed one of his most acclaimed roles: Shylock, from *The Merchant of Venice*. The monologue Murray chose is one he frequently invokes in making his plea for humane policies toward displaced Syrians. In that context, he adapts this, one of Shakespeare's most memorable monologues:

"Hath not a Jew eyes? Hath not a Syrian eyes? If you prick us do we not bleed? If you poison us do we not die? Why does he hate me? Because I am a Jew. Why do they hate me? Because I am a Syrian, because I am Muslim, because I am Mexican, because I am…endless."

Murray's plea for humanizing the other is at the heart of MFA's bridge-building work—and dehumanization is at the heart of the anti-refugee rhetoric that is pervading the public discourse.

Over the past few years, we've seen a shutdown of Syrian refugee entry into the US and other host countries, a decrease in funding for refugee agencies, and a bolstering of the Assad regime due to US diplomatic withdrawal and new relationships with Russia. This has triggered an increase in Syrian refugees massing at borders, trying to flee to Jordan, Iraq, Turkey, and Europe. The next few years must usher in increased refugee admissions, more aid in place, and the skillful exercise of humanitarian diplomacy.

Given the scale of destruction and the regime's recent actions, there's very little likelihood that most Syrians will ever be able to return home. Absent a diplomatic solution to the Syrian war, the massive displacement it has spawned must be confronted with more imagination and courage than we've seen to date.

UNHCR is the principal agency responsible for the protection of refugees and the first line for resettlement referrals. UNHCR refers only those who are the most vulnerable and pose no threat to their host countries.

UNHCR is the only source of refugee referrals that the US currently accepts. However, the State Department is authorized to certify NGOs to make referrals once they've undergone training. It has been many years since any such training has been held. It would be simple to reactivate State Department training and certify NGOs in the Middle East and North Africa (MENA) region—such as the International Refugee Assistance Program— to make Priority-1 ("P-1") resettlement referrals directly to the US Refugee Admissions Program (USRAP).

The number of refugees the US admits each year is determined by the president in consultation with Congress. Any unilateral attempt by a president to suspend the refugee program or reduce the number of refugees in the middle of a fiscal year— as Trump attempted to do in his first year in office—violates the statutes. Because the rest of the world follows the lead of the US in refugee admissions, the president's decisions have an impact far beyond our borders. The failure to do our share damages our national interests by impacting the stability of our allies in Europe and the Middle East and contributes to the crises they face.

It has been years since the US has met its refugee admissions targets. The agencies that keep the pipeline flowing are being starved of funds. The Office of Refugee Resettlement (ORR) at the Department of Health and Human Services is responsible for resettling and integrating refugees upon arrival. With razor-thin funding, it's also responsible for caring for unaccompanied minors. Children's program funds are co-mingled with those of the refugee program. The recent heart-wrenching influx of unaccompanied children from Central America has depleted the funds for refugee resettlement. Funds for ORR need to be increased and segregated from those of the children's program. An investment in ORR creates a glide path for refugees to successfully integrate and start making contributions to the US economy.

United States Citizen and Immigration Services (USCIS) administers the country's naturalization and immigration system. Unlike other federal agencies, it is funded almost entirely by user fees rather than congressional appropriations. But its new ideological direction is evident from the phrase that was removed from its mission statement in 2018: "America's promise as a nation of immigrants." Hopefully, a new Administration will reverse that change.

Refugee processing and resettlement is a complicated process—too complicated. What's needed is a holistic approach. Federal agencies lack a uniform protocol for conducting background checks. They could streamline the process by developing standardized guidelines for all the separate agencies that are part of the Interagency Check (IAC). The process would also benefit from hiring more DHS staff with experience in the Middle East.

In 2016–17, MFA had the privilege of working with the Harvard Law School Immigration and Refugee Clinical Program on a bedrock report funded by its alum, Howard Milstein. That report, "Fulfilling U.S Commitment to Refugee Resettlement," deserves the widest possible distribution and should be a policy primer for all legislators addressing the Syrian refugee crisis in particular and refugee issues in general. The report's recommendations advance the goals of national security, job creation, and compliance with international and domestic humanitarian and legal obligations.

A Harvard Kennedy School white paper, authored by Michael Ignatieff, recommends building up the US processing facilities in

Lebanon, Jordan, and Turkey. Consistent with that recommendation, the Harvard Law School report advises the Department of Homeland Security to expand the deployment of Refugee Affairs Division officers for screening. But when travel to regional sites—Jordan, Lebanon, and Turkey—is not possible, due to local instability or a COVID-19 pandemic, make use of video technology for refugee interviews.

The Harvard Law School report demonstrates that admitting more Syrian refugees serves US national security interests. It increases our leverage in the Middle East and enhances cooperation from regional actors. It underscores the importance of that cooperation in Turkey, Jordan, and Iraq—all of which host US military bases. All three of those countries, along with Lebanon, are straining under the burden of Syrian refugees. For the sake of their stability, the US and other wealthy countries must provide them with more support and relieve them of some of these dependents. Stability is the enemy of extremists and undercuts their ability to recruit. One intangible result is the goodwill that comes from demonstrating that the US is not hostile to Muslim-majority countries. That, too, pulls the carpet out from extremist groups that tout the West's hatred of Islam as a way to enlist impressionable and angry young Muslims to their cause.

Further, as this chapter amply demonstrates, refugees—and Syrians, in particular—make significant contributions to our economy. The Harvard Law School report gives compelling examples. Here are two: Cleveland, where the government's $4.8 million investment in services for refugees catalyzed almost $50 million circulating through the local economy from refugee-owned businesses and household spending. And Buffalo, whose mayor is quoted as saying: "One of the reasons that Buffalo is growing stronger, that Buffalo is getting better, is because of the presence of our immigrant and refugee community." This is precisely what the Basha brothers hoped to achieve in their efforts to repopulate and rejuvenate dying industrial cities like Pontiac, Michigan with Syrian refugees.

The US has, for years, had trouble filling its skilled-labor needs from the domestic labor pool. Refugees provide a much-needed source of labor. As shown in this chapter, they also create jobs with the businesses they start.

- *Many cities are dying.* We should bring in refugees to rebuild them with their resilience and entrepreneurship.

- *Airlines are floundering.* We should recruit them to rescue refugees and transport them to new homes.

- *Many parts of our country are desperately short of health-care workers.* Put the doctors who have fled Syria to work as paramedics or nurses' aides while they go through their relicensing process.

- *The US population is aging.* Putting the elderly in nursing homes is much more expensive than keeping them at home. Refugees can work as their aids and companions and help them stay in place.

- *More Americans are unemployed than at any time since the Great Depression.* Give some of them work helping refugees acclimate to a new country. They can teach them the language; they can help them restore a home; they can teach them a new trade.

Some people fear that refugees, equipped with skills their American hosts impart, will take their jobs by working for lower wages. But as previously shown in the section on fear of negative economic impact, refugees tend to be entrepreneurial. They are net job creators, not job takers.

Once in the US, refugees are placed by nine agencies—of which IRC is one. Two-thirds are faith-based—Church World Service, Episcopal Migration Ministries, HIAS, Lutheran

Immigration and Refugee Service, US Conference of Catholic Bishops, World Relief—which demonstrates the crucial role that religious communities play in aiding refugees. Each agency is under contract with the government to handle different regions of the country. But because of the devastating cutback in admissions, the resettlement budgets of these agencies have been decimated, causing hundreds of layoffs and at least twenty office closures across the country.

Once resettled, the focus needs to be on successful integration. As outlined above, the five elements of successful integration are housing, work, language, education, and trauma treatment. This is where public/private partnerships play a big role.

Education is a serious issue for Syrian refugees—more serious than for most because of years of displacement and attacks on schools. They need extensive remedial work to catch up. A college education is the launching pad to enable young refugees to contribute to our economy and perpetuate our values. To these ends, the federal government and private sector should fund college scholarships. The US State Department's small scholarship program needs to be expanded, and more institutions need to follow the example of Johns Hopkins University and the Jesuit Refugee Services in providing scholarships for Syrian students. The philanthropic community can play a central role here by funding scholarships for Syrian refugees at their own alma maters and elsewhere.

When the Trump administration dramatically curtailed Muslim admissions to the US, those with student visas, who had been planning to attend American universities, found themselves academically stranded. Bard Berlin, which also enrolls refugees, invited them to pivot to Germany, where they would be able to graduate with both a US and German degree.

In an earlier chapter, I mentioned Orient's innovative curriculum tablets, which provide mobile education for Syrian children whose schools have been destroyed or who have been repeatedly displaced. These need to be widely distributed and, of course, that takes money.

Citing the Syrian crisis, in June 2016, President Obama issued a call to action for private sector investment. In response, fifty-one US companies made significant commitments to aid refugees. Among these: Airbnb, Chobani, Facebook, Goldman Sachs, Google, Uber, UPS. Soros Fund Management alone pledged $500 million to help refugees start businesses. The corporate initiatives focused on three impact areas: education, employment, and enablement. When the US economy recovers, the business community must again be mobilized on behalf of refugees.

Impact investing, which converts financial returns into social returns, has a role in integrating refugees. One example: SPEAK, a social tech start-up, tackles the social exclusion of the displaced by taking on the barriers they face in a new city: language, racism, xenophobia, and the lack of a support network. SPEAK connects migrants and refugees with locals through language courses and cultural events that promote informal learning, common interests, and building friendship networks. The start-up cites success stories that include finding a guarantor for a lease agreement, helping to put together a CV, and helping to secure job offers.

Having been successfully piloted in several cities in Portugal, SPEAK closed a seed impact investment round of €500K to expand internationally. SPEAK has started operating in Italy and had planned to bring the program to multiple cities in Europe by 2020. Why not bring SPEAK to the US as well?

Such private initiatives should *supplement* rather than replace agency services and government coordination and funding. That's where Congress comes in. Members of Congress must be vocal in explaining why resettlement will not endanger national security. They must resist Islamophobia and calls to resettle only Christians. To distinguish which refugees will or will not be resettled based on their religion or national origin raises constitutional and legal problems. States can't pick and choose among refugees—and neither should Congress. That said, Syrian Christians have been underrepresented among resettled refugees. With Christians being persecuted in so many Arab countries, they should get their pro-rata share of resettlement slots.

Legislative efforts to suppress resettlement over the past few years—in Congress and the states—must be reversed, especially the repugnant tactic of some thirty governors seeking to withdraw entirely from the federal government refugee relocation program. Governors do not have the authority to ban refugees from their states. The US government has sole authority over whether immigrants and refugees of any nationality enter this country.

I recognize that elected officials are largely driven by public opinion. As discussed in this chapter, public acceptance of refugees is, to a great extent, contingent on messaging. We must fund social media campaigns that provide facts to counter xenophobia and Islamophobia. We must support anti-hate groups such as ADL, ACLU, America's Voice, and the American Immigration Council. The antidote to radicalization is to do our share of resettlement and provide generous aid in place.

The pandemic will ease, and it's time to again open our hearts and borders to refugees. We need to stop perceiving the victims of terror as terrorists. We need to come to our senses about the vast contributions that refugees have made to our economy and regional stability abroad. We need to respect their resilience and give them a lifeline with which to rebuild their lives. In short, we need to start implementing rational policies for resettling refugees in the US and elsewhere.

With the election of a new administration, the US has an opportunity to renew its leadership as a beacon for refugees. The platform on which President Joe Biden ran included a pledge to "immediately reverse the Trump administration's cruel and senseless policies": the separation of parents from their children at the US border, inhumane asylum rules, and the travel ban. He also ordered a review of Temporary Protected Status for vulnerable populations and pledged to set annual refugee admissions at 125,000, seeking to raise it over time, "commensurate with our responsibility and our values." All of this provides new hope for Syrian refugees.

If there's one point I need to hammer home, it's this: displaced Syrians must be rescued one way or the other. If we don't resettle them, we need to provide enough aid to give them some kind of life and some kind of hope. If we don't do that, David Miliband's admonition will come back to haunt us: "What starts in Syria does not end in Syria."

* * *

Not many of us get to contribute our two cents to foreign policy, operate on the level of massive international agencies, recruit wealthy corporations to a cause, or implement grand solutions. But there is much we can do on a smaller scale and a new, more sympathetic administration can ease the way forward.

Earlier, I cited F. Murray Abraham's plea to resurrect private sponsorship of refugees.

Driven by the flood of refugees from Southeast Asia at the end of the Vietnam War, the US replaced private sponsorships with the Refugee Act of 1980. The purpose was to centralize and regularize the system of refugee admission and resettlement. That is a role that the federal government must not be permitted to abdicate. But private sponsors—especially the faith-based community—can play a big role in the successful integration of refugees. With training from the professional resettlement agencies, they can cover pre-arrival travel costs and post-arrival financial support for the first year, provide language classes, secure educational enrollment and employment, assist with cultural orientation, and provide housing and furniture.

Religious congregations are particularly well organized to form welcome committees and assist with supports for refugees. The "Good Neighbor" Teams of World Relief, a Christian humanitarian aid organization, supplement government aid during the transition period with mentoring, language classes, and social services.

Perhaps the most important role for faith leaders is to prepare the ground through multifaith dialogue. The legal framework for private sponsorship already exists in the actions taken by US President Ronald Reagan: Under his authority to determine the number of refugees to be resettled in the US, a separate, *additional* quota of 10,000 privately sponsored newcomers was created. Under this system, sponsors are matched with refugees in three ways: naming a refugee already in the pipeline for resettlement, naming an unrelated refugee overseas, or naming a refugee relative overseas; and then an application for resettlement is submitted. That's how my parents and I were admitted to the US in 1952: my father's cousin, Eugene, sponsored us. But private sponsorship has fallen by the wayside. It needs to be revived.

IRAP has put forth an approach for doing so in a 2020 report:

- Create an FY 2021 Private Sponsorship Initiative to allow up to 5,000 refugees to be resettled to the U.S. through a co-sponsorship model.

- Create a P-6 category for future private sponsorship admissions to ensure efficient processing and additionality.

- Create a permanent Private Sponsorship Initiative beginning in FY 2022, with the first year acting as a bridge from the co-sponsorship model to a more fully private scheme.

- Establish a fixed percentage of the PD that will be set aside as additional private sponsorship slots (i.e., if the percentage is 10 percent and the PD is 100,000, there will be 10,000 private sponsorship slots, for a total of 110,000).

California, Michigan, Texas, Arizona, and Pennsylvania are the US states where one finds the most resettled refugees. In states with governors who are refusing to resettle Syrian refugees, private donors are needed to replace a reduction in state funds.

In those places that have welcomed the most refugees, there's a gap between needs and services. There is an urgent demand for affordable housing, trauma services, and medical care. Offer up an empty apartment or volunteer your skills as a psychologist or doctor. Or sponsor a Syrian refugee family for a year in which you provide housing, mentoring, and support.

But what can be done in the meantime, while we wait to crank up the resettlement machinery? Displaced Syrians have immediate needs for food, clothing, medicine, and hygiene. Religious congregations, social clubs, and affinity groups can host packing events to gather goods that are needed on the ground.

Just as important, lift up Syrian voices so the displaced become visible and real. Reading about 13 million displaced people has nowhere near the impact of one human story.

* * *

In 2020, I became part of a council of religious leaders co-organized by UNHCR and Religions for Peace, where I serve as an honorary president. In our initial meeting, Filippo Grandi, the UN high commissioner for refugees, called on us to organize our efforts around three tasks related to refugees: acceptance, inclusion, and solutions. Acceptance means welcoming the stranger, changing the narrative about the displaced, influencing opinion, and countering the demonization of refugees for short-term political gain.

Inclusion means prioritizing poverty and education and advocating for including refugees in the host countries' existing institutions—schools, health systems, and so on—rather than isolating and segregating refugees.

Solutions means preventing and solving forced displacement, addressing its root causes through dialogue and reconciliation work, addressing the causes of flight, and working toward a peaceful return home.

Those tasks are at the heart of what this chapter—and much of this book—has been about.

For those who feel moved to alleviate Syrian suffering, but don't know where to begin, this chapter offers some paths for you to follow. In this book, I've shared my own path—the people and organizations I encountered along the way, the ideas that impelled me, the obstacles that had to be circumvented, and the good that my partners helped me achieve.

At times, we were buffeted by external politics, hamstrung by cultural misunderstandings, torn by turf battles, and mired due to deferred decisions.

But it's all worth it. Everything we did is captured in a gift I received from Poly, one year after we began our work together. It was a small but deeply meaningful plaque from the IDF inscribed with the powerful words of the great sage, Hillel: "Whoever saves a life, it is considered as if he saved an entire world." Poly then added his own inscription: "Thank you for your contribution to bringing light into darkness." Those words—Poly's and Hillel's—moved me deeply as a Jew and as a person trying to find an entry point for doing some good. It never fails to bring tears to my eyes because it's my reminder that one person can do something real to alleviate massive suffering. In the case of MFA, we were able to relieve the suffering of more than two million individuals as of this writing.

MFA spokesperson F. Murray Abraham captures the aspiration of all of us "do-gooders" who want to overcome this massive tragedy: "I've always thought the slogan 'Never again' should be amended slightly. I would like to see it become 'Never again to anyone.'"

ACKNOWLEDGMENTS

Most author acknowledgments end with their families. But mine begins with my family. Neither this book, nor the work that it describes, would have been possible without my late husband, Rabbi Marc Tanenbaum, or my current husband, Dr. Leonard Polonsky C.B.E. Marc inspired it, and Leonard supported it. He was patient with my frequent overseas trips and unfailingly generous in backing my commitment to the Syrian cause. Next is my son, Joshua-Marc Bennett Tanenbaum, who is thoroughly both his father's and stepfather's son. Although Joshua's father died seven weeks before my son was born, a commitment to interreligious understanding and human rights is hard-wired into his DNA. From his stepfather, he acquired his intense commitment to impactful philanthropy. Accordingly, between the time that Joshua-Marc graduated college and began his first full-time job, he worked with me in getting the Multifaith Alliance for Syrian Refugees (MFA) off the ground. His strategic thinking and digital savvy gave MFA a presence when we were just a few volunteers and interns working out of my home office. Among these, Frank Kinard, Eric Greenberg, Allyson Zacharoff, and Gabrielle Charnoff.

Some moved on to become part of MFA's core team, along with Bennett Gross, who led MFA for several crucial years, Marlene Adler, Betsy Dribben, Ahed Festuk, Ionut Gitan, Emily Kay, Avi Rothfeld, Sana Shtasel. Over the years, some have come and some have gone, but whether still with us or not, they made enduring contributions to our work.

Among other cherished colleagues, this book relates the voyage that Gal Lusky, Shadi Martini, Ghassan Aboud, General Yoav "Poly" Mordechai, Mohammed Ammar Martini, Colonel Sharon Biton, and I took together. They are the heroes of this story. My acknowledgment of, and gratitude to, them finds full expression in the pages of this book.

Of course, the work MFA did couldn't have taken place without the backing of those who took the plunge with us into unknown territory. The first to step up were members of the Jewish Funders Network. Among these: Arnow Family Fund, Becker Charitable Trust, Alisa & Dan Doctoroff and Bloomberg Philanthropies, Genesis Prize Foundation, Leichtag Foundation, Kirsch Charitable Foundation, and Russell Berrie Foundation. But I must give a special shout-out to Howard Milstein, who provided financial backing both for MFA and the collaboration with Harvard Law School for its seminal report on policy aspects of the Syrian refugee crisis. He also donated prime office space to house MFA and hotel lodging for our far-flung staffers when they needed to be in New York. These in-kind contributions allowed us to devote more of our resources to advocacy and humanitarian aid.

And now, *aharon aharon haviv*, a poignant Hebrew expression that translates loosely into "the last is the most beloved"—or, in more common vernacular, "last, but not least." I deeply appreciate my agent, Karen Gantz, for her profound belief in this book and for making the *shiddach*—match—with my editor, Adam Bellow. From the moment we met, I felt as if Adam and I were completely in sync. Adam's sincere interest and hands-on engagement gave me the motivation to share this story. Although I have written dozens of articles and given countless public speeches, this is the first book that I've written since 1989. Adam was a full partner in bringing it to fruition.

GLOSSARY OF ACRONYMS

ACLU American Civil Liberties Union
ADL Anti-Defamation League
ARCS American Relief Coalition for Syria
CIFIA Correct Islamic Faith International Association
CNAS Center for New American Security
COVID-19 Coronavirus 2019
DHS Department of Homeland Security
EC European Commission
ECHO European Commission Humanitarian Aid and Civil
Protection Department
EFD European Foundation for Democracy
EU European Union
FSA Free Syria Army
GCR Global Covenant of Religions
GNA Global Needs Assessment
HIAS Hebrew Immigrant Aid Society
IAC Interagency Check
IDF Israeli Defense Forces
IDP Internally Displaced Person
IFA Israeli Flying Aid
INSS Institute for National Strategic Studies
IRA Irish Republican Army
IRAP International Refugee Assistance Program
IRC International Rescue Committee

GLOSSARY OF ACRONYMS

ISIS Islamic State in Iraq and Syria
ISOP International School of Peace
JCC Jewish Community Center
JCPA Jewish Council for Public Affairs
JDC American Jewish Joint Distribution Committee
JFN Jewish Funders Network
JICRC Jordanian Coexistence Research Center
KRI Kurdish Regional Government in Iraq
MENA Middle East and North Africa
MEP Member of European Parliament
MFA Multifaith Alliance for Syrian Refugees
MK Member of Knesset
MP Member of Parliament
NATO North Atlantic Treaty Organization
NGO Non-Governmental Organization
NIS New Israeli Shekel
OCHA United Nations Office for the Coordination of Humanitarian Affairs
ORR Office of Refugee Resettlement
PDC People Demand Change
SAC Syrian Action Committee
SAMS Syrian American Medical Association
SETF Syria Emergency Task Force
SDF Syria Democratic Forces
TIP The Israel Project
UAE United Arab Emirates
UNDOF United Nations Disengagement Observer Force
UNHCR United Nations High Commission for Refugees
UNICEF United Nations Children's Fund
USCIS United States Citizen and Immigration Services
USRAP United States Refugee Admissions Program
WFP World Food Program
WHO World Health Organization

SOURCES

Abu Ahmad, Ibrahim, "Assad's Law 10: Reshaping Syria's Demographics," Fikra Forum, The Washington Institute for Mideast Policy, September 2018.

Affordable Housing Institute, "Zaatari: The Instant City," 2014.

Al-Khuder, Khalifa, "The Conflict Has Torn Apart Syrian Tribes, But They Must Remain an Important Player," *SyriaSource*, The Atlantic Council, July 2019.

Al Musarea, Ammar, "The Role of Syrian Tribes: Betting on a Lost Cause," The Washington Institute for Near East Policy, March 2019.

Al Wazani, Khalid, "The Socio-Economic Implications of Syrian Refugees on Jordan," Konrad Adenauer Stiftung, April 2014.

Ali, Dr. Sundas (Lead Analyst), "British Muslims in Number," Muslim Council of Britain, January 2015.

Assaad, Ragui, Thomas Ginn and Mohamed Saleh, "Impact of Syrian Refugees in Jordan on Educational Outcome for Jordanian Youth," Economic Research Forum, Working Paper 1214, September 2018.

Beir, David, "Muslims Rapidly Adopt U.S. Social Values," Cato Institute, October 2016.

Bolton, John, *The Room Where it Happened*, Simon & Schuster, 2020.

Camarota, Steven, "The High Cost of Resettling Middle Eastern Refugees," Center for Immigration Studies, November 2015.

Dukhan, Haian, "Tribes and Tribalism in the Syrian Uprising," Centre for Syrian Studies, University of St. Andrews, 2014.

Fache, Wilson, "West Looks for Ways to Combat Assad's Latest Weapon: International Aid," *Haaretz*, July 14, 2020.

Geneva Peacebuilding Platform, "White Paper on Peacebuilding," 2015.

Hardman, Nadia & Gerry Simpson, "Greece: Violence Against Asylum Seekers," Human Rights Watch, March 2020.

Harvard Immigration and Refugee Clinical Program, "Fulfilling U.S. Commitment to Refugee Resettlement: Protecting Refugees, Preserving National Security & Building the U.S. Economy through Refugee Admissions," May 2017.

Heras, Nick and Kaleigh Thomas, "Solving The Syrian Rubik's Cube: An Instruction Guide for Leveraging Syria's Fragmentation to Achieve U.S. Policy Objectives," Center for New American Security, April 2019.

Hussein, Akil, "Division Defines Syria's Tribes and Clans," Chatham House, January 2018.

Ignatieff, Michael, "The United States and the Syrian Refugee Crisis," Shorenstein Center on Media, Politics, and Public Policy, Harvard Kennedy School, January 2016.

International Refugee Assistance Project, "Expanding Complementary Pathways for

Refugees and Displaced Persons: A Blueprint for the U.S. Government," November 2020.

International Rescue Committee, "Are We Listening: Acting on Our Commitments to Women and Girls Affected by the Syrian Conflict," September 2014.

International Rescue Committee, "Syria: A Regional Crisis," IRC Commission on Syrian Refugees, January 2013.

Kallick, David, Cyierra Roldan, Silva Mathema, "Syrian Immigrants in the United States: A Receiving Community for Today's Refugees," December 2016.

Little, David ed., *Peacemakers in Action: Profiles of Religion in Conflict Resolution*, Cambridge University Press, 2007.

Megally, Hanny and Elena Naughton, "Gone Without A Trace: Syria's Detained, Abducted, and Forcibly Disappeared," NYU International Center for Transitional Justice, May 2020.

Mogelson, Luke, "America's Abandonment of Syria," *The New Yorker*, April 27, 2020.

Motaparthy, Priyanka and Nadim Houry, "If the Dead Could Speak," Human Rights Watch, December 16, 2015.

Netherlands Ministry of Foreign Affairs & Canadian International Development Agency, "Review of the World Food Programme's Humanitarian and Development Effectiveness 2006–2011," April 2012.

Pourchot, Georgeta, ed., "International Refugee Research: Evidence for Smart Policy," Virginia Tech School of Public and International Affairs, September 2018.

Ross, Dennis, *The Missing Peace*, Farrar, Straus and Giroux, 2004.

Sosnowski, Marika and Jonathan Robinson, "Mapping Russia's Soft Power Efforts in Syria Through Humanitarian Aid," The Atlantic Council, June 25, 2020.

Tabrizi, Aniseh Bassiri and Raffaello Pantucci (eds), "Understanding Iran's Role in the Syrian Conflict," Royal United Services Institute for Defence and Security Studies, August 2016.

Talla, Vasudha, "Private Sponsorship of Refugee Resettlement in the United States: Guiding Principles and Recommendations," Urban Justice Center, International Refugee Assistance Project, and Human Rights First, October 2016.

UNHCR, "Syria Regional Response Plan, January to December 2013."

UNHCR, "Regional Strategic Overview 2020-2021," December 2019.

UNHCR, "UNHCR Global Appeal 2019 Update, Overview: UNHCR's 2019 Financial Requirements," 2019.

Youssef, Shiar, "Iran in Syria: From an Ally of the Regime to an Occupying Force," *Naame Shaam*, September 2014.

UK

BBC News, "Attitudes Harden Towards Refugees from Syria and Libya, BBC Poll Suggests," February 2016.

BBC News, "UK to accept 20,000 refugees from Syria by 2020," September 2015.

SOURCES

Brokenshire, James, "Vulnerable Persons Relocation Scheme for Syrian Nationals," Written Statement to UK Parliament, March 2014.

Capital Mass – Diocese of London, "Refugee, Migrant and Modern Slavery Response," 2020.

Chater, James, "What are the Consequences of Brexit for the Refugee Crisis?" *NewStatement,* June 2016.

Divya Talwar, "UK Attitudes Towards Islam 'Concerning' After Survey of 2,000 People," *BBC Newsbeat,* May 2016.

European Resettlement Network, "First Syrians Arrive Under in the UK Under the Vulnerable Persons Relocation Scheme (VPRS)," March 2014.

Frazer, Jenni, "Holocaust Survivor Repays Ultimate Debt via Rescue of Syrian Christians," *The Times of Israel,* July 2015.

GOV.UK, "Immigration Statistics," July to September 2016; and January to March 2016.

Interfaith Refugee Initiative, "Faith Leaders' Open Letter to the Prime Minister," September 2016.

Katwala, Sunder, Jill Rutter, and Steve Ballinger, "Immigration and Integration in Post-Referendum Britain: What next after Brexit?" *British Future,* August 2016.

Katwala, Sunder, Jill Rutter, and Steve Ballinger, "How to Talk About Immigration," *British Future,* 2014.

Khomami, Nadia and Chris Johnston, "Thousands Join Solidarity with Refugees Rally in London," *The Guardian,* September 2015.

Lipka, Michael, "Muslims and Islam: Key Findings in the U.S. and Around the World," Pew Research/Fact Tank, August 2017.

Sherwood, Harriet, "Archbishop of Canterbury Takes in Syrian Refugee Family," *The Guardian,* July 2016.

UK National Audit Office, "The Syrian Vulnerable Persons Resettlement Programme," September 2016.

UNHCR, Syria Regional Refugee Response Data, May 2020.

UNICEF, Syrian Refugees and Other Affected Populations in Turkey, Lebanon, Jordan, Iraq and Egypt, December 2019.

World Jewish Relief, "Refugee Crisis: One Year On," 2016.

Three Great Fears

Aiyar, Shekhar, Bergljot B Barkbu, Nicoletta Batini, Helge Berger, Enrica Detragiache, Allan Dizioli, Christian H Ebeke, Huidan Huidan Lin, Linda Kaltani, Sebastian Sosa, Antonio Spilimbergo, Petia Topalova, "The Refugee Surge in Europe: Economic Challenges," International Monetary Fund, January 2016.

Carrion, Doris, "Syrian Refugees are not the Security Threat They are Feared to be," Chatham House, September 2015.

Emergency Relief Coordinator "Humanitarian Needs Overview," Briefing for Security Council, November 2018.

Evans, William N. and Danial Fitzgerald, "The Economic and Social Outcomes of Refugees in the United States: Evidence from the ACS," National Bureau of Economic Research, June 2017.

Heimlich, Russell, "Muslim Americans: No Signs of Growth in Alienation or Support for Extremism," Pew Research Center, September 2011.

Human Rights First, "The Syrian Refugee Crisis and the Need for U.S. Leadership," February 2016.

International Rescue Committee, "The Disruptive 'New Normal' of Displacement," final report of the Forced Displacement and Development Study Group, April 2017.

International Rescue Committee, "Survey Shows Sympathy for Syrian Refugees Across Europe; Economic Pressures Frequently Cited as a Concern," Press Release, September 2016.

International Rescue Committee, "Emergency Economies: The Impact of Cash Assistance in Lebanon," August 2014.

IPSOS MORI, "Perceptions are not Reality: What the World Gets Wrong," IPSOS Perils of Perception Survey, 2016.

Kallick, David Dyssegaard, Cyierra Roldan, and Silva Mathema, "A Receiving Community for Today's Refugees," Center for American Progress, December 2016.

Koser, Khalid, "IDPs, Refugees and Violent Extremism: From Victims to Vectors of Change," Brookings Institute, February 2015.

Long, Katy, "Why America Could – and Should – Admit More Syrian Refugees," The Century Foundation, December 2015.

SOURCES

McGuinness, Terry, "The UK response to the Syrian Refugee Crisis," House of Commons Library, June 2017.

McHugh, Margie, "The Integration Outcomes of U.S. Refugees: Successes and Challenges." Migration Policy Institute, 2015.

Miliband, David, "From Sector to System: Reform and Renewal in Humanitarian Aid," speech given at Georgetown University, April 2016.

New American Economy, "From Struggle to Resilience: The Economic Impact of Refugees in America," June 2017.

Newland, Kathleen, "The U.S. Record Shows Refugees are not a Threat," Migration Policy Institute, October 2015.

Nowrasteh, Alex, "Terrorism and Immigration: A Risk Analysis," Cato Institute, September 2016.

Organisation for Economic Co-operation and Development, "Economic Survey of Turkey," July 2018.

Pew Research Center, "U.S. Muslims Concerned About Their Place in Society, but Continue to Believe in the American Dream," Report, July 2017.

Pew Research Center, "The Future of Worlds Religions: Population Growth Projections, 2010-2050," Report, April 2015.

Pew Research Center, "The Future of the Global Muslim Population in Europe," Demographic Study, January 2011.

Anti-Defamation League, "Myths and Facts About Muslim People and Islam," 2017.

Tent.org, "Global Reports" 2016 and 2017.

UNHCR, "Refugee Resettlement Facts," March 2020.

UNHCR, "Syria Conflict at 5 years: the Biggest Refugee and Displacement Crisis of Our Time Demands a Huge Surge in Solidarity," March 2016.

UNICEF USA, "How to Help Syria and Its Children," 2020.

U.S. Committee for Refugees and Immigrants, "Security Screening of Refugees Admitted to the U.S.," 2019.

Wike, Richard, Bruce Stokes and Katie Simmons, "Negative Views of Minorities, Refugees Common in EU," Pew Research Center, July 2016.

World Bank, The "Jordan Economic Overview," October 2019.

World Bank, The "Lebanon Economic Overview," April 2019.

Zong, Jie and Jeanne Batalova, "Syrian Refugees in the United States," Migration Policy Institute, January 2017.

Zong, Jie, "Profile of Syrian Immigrants in the United States, Migration Policy Institute," 2015.

INDEX

INDEX

INDEX

Syrian civil war role of, 19, 20–21,
50–52, 86–87, 90, 123–125, 181,
205–206, 209, 215–216
Islamic Action Front, 48
Islamic Front, 98
Islamic Society of North America, 162
IsraAid, 62–63, 212
Israel
Aboud's leadership support by,
203–205
Arab Council for Regional Integration with, 69, 76–79, 105
Bahraini relations with, 78–79
Bennett's humanitarian diplomacy
and, 26–27, 38–44, 62–63, 64–82,
83–94, 96–113, 114–136, 154–
180, 195–208, 222–223, 248
conflicting agendas with, 113,
114–136
COVID-19 in, 203
Egyptian relations with, 28, 78–79,
101, 109
geopolitics of, 222–223
Hezbollah and, 31, 98, 102, 104,
109, 121, 133, 184, 186, 200, 203
humanitarian aid by, 38–40, 42,
62–63, 64–82, 84–94, 103, 108–
113, 128–130, 132–136, 154–155,
174–177, 195–208, 212, 222
Israel Defense Forces of, 39–40,
70, 89, 93, 103, 111–112, 127,
128–129, 154–155, 157–158, 160,
164–168, 175–176, 186–187, 248
Jordanian relations with, 27, 28–31,
35–36, 40, 43–44, 48, 62–63, 78,
89, 101, 109, 197, 222–223
Judaism and, 14, 16, 26, 71
Kuwaiti relations with, 79
Lebanonese relations with, 26, 28,
29, 96, 109, 119
medical support for Syrian hospital
through, 154–180
medical technology as aid from,
196–198
medical treatment for Syrians by,
38–40, 42, 63, 65–66, 70–71, 79,
89, 93, 103, 112, 132, 174–177
Moroccan relations with, 78

multifaith collaboration with, 35–36,
62–63, 64–82, 83–94, 96–113,
114–136, 154–180, 195–208, 248
Omani relations with, 79
Palestinian relations with, 28–31,
68–69, 70, 75, 77, 107, 121, 170,
173
people-to-people diplomacy with,
78, 82, 84, 96–113, 121–122
Russian relations with, 121, 125–
126, 184–185, 186, 221
Saudi relations with, 78–79
statehood of, 28, 68, 96
Sudanese relations with, 78
Syria comparison to, 115
Syrian government relations with,
28, 29, 71–72, 84, 91–93, 96–97,
101–102, 174–175
Syrian perception of, 74–76, 80–82,
179–180 (*see also* people-to-people diplomacy)
Syrian refugee refusal by, 185
UAE relations with, 78, 208
US relations with, 28, 131, 203
visas by, 123, 125–130, 155, 161, 164
water rights in, 44
Israeli Flying Aid (IFA), 62, 63, 67,
70–72, 80, 85, 89, 112, 123, 134,
156–157, 159. *See also* Lusky, Gal
Israeli Trauma Coalition, 62

J
Jabhat Fatah al-Sham, 50
Jennings, Peter, 34
Jesuit Refugee Services, 242
Jewish Coalition for Syrian Refugees in
Jordan, 42–43, 49, 72
Jewish Council for Public Affairs
(JCPA), 42
Jewish Funders Network (JFN), 61, 75,
81, 111
Jewish population. *See also* Israel
anti-Semitism among refugees
toward, 214
Bennett's humanitarian diplomacy
through, 41–44, 48–49, 61–63,
64–82, 83–94, 98–99

INDEX

Refugee Act (1980), 230, 245
refugees
  Bennett's work for (*see* Bennett,
    Georgette, humanitarian
    diplomacy)
  community policing among,
    57–58
  contributions of, 73, 226–227,
    228–229, 232–234, 240–241, 244
  COVID-19 and, 213–214, 232
  displacement of (*see* displacement)
  geopolitics affecting, 209–225
  humanitarian aid for (*see* humani-
    tarian aid)
  immigrants distinction from, 229
  integration of, 45, 208, 231, 233,
    238–239, 242–243, 245–246
  IRC report on, 3–4, 14
  living conditions for, 55–60, 73
  Muslim, fear of, 232, 235–236,
    243–244
  post-World War II, 6, 8–9, 15, 88,
    230
  private sponsorship of, 231, 233,
    245–247
  public opinion on, 230–231, 244
  recruitment and radicalization of,
    59–60, 235, 240
  "refugee tourism" offending, 55
  resettlement of, 25, 43, 45–46, 49,
    59, 155, 162, 182, 212, 226–249
  return to Syria, 45–46, 173, 180–181,
    208, 210, 237–238
  state actors and admissions of, 22
  Syrian statistics on, 21, 209
  Tanenbaum's work with, 1, 12–13
  terrorism fears and, 84, 182, 211,
    232, 235–236, 244
  urban, 4, 46, 85, 181
  violence toward, 3–4, 46, 58–59,
    62–63, 212–213
  weaponizing plight of, 211–212
  work options for, 46, 57, 232–233,
    241, 243
Reid, Alec, 69
religion
  Amman Message on, 36
  commonalities among major, 48

geopolitics and, 217
  humanitarianism and, 12, 15–16, 25,
    26, 48–49, 71, 229, 246
  Judaism as, 14, 15–16, 26, 71 (*see also*
    Jewish population)
  moral authority and, 49
  multifaith collaboration (*see* multi-
    faith collaboration)
  of refugees, 235–236, 243–244
  religicide as genocide based on,
    52–54, 60
  Syrian civil war origins and, 18–19
  values-driven policy reflecting, 179
Religions for Peace, 247
Reut Group, 70, 198
Revolutionary Action Movement, 10
Revolutionary Guard Corps Quds
  Force, 19, 86
ReWalk Robotics, 196
Rivlin, Reuven, 110
Rockefeller, Happy, 10
Rose Castle Foundation, 55
Royal Institute for Inter-Faith Studies,
  33
Rupp, George, 2, 40
Russia. *See also* Soviet Union and Soviet
  bloc
  geopolitics of, 211, 215–218,
    219–221
  humanitarian aid through, failure
    of, 184, 202, 216
  Israeli relations with, 121, 125–126,
    184–185, 186, 221
  Jordan's stability and influence of,
    31
  MFA obstacles from, 113
  religicide resolution opposition by,
    53–54
  Saudi relations with, 220
  Syrian civil war role of, 19–20, 21,
    86, 103, 121, 131, 173, 177,
    184–185, 199, 201–202,
    205–206, 209, 211, 215, 216–218,
    219–221
  UN Chapter 7 resolution opposition
    by, 23, 216
Russian Orthodox Church, 217
Rustin, Bayard, 12